W9-AVR-960

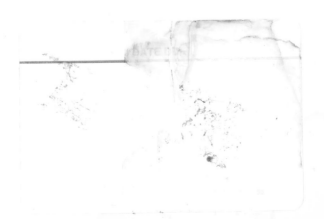

Language in Motion

Language in Motion

Exploring the Nature of Sign

Jerome D. Schein and David A. Stewart

Gallaudet University Press   *Washington, D.C.*

Gallaudet University Press
Washington, DC 20002

Library of Congress Cataloging-in-Pubication Data

Schein, Jerome Daniel.
    Language in motion : exploring the nature of sign / Jerome D.
Schein and David A. Stewart.
      p.   cm.
    Includes bibliographical references (p.   ) and index.
    ISBN 1-56368-039-4
    1. Sign language.   2. American Sign Language.   3. Deaf—Social
conditions.   I. Stewart, David Alan, 1954-   . II. Title.
HV2474.S34 1995
305.9'08162—dc20   95-12553
                                                              CIP

Contents

Preface

$\boxed{A}$ world with no sounds. Phones don't ring. Thunder doesn't clap. The radio's just another piece of furniture. Automobiles glide silently past. Imagine, a soundless environment. Does such a world exist? And in that world, how would you communicate? Without sound, how would you get the news of the day? Would you be able to order pizza and have it delivered to your house? How would you invite friends to a barbeque? Could you explain to a colleague why you were late for your meeting?

You may immediately recognize that such a world—a world without meaningful hearing—already exists. It is not a special place; it is not hidden in an enclave marked only by road signs restricting access. It is all around you, and yet few ever see it. Simply stated, it is the world of deaf people.[1]

That the deaf world tends to be invisible stems from two facts. First of all, deaf people are a small minority within the general population. How much of a minority is something we will discuss in chapter 7. Second, deaf people have no obvious indications of their lack of hearing—until you try to communicate with them. They don't wear dark glasses, carry canes, or sit in wheelchairs. Hearing aids, if they wear them, are not distinctive because persons who are hard of hearing also use them. But talk to a deaf person and their lack of hearing becomes apparent.

"What a tragedy," you might say. "No sound; no way to communicate." Not really. Most deaf people have developed a lifestyle detached from sounds. They communicate with signs, rather than speech. For that reason their social lives revolve around other people who use sign language. The majority of those who marry choose deaf spouses. Ask a deaf couple if they would rather have a hearing or a deaf child, and more than likely they will say deaf. It is not that they do not like hearing people; it is just that as social creatures, the value of communication is deeply ingrained in them. They know that communicating and socially identifying with a deaf child who signs will be much easier than with a hearing child who depends on speech. They love their children equally, hearing or deaf. It is simply a matter of communicating.

Language and Communication

Can we exchange information without a shared language? Yes, we have many examples of people communicating without having a common language. We do not have to go farther than the initial encounters between the Europeans who emigrated to the New World and the indigenous population. Columbus communicated with the natives, whom he misnamed Indians because he thought he had reached India. But he did not know their language nor they his. The pioneers who came to North America communicated with the local people they encountered before they knew each other's languages. In the Pacific explorers gathered information from natives—information that was accurate enough to save their lives as they sailed in the directions and for the times indicated by the natives—without the benefit of a common language.

What Is Language?

Since this book is about language, we should establish a definition of it at the outset. You may already know that experts do not agree on what language is. But we are not linguists, so, like Humpty Dumpty, we can proclaim, "When I use a word it means just what I choose it to mean—neither more nor less." Actually, we will be concurring with the majority of language experts if we adhere to the following definition:

> Language is a systematic means of communicating ideas and feelings by the use of conventional symbols.[2]

The term *systematic* refers to the rules for combining the elements of the language—the grammar. The word *symbols* in the definition conveys another critical aspect of language: it is referential. Symbols refer to something that need not be present to be discussed. Symbols allow us to communicate about events in the past or future and at a distance or hidden from the sender or the receiver. The symbols may be of any kind: auditory, visual, tactual, or whatever, so long as they can be transmitted by one person and received by another. *Conventional* implies prior agreement about the meaning of the symbols between two or more people.

Our definition of language avoids some of the controversial issues, though not all. It tells what language can do—communicate thoughts and emotions—not what it must do. It makes clear that a set of symbols, a collection of signs, does not make a language if there are no rules for putting the symbols together. The concept of language expressed here is a social one; it requires that others (at least one other) share an understanding of the language elements (grammar and vocabulary) before the system achieves linguistic status. Sender and receiver may not be able to explicate the rules, but they demonstrate their internalization of them by their consistent behavior in relation to them.

Some linguists require that the symbols be arbitrary rather than iconic (representations of the form of that which is being described, like a picture of an object, an icon). An arbitrary symbol could not be understood by someone unfamiliar with the language. An iconic symbol could. Our definition of language does not address this point, but our discussion of sign language will.

We do not include the dynamics of languages in the definition—the fact that as languages are transmitted they tend to alter somewhat, usually in predictable ways. For instance, the original word for a flying machine that carries passengers was *aeroplane*; now *plane* means the same thing. The tendency to shorten or to prune words is one predictable feature of most languages, including sign languages. We will take up this latter point in the second chapter, when we discuss the structure of sign language.

Having said that, it should be noted that communication by pointing, pantomiming, drawing, and other nonlinguistic means is limited. For wide-ranging communication, especially for discussions about things not present and events not experienced in common, language is essential. We conclude that you can have communication without language, but the communication you will have will be thin gruel compared to the rich stew that comes with language.

Must languages be spoken or written? Are there forms of language other than the one with which most people are accustomed? The answer, of course, is yes: sign language. Like all languages, it consists of symbols that are combined according to rules (syntax) in order to convey thoughts and feelings. What are the symbols of a sign language? Instead of sounds or printed figures, they are the images made by fingers, hands, and arms—images that are linguistically shaped by movements of the eyes, eyebrows, lips, and cheeks, by the hunching and twisting of the shoulders, by the signer's posture. In the United States and in most of Canada the language of signs is called American Sign Language or, as it is commonly abbreviated, ASL. For deaf people ASL is fundamental to communication. It is their language.

Speech and Language

That the word *language* derives from *lingua* ("tongue") betrays the common confusion about the relation between speech and language. For many earlier linguists, the words were synonymous[3]. The notion of a language not arising from spoken communication received little attention from leaders of language-development studies, and they in turn heavily influenced educators of deaf children. Because sign languages are not spoken, educators until recently did not accept the signing behavior prevalent in the Deaf community as a language. This gave them a reason for barring sign language from the classroom and, to the extent possible, from the schoolyard. Thus, the failure to separate speech from language had a profound influence on the education of deaf students. To avoid repeating that error, consider our definition of speech: *Speech consists of vocal utterances that may or may not be meaningful to others.* The key difference between speech, as we have defined it, and language is the requirement of meaningfulness. Speech does not need to be meaningful; language does.

Are speech and language independent of each other? If they are, we should find speech without language as well as language without speech. To illustrate speech without language, we could point to talking birds. A parrot's utterances lack meaning and do not intentionally express thoughts and emotions. The bird does not necessarily want to eat when it says, "Polly wants a cracker!" It is merely repeating words it has been taught to say.

Turning to human examples of speech without language, consider *glossolalia* (speaking in tongues), which is sometimes heard in Pentecostal churches. It is speech without discernible meaning. Patients with certain forms of aphasia may speak but their words make no sense. Likewise, deaf persons with aphasia have been found to produce strings of signs that have no meaning to others[4].

What about language without speech? Some people are born with anarthria (nonfunctioning vocal apparatus) and other conditions, such as cerebral palsy, and are unable to speak, but nonetheless can understand and develop language. They are able to express themselves through sign language or communication boards and other devices. Speech pathologists have noted other cases of normally hearing children who were unable to speak but who, nonetheless, understood language.

Accepting the independence of speech and language is essential to appreciating ASL as a fully developed language, not a manual version of English. The fact that ASL and all other sign languages are natural languages partly accounts for the mushrooming interest in them—an interest that has exerted considerable influence on the education of deaf children and the rehabilitation of deaf adults. Furthermore, separating speech from language encourages a broader approach to research on both—an approach with potential for advancing our command of communication.

Hearing and Seeing

Our two distance receptors, sight and hearing, work together so well that we may not have given much thought to their coordination. When both are intact, they work in tandem like a pair of well-trained coach horses. The two senses function so smoothly it is difficult to appreciate the effort of one or the other alone. But when either sense is seriously impaired or absent, we become sharply aware of differences in the way they operate.

A critical difference between hearing and seeing is that we hear *sequentially*, but we see *simultaneously*. That difference in temporal relations unlocks a distinction between spoken and signed languages that we will want to remember. If two words are simultaneously spoken, one contributes noise relative to the other. The sounds of language must occur one after the other if we are to hear and understand them. But when viewing a scene, we can grasp at once many of its features. When we describe the scene, we are forced to recite the features sequentially, but that is characteristic of our spoken language. In sign language more than one idea can be expressed at the same moment. We will find this characteristic aids in classifying sign communication and in understanding its impact on the development of visual-gestural languages as opposed to those that are sound based.

Attitudes toward Language

Language is a very personal attribute. How we use language is taken as an index of our intelligence and clearly marks our social position. George

Bernard Shaw makes that point in his classic drama about language, *Pygmalion*. Early in the play, Professor Higgins points to Eliza Doolittle, standing in Covent Garden in her flower-girl rags, and says:

> You see this creature with her Kerbstone English: the English that will keep her in the gutter to the end of her days. Well, sir, in three months I could pass that girl off as a duchess at an ambassador's garden party. I could even get her a place as a lady's maid or a shop assistant, which requires better English.[5]

In his preface to the play Shaw comments, "Finally, and for the encouragement of people troubled with accents that cut them off from all high employment, I may add that the change wrought by Professor Higgins in the flower-girl is neither impossible nor uncommon."[6] Shaw cannot resist this added bolstering of his argument, nor would many knowledgeable persons disagree with his fundamental claim, if not his hyperbole, about the critical determination of social status by language.

In 1866 the Linguistic Society of Paris would not permit the presentation of papers that raised questions about the origin of language. To raise the issue at all was blasphemous. Language was the exclusive property of humans, the basis for our uniqueness. To question its origins was to imply that it might not have been handed down from above. Even now there are theorists who react emotionally to any questions about language existing in forms other than human. To them the very attribution of such a complex function to "lower" forms of life seems to demean our own. To readers who hold similarly exalted views of language, some of what follows could be upsetting.

Are we occasionally chauvinistic about our language? The present acceptance of English as essential to the study of most sciences reinforces such attitudes. The worldwide acceptance of English, however, is of recent origin. Until World War II German was accepted as the language of science and French the language of diplomacy. We should remind ourselves that in Shakespeare's time English was regarded as a "barbarous, vulgar, and rude tongue without logic."[7] It was considered unfit for scientific, let alone for polite, discourse. Four hundred years ago Sir Thomas More commented on the subject of the English language.

> That our language is called barbarous is but a fantasy, for so is, as every learned man knoweth, every strange language to any other. And though they would call it barren of words, there is no doubt that it is plenteous enough to express our minds in anything whereof one man hath used to speak with another.[8]

Thus Spake the Lord

Writing in a sardonic vein, Flora Lewis, *New York Times* columnist (7 May 1982, p. A33), tells a joke to make a point about linguistic insularity.

> Refusal to accept anyone else's language as worth knowing reflects the same narrow-gauge kind of head, the same stubborn ignorance, as that of the fundamentalist I heard about who denounced people speaking in other tongues, saying, "If English was good enough for Jesus Christ, it's good enough for them."

The story is apocryphal in both senses.

Governments have seen control of language as a means of dominating the citizenry. The idea is not in the least absurd. If all government is conducted in a language other than your own, then you do not have ready access to that government. If you cannot understand what is said about you in court, you cannot adequately answer your accusers. If you cannot read the placards, fill out the forms, and in other respects communicate with the government, then you are the government's vassal. You will not be able to advance your status in a country whose language you cannot use. Your livelihood, and possibly your life, will be in jeopardy should a language not known to you become the basis of commerce. In addition, think of what it means when the sovereign language, whatever it might be, is touted as a superior vehicle for thought. We shall see that this idea has continually been broached by adherents of particular cultures to denigrate those over whom they wish to impose their will.

Remember furthermore that wars have been fought over language. For example, in Belgium the Flemings and the Walloons have fought for nearly three centuries about whose language should prevail and now have only an uneasy truce. In 1980 the citizens of Quebec barely defeated a proposal to secede from Canada, a move some Quebecois believed necessary to protect their French language. Still, the decision not to secede did not stop fears of the disintegration of French culture in Quebec. To assist in protecting French as its dominant language, the provincial government enacted a law that required all signs to be printed in French only. Even bilingual signs became illegal. The Supreme Court of Canada ruled that the law violated freedom of speech, which includes the use of any language,

Dumping Mental Garbage

A linguist strongly attacks earlier conceptions of the role of language in culture, especially its use as a tool of oppression by colonialists, as follows:

> According to 19th-century racists, languages and people alike were ranged along a scale of being from the primitive Bushman with his clicks, grunts, and shortage of artifacts, to the modern Western European with his high pale brow and plethora of gadgets. That was when everyone, racist or anti-racist, did believe that Western Man was superior; the only argument was about how nasty this superiority permitted him to be toward "lesser" breeds. Now that we are rapidly disabusing ourselves of this kind of mental garbage, it becomes possible to uncouple language from "level of cultural attainment" and look at it developmentally without any pejorative implications.[9]

temporarily settling that dispute. Quebec's attitude notwithstanding, Canada remains an officially bilingual country, with every federal document printed in both French and English.

So, at national levels and at personal levels decisions about language provoke controversies. No wonder then that discussions of it can stir strong emotions—emotions that sometimes pervert reason. You therefore need to approach what follows with an open mind. The conclusions to be drawn from revised views of our world may prove to be much more fruitful for you than any perspectives they might replace. And even if you make no conceptual reorganizations, you will likely enjoy meeting your deaf neighbors—in their language.

What Lies Ahead in This Book

This book takes a not-too-technical look at sign languages. It is for all those who meet with deaf people, share homes with them, work alongside them, have them as students in class or as clients, friends, and customers. Increasingly, your chances of encountering deaf people grow. So do your chances of becoming deaf or hard of hearing. Furthermore, what follows should interest students of language and culture. In one way or another, all of us use our hands when we communicate.

Our focus will be on communication by deaf people, especially those who live in the United States and Canada, though we will consider sign languages that exist in almost every country throughout the world. Today, most people have seen someone signing—on a bus, in a store, at public meetings, on television. Since Jimmy Carter's successful bid for the U. S. presidency in 1976, many politicians have employed interpreters to sign their public addresses for the benefit of deaf people in the audience. In the popular movie *Children of a Lesser God,* the heroine is deaf and signs her part. Sign language appears frequently on television. A whole generation of children has grown up watching Linda Bove sign on *Sesame Street,* and millions of television viewers have seen *Reasonable Doubt,* a series in which a deaf attorney uses ASL in the courtroom.

How did sign language become so popular? Why is there a sudden interest in it and why did interest emerge so slowly? When and where did sign languages originate? How did they develop? Are they easy or difficult to learn? Who teaches them and where? How are they used for day-to-day interactions among deaf people and between deaf and hearing individuals? Is there an international sign language? Are there other forms of signed communication, other ways to convey messages with one's hands alone?

Answering these questions will take us through art into science and back again, seeking to solve the mysteries of sign langugage. Some questions about sign language have no firm answers at present. Research in many aspects of sign language has begun only recently. But what has already been observed, studied, validated, and catalogued provides a thorough restructuring of some well-established beliefs about sign language and deaf people—and about language itself. Such cognitive restructuring forces a weakening, if not a complete rejection, of a few cherished ways of thinking—not only about our language, but about our culture. This survey of sign language will take us to the theater, to industry, into courtrooms, among educators and rehabilitators, and, most fascinating of all, into the lives of deaf people.

So much for what this book is about. What it is *not* is a sign glossary. It has a great deal to say about how to make oneself understood in sign language; it offers information about where to get sign language instruction and how to identify good teachers; it will help the reader sort through the recent plethora of sign dictionaries. But this book is not a dictionary, nor is it a lesson book. It introduces you to an intriguing language and to the people who use it and, if the book succeeds, it will open your mind to possibilities as yet unrealized for an ancient form of communication that has only recently been accorded its correct place in the linguistic spectrum.

Disciplines

The study of sign language is not the sole province of linguists. Anthropologists, educators, neurologists, psychologists, sociologists, and others have begun to look at sign language to provide enlightenment on language and on human interactions. Ever since the revolution in physics, scientists have recognized the centrality of language to their activities. One of the major contributions of Einstein and the philosophers who interpreted his revolutionary thinking about physics was to explain how our definitions of research terms influence the results.[10] Thus, the newly aroused interest in sign language comes naturally to educators, scientists, and the general public. They have all recognized the centrality of language to our thinking.

Our treatment of the subject of sign language will try to avoid the jargon of the disciplines that have now embraced sign language—linguistics, psycholinguistics, sociolinguistics, education, rehabilitation, psychology, anthropology—and will try to find common paths through the academic maze. As we examine some of the technical terms used, we will assume that the reader is not acquainted with them, so each will be explained as it is introduced. What is more, we will attempt a comprehensive view of sign language, eschewing detail in favor of breadth. To compensate for the lessened detail, we include a sizable list of references from the growing literature to guide readers who wish to pursue their interests in further depth.[11]

About the Authors

Because modern study of sign languages used by deaf people only began in the 1960s, and because much of what is written depends on informed opinion rather than systematic research, readers have a right to demand more than the usual knowledge about the authors of a book about sign. Our combined experience with and research on sign language exceeds 75 years, but we approach it from different perspectives.

For one of us signing is a way of life; he is deaf, and ASL is his language. The other author learned to sign in adulthood and can hear normally, and English is his language. Both of us have taught sign classes, done research on sign language, and written at some length about sign and about deaf people. Both hold doctorates in psychology, and both have had the honor of being chosen for the University of Alberta's David Peikoff Chair of Deafness Studies, one of only two such university chairs in the world.

While we have been involved with sign language for many years, we retain our fascination with it and our enthusiasm for passing along what we have learned about it and those who use it.

Notes

1. For our definition of *deaf*, see chapter 7. Here we note only that by deaf we do not mean a complete inability to hear any sound—an extremely rare condition. Rather, deaf refers to the severely reduced ability to hear and understand speech. For communication deaf people are visually dependent. They may be able to hear some sounds, but what they hear is insufficiently clear for effective verbal communication.

2. Schein 1984.

3. Refer to definitions of *language* in dictionaries published prior to 1980; for example, "the expression or communication of thoughts and feelings by means of vocal sounds and combinations of such sounds, to which meaning is attributed; human speech" (*Webster's New Twentieth Century Dictionary*, 2d ed., 1970. New York: Simon & Schuster).

4. Aphasia is a condition in which ability to express language is lost due to disease of or injury to the brain.

5. Shaw 1912, 6.

6. Shaw 1912, p. vi.

7. Brennan & Hayhurst 1980, 234.

8. *Ibid.*

9. Bickerton 1981, 299.

10. For a discussion of this point, begin with Feigl and Brodbeck, 1953. The philosophers who pursued Einstein's theories belonged to what became known as "the Wiener Kreis" ("the Vienna Circle") after their habit of meeting in that capital's coffeehouses for their debates.

11. If we had to select a name for the discipline devoted to the study of sign it would be *semiology*. The *Oxford English Dictionary* and *Webster's New World Dictionary*, both distinguished lexicons, do not agree as to the meaning of this useful but seldom-used word; nor do they agree as to its spelling (*semeiology* in the former and *semiology* in the latter). *Oxford*'s first meaning for the word is "sign language." *Webster's* sole definition is "the science of signs in general." They do agree on the Greek root, *semeion* (sign). It would appear that semiology could accommodate our interest in sign language as well as in sign codes, a distinction that, if not clear now, will become so in the chapters to follow. Semiology also seems to fit our concern with both the scientific and the cultural aspects of sign. It is offered here without foreboding but with some anticipation of minor controversy. If controversy arises, that will be to the good, for such debates typically stir increased attention to a subject.

1
A Brief History of Sign Language

*W*e may never know when sign language first came into being nor whether its first users were deaf or hearing. But evidence suggests signing is as old as the human species—and possibly older. Anthropologists who have speculated about the origins of language and who accept an evolutionary concept of its development now theorize that gesture preceded vocal utterance in human communication.[1] That is why studies of animal communication have such strong implications for linguists. They suspect that our ancestors communicated with their hands long before they communicated with their voices.

The view opposing the evolution of language is that it came full blown from the mouths of prehistoric humans. These theorists have even brushed aside questions of language origins with reference to a "mutation" that accompanied the emergence of the earliest humans. To the contrary, we posit that languages, signed and spoken, have followed an orderly development. It may even be that the linguistic link between humans and other life forms is "in their hands."

The Evidence for Signs

Several disciplines—anthropology, biology, paleontology, and psychology—contribute to the reconstruction of early forms of communication. Taken together, their separate findings support the conclusion that sign preceded speech in human communication.

Fossil Evidence

Paleontologists study the anatomy of early humans and their immediate ancestors using bones from specifically dated eras. Their examinations suggest that the vocal space of early humans (e.g., australopithecine and ramapithecus) would not accommodate the complex speech apparatus we now have. At the same time the skeletal structures are consistent with having facile hands.[2]

Anthropologists have interpreted some cave paintings and early writing as depicting people signing.[3] Pictographic writing, like Egyptian hieroglyphics and Minoan Linear B, indicate an initial attempt to translate gestures, either in addition to or in conjunction with speech. While hardly conclusive in themselves, such pictorial and graphic evidence contributes to theorizing about earliest language origins.[4]

Animal Communication

Current studies of animals by psychologists provide another link between human precursors and ourselves. If other primates—gorillas and chimpanzees, particularly—can communicate gesturally, that would suggest a similar capacity in our ancestors and would strengthen the argument that they used sign. The issue of animal communication, however, has not been fully resolved. To some extent experimental results are influenced by the experimenter's approach. Some who have found what they regard as substantial evidence of chimpanzees' ability to learn and use sign have credited their success to the way they arranged conditions: "Indeed, it seems that the more freedom we allow in our experiments for the subject to participate, rather than constraining the subject either in a confining apparatus or experimental procedure, the more interesting are the results, and the more impressive is the evidence for apparently higher-order kinds of cognitive operations in the chimpanzee."[5]

One of the most exciting demonstrations of the use of signs by a chimpanzee is also highly controversial, largely because the investigator in charge of the experiment denies the interpretation placed on his data. Nim Chimpsky's exposure to sign came shortly after his birth and proceeded through his first four years or so. Nim did use signs consistently, but Herbert Terrace, the animal project's director, concluded that Nim's signs were imitative and did not reflect a grasp of language principles.[6] Gregory Gaustad reviewed Terrace's book and countered that Terrace's initial bias against the idea of animal communication blinded him to Nim's accomplishments.[7] Terrace retorted: "In searching for evidence that Nim was using sign language, Gaustad apparently fails to grasp that both speaking and signing children, but not apes, provide rich corpora of spontaneous

Challenges to Animal Communication

A nineteenth-century linguist pontificated that "The one great barrier between the brute and man is Language. Man speaks, and no brute has ever uttered a word. Language is our Rubicon, and no brute will dare to cross it."[10] By contrast a modern linguist, reviewing studies of apes' attempts to sign, concedes that, though all the evidence is not in, "perspectives on the nature of man's relationship to other animal species have changed dramatically."[11] Certainly today a philosopher is hardly likely to assert that animals "would not dare to cross" the language barrier!

utterances that allow one to ascertain the degree to which a child's utterances are rule governed."[8] Gaustad responded: "It is a wonder that any spontaneity was exhibited by Nim. However, when chimpanzees are raised in a way that more nearly resembles the rearing conditions of human children, the chimpanzee's utterances are spontaneous. . . ."[9] And so the debate between scientists continues.

Jane Hill, an anthropologist, urges that we take an evolutionary view of language development. "It seems clear that human languages, like other behavioral systems, are the products of evolutionary processes. To make such a statement does not degrade human language any more than it degrades the beauty of the colors of butterflies if we point out that they function in defense or in sexual attraction."[12] To accept the ability of animals to use language does not degrade human language. That word, *degrade*, provides a clue to the reasons for the anger that the very idea of animal communication arouses in some individuals, laymen and scientists alike.

A Biological Approach

The problem of language beginnings can also be addressed by applying the principle from biology that *ontogeny recapitulates phylogeny*. The notion that individual development from conception follows an evolutionary course is a powerful research tool, bringing the irretrievable past under present scrutiny. By studying the development of individuals from fetal stages through infancy and early childhood into adulthood, scientists can test ideas about the probable behavior of humans in prehistoric times.

The Language of Bees

The controversy over animal communication is not fueled solely by animals who closely resemble ourselves. James Gould points out that, despite impressive evidence of language in bees, some scientists cannot accept that notion. Gould might as well have been speaking about primates when he says:

> Some of the resistance to the idea that honey bees possess a symbolic language seems to have arisen from a conviction that "lower" animals, and insects in particular, are too small and phylogenetically remote to be capable of "complex" behavior. There is perhaps a feeling of incongruity in that the honey bee language is symbolic and abstract. . . . Especially in ethology, it is difficult to avoid the unprofitable extremes of blinding skepticism and crippling romanticism.[13]

This observation has been echoed by others who question the very essence of the issue: "What has, in effect, stopped us has been a firm belief in the uniqueness of man as the only creature with language. How could we know that?"[14]—a doubt well worth expressing in view of all the evidence rapidly coming to hand.

Linguists are now paying keen attention to the earliest language behavior of very young children and have noted some fascinating regularities. These regularities also appear in the development of sign language by deaf children.[15] The adult forms of languages, as we know them, emerge from considerable social buffeting. The childlike forms appear to be wired into the organism.

Linguists agree that there is a "universal development sequence" in the acquisition of language. The extent of this universality caused one linguist to comment wryly that the "quite surprising degree to which results to date support this vision has sustained the researcher when he gets a bit tired of writing down Luo, Samoan, or Finnish equivalents of 'That doggie' and 'No more milk.' "[16] Studies are also showing that gestures play a role in the language development of all children: "Both words and gestures show a similar course of development from context-bound routines to generalized use for an increasingly broad set of referents and situations."[17] Research has also revealed that universal characteristics may exist across sign languages, as shown in the examination of marked and unmarked hand shapes, which suggests that there may be a "natural theory of phonology for all sign languages."[18]

By studying both the acquisition of sign languages by deaf children and spoken languages by hearing children it may be possible to delineate language universals that cross modalities (i.e., speech and signs) as well as those that are modality specific.[19] Thus, the observed similarities in the development of gestural behavior in deaf children and the development of gestural and vocal behavior in hearing children is indicative of the role gestural expression has in both deaf and hearing children's communication with adults during the early stages of the communication process.[20]

Nature's Experiment

Occasionally, researchers stumble on natural experiments that they would not, or could not, set up. Rolf Kushel found a deaf man on the remote Polynesian island of Rennell, where the inhabitants' oral history covering twenty-four generations had no previous record of a person who had been deaf since birth. The deaf man, Kangobai, had developed systematic signs that he had been able to teach to his hearing compatriots and thus established communication with them. Kangobai's signs parallel the island's spoken language. The Rennellese have no one term for fishing; it is an activity too vital to their economy to be left unspecified, except, as Kushel points out, when a Rennellese is speaking to "an ignorant anthropologist." Kangobai, similarly, has no general sign for fishing. Instead, he has at least ten distinct signs that range in meaning from "to catch a fish with a spear" to "to net flying fish by torchlight."[21] The study of this isolated man's naturally developed signs can be as provocative to the linguist as the studies of first signs in children. Both approaches provide strong evidence of the innate human capacity to acquire language.

Cultural Anthropology

Much can also be learned about language origins by studying first contacts between people from cultures that have had no prior communication. Gordon Hewes reviewed accounts of early explorers' interactions with the indigenous people they encountered. He was interested in how they managed to establish meaningful intercourse without knowing each other's languages. He found that through signs they communicated with a high degree of accuracy: "Thus, when some Eskimos indicate by signs that they will return to a particular place after three days, and they do in fact show up as they promised, both parties appear to have understood the message in the same way. Navigators, including Christopher Columbus, acting on signed information, have found islands in the direction and at distances indicated."[22] Hewes regards the study of these initial encounters between people who have no shared language as highly important to our understanding of language origins. You could probably identify with this notion if you have ever traveled to a country where a foreign language was spoken. Without access to a common language and without the services of an interpreter, you might very well have relied on gestures to obtain information.

Neurology

Where in the brain is language located? Pierre Paul Broca determined that the left side of the brain had primary control of speech in right-handed people. Recent experiments show that for the right-handed majority the primary language function is located on the left side of the brain and the secondary one on the right side.[23] The left side of the brain is thought to be more accessible to meaningful auditory stimuli, the right to pictorial materials.[24]

How does this relate to sign language? Because ASL operates in a visual-spatial medium, and spatial operations appear located in the right hemisphere, a reasonable hypothesis would be that damage to the right hemisphere will affect signing ability. That, however, is not the case. Signers with damage to the right hemisphere showed "severe spatial disorganization, were unable to indicate perspective, and neglected the left side of space, reflecting the classic visuospatial impairments seen in hearing patients with right hemisphere-damage."[25] Yet these same signers were not aphasic, in that they showed no impairment of their language abilities. Signers with damage in the left hemisphere on the other hand "were not impaired in nonlanguage visuospatial tasks, but were very impaired in language functions."[26] Deaf signers who had damage in the right side of their brain did not show any linguistic or signing deficits, while deaf signers with left-brain damage revealed severely impaired language functions.[27] Such studies provide further support to the claims for sign languages as true languages. As one prominent group of researchers conclude, "[T]he left hemisphere . . . is dominant for sign language, even

Why Study the Origin of Language?

In uncovering the mysteries of ASL and other sign languages we may be contributing to our understanding of how language became such an invaluable part of our existence, how it took its present shape, and how we might continue to shape it more effectively in the future. The anthropologist Gordon Hewes has summed up the arguments for more intensive study of this topic.

> The problem of language origins is one of the most important in the study of human evolution, not only because the use of language is the sharpest behavioral difference between man and other animals, but because language underlies so much of human cultural achievement, including man's efforts to understand the world.[29]

though processing sign language involves processing spatial relations at all linguistic levels."[28]

Prehistoric Communication

One critical aspect of anatomy is posture. Until an organism is erect, it must use its four appendages for mobility; so chimpanzees are considered especially good subjects for learning sign language, but other apes are not because they propel themselves on all fours. When hominids (including humans) became erect, their hands were freed for tool use as well as communication. Consequently, anthropologists regard the onset of *homo erectus* as a probable date for the beginning of sign language.

The conditions surrounding early humans also had to affect their choice of a language modality. When they hunted on relatively open plains, it is safe to assume they could and would use signs. They could see each other, and the silent communication would not alert their prey. But when they entered the woods or hunted in high grass, verbal signals may well have become more important. To communicate in sign requires good visual conditions, adequate light, and unobstructed views.

Of course, there is no convincing reason to believe that using gesture precluded using speech or vice versa. The factors favoring and shaping language development are likely to be complex: acting, reacting, and interacting. In prehistoric times, as now, people probably used both speech and gesture. Whether or not their use of gestures reached the stage of formal language, permitting full communication without vocalization, is an unanswered and, likely, unanswerable question. Although some evidence supports the notion that sign languages have existed among humans since very early times, the crucial data, the unequivocal findings, have not yet appeared.

Sign Language: B.C. through the Middle Ages

Aristotle's assessment of the effects of being deaf cursed deaf people for two thousand years. Reasoning that speech and language are one and the same, Aristotle concluded that those who could not speak were unteachable. Children who were deaf at birth were often exposed to the elements and left to die by the ancient Greeks, and deaf children's minds were similarly left unexplored by other nations influenced by Aristotle.[30]

Aristotle's influence on attitudes toward deaf people extended well beyond Hellenic culture. Rome, for one, denied citizenship to individuals who were born deaf. The ancient Hebrews denied full religious standing to deaf people who did not speak. The proscriptions were largely parentalistic, an attempt to keep unscrupulous people from taking advantage of those presumed to be intellectually incapable of managing their own affairs. Thus, in the Talmud, Jews who are born deaf are lumped together with mentally retarded persons in the category of those who cannot legally make a contract. Such laws must be considered in their two-thousand-year-old context: they were promulgated at a time when deaf children were not educated. The attempt to circumvent the exploitation of deaf people made them, in effect, wards of the state, with all the protections intended by that status. Today, most Jewish religious liberals ignore or reinterpret this bit of tradition. Deaf Israelis are educated in excellent facilities and enjoy the benefits of citizenship, much as deaf people do in Greece and Italy.

The benefits of sign language were not unknown at this time. The thinking of Aristotle (384–322 B.C.) was in large part influenced by the Greek philosopher Plato (428–348 B.C.) who in turn was a student of Socrates (470–399 B.C.). It was Socrates who, upon contemplating language in the absence of speech, stated: "If we had neither voice nor tongue, and yet wished to manifest things to one another, should we not, like those which are at present mute, endeavor to signify our meaning by the hands, head, and other parts of the body?"[31] Whether Aristotle was aware of this observation or not, it is unfortunate that through much of written history, positive observations about sign language and deaf people tended to be shuffled into obscurity by the weight given to negative observations.

While attitudes toward those who could not hear and did not speak were, from our perspective, harsh in those early days, sign language had gained (or regained) a fair measure of acceptance. Luigi Romeo points out that records exist of signs used by religious orders during the twelfth century and even earlier. Recognizing the difficulties of obtaining and translating ancient texts, Romeo nonetheless believes that "sporadic studies so far have not yet tapped what could be a cache of treatises on gesture languages used during the Graeco-Roman era of inquiry and even more productively during the Middle Ages. A systematic investigation would uncover a gold mine of texts, which in part could contribute to the understanding of the nature of signs and their 'universals' as well as of 'diachronic' generalities, at least for Western cultures."[32]

The Renaissance

Not until the sixteenth century did educators call into question the wisdom of Aristotle. The Italian physician Girolamo Cardano is not known to have treated a single deaf patient himself, but in his writings he countered the Aristotelian dogma on the status of being deaf. His influence in contrast to that of the mighty Greek philosopher was inconsequential, so our mention of Cardano is rather to acknowledge his courage, historically, than to mark any great accomplishments on his part. Still, he set forth what might have been a Magna Carta for deaf people when he said that "the mute can hear by reading and speak by writing."[33] Putting those revolutionary ideas into practice fell to the credit of two Spanish priests, Juan Pablo Bonet and Pedro Ponce de León.

Silent religious orders have used some form of signed communication for centuries. Originally developed as signals for particular situations, over time these signs have begun to take the shape of formal languages. Robert Barakat has studied communication in Cistercian monasteries, in which silence is a required part of life but in which signs have been permitted since at least A.D. 328.[34] The resulting sign language is a peculiar mixture of natural and arbitrary characteristics, some aspects resembling sign languages in general, and others the spoken language of the country in which a particular monastery is situated. The existence of sign language in religious retreats eventually led to modern education for deaf children.

Signs of the Cistercian Monks

Cistercian monks still take vows of silence and, like every sign language in the world, theirs is undergoing changes and additions to expedite their conversations about a world that differs from the past as well as to accommodate new terms that have crept into their spoken language. Cistercians have combined the sign for RED and HORSE to indicate TRACTOR; BULL and PUSH to get BULL-DOZER—two things they didn't have to worry about one thousand years or even two hundred years ago. Cistercian signs can also get complicated, as in the production of the sign for STAR, which is the sequence of the signs LITTLE + NIGHT + TIME + LIGHT + UP. And perhaps in a moment of good humor, the Cistercian sign for "Oh dear" was conceived as the compound sign for the letter O and the sign for DEER.[35]

A silent environment, such as the Cistercian monasteries provided in ancient times, made a hospitable residence for deaf children. However, with the evidence contained in written historical documents at hand, the conjunction of those virtues produced no known benefits in the education of deaf children until the middle of the sixteenth century.

Pedro Ponce de León entered the Monastery of San Salvador de Oña in 1526. Inadvertently, in 1545 the monastery became the first school for deaf children in recorded history. That year, the powerful head of a well-placed Castilian family, the Marquis Juan Fernández de Velasco, brought his two deaf sons to live at the monastery. Don Pedro was about eight years old, and his brother Don Francisco was about twelve. Their parents had eight children, five of whom were deaf. The three deaf girls all spent their lives in convents. Placing their deaf children in these religious retreats served to prevent their procreating and to put them out of sight. When their father placed Pedro and Francisco in the monastery, he very likely had no plans, no hopes, for their education. But the kindly priest Ponce de León almost immediately and instinctively took charge of them and began their education.

Ponce de León wrote a book describing his methods, but the manuscript—which was never published—was lost, possibly burned or mislaid in some storehouse of ancient documents. All that is known (based on a great deal of supporting evidence) is that he succeeded. Both of the deaf boys learned to read and to speak—Francisco who died at an early age, spoke a little; Pedro, who lived past thirty years of age, not only spoke, he reportedly sang in the monastery choir! He also read and wrote, not only Spanish, but also Latin and to a lesser degree Greek. After hearing of Ponce de León's success, many noble families brought their deaf sons to the monastery.

Secondhand reports (one from the physician to Spain's King Philip II) confirm that Ponce de León began his pupils' education with instruction in reading using fingerspelling. A fingerspelled alphabet was already available to Ponce de León in his religious order. After establishing the concepts of language he attempted to teach his students to speak. Not all did so, but all who are known to have studied with him did gain some competence in Spanish, at least. It is almost certain that Ponce de León used signs, as they also were a part of the monastic environment. An eleventh-century text, Wilhelm's *Constitutiones Hirsaugienses*, gives directions for making over four hundred signs. In one of the rare surviving documents that he is known to have written, Ponce de León told what, but not how, he taught his deaf charges ("the sons and daughters of great noblemen and important people"):

> I taught them how to read and write, count, pray, serve at Mass, understand the Christian doctrine, confess orally, and to some Latin and others Latin and Greek and to one even Italian. . . . Besides, they were very knowledgeable in the history of Spain and other lands and they made use of the doctrine, politics and the discipline that Aristotle denied them.[36]

Those last words, "the discipline that Aristotle denied them," indicate Ponce de León's awareness of his iconoclasm. He challenged established wisdom. When he died, after serving fifty-eight years as a monk, he was accorded honors usually reserved for heads of monasteries. On his headstone is the inscription, "Here lies the venerable Fray Pedro Ponce worthy of eternal remembrance for the gift bestowed upon him by God of making the mutes speak."

The pioneering work of Ponce de León might have gone to waste had it not been for another Spanish priest, Juan Pablo Bonet. Bonet did publish his methods, and that work survives to this day. Like his predecessor, Bonet drew his pupils from the noble and wealthy families of Spain. He taught them to read, speechread, and speak. To do so, he used fingerspelling and signs. In fact, the fingerspelled alphabet that he used is little changed to this day (see chapter 3). Though Ponce de León holds precedence in the education of deaf children, Bonet's work is more widely recognized because of his publications.[37]

Instructional methods have been altered over the last three centuries. What survives—the great legacy—is the faith of Cardano, Ponce de León, and Bonet in the ability of deaf persons to acquire language. Not necessarily speech, but definitely language. The intellectual courage of these Renaissance men stands as a bulwark against the Aristotelian views of the capabilities of deaf people. Their labors on behalf of deaf people produced encouraging results, results we seek to emulate to this day. Their message was that a hearing loss per se does not preclude language development, a message that spread from Italy and Spain into France, Germany, and England, and eventually to the United States.

From the Eighteenth Century to 1880

The name that lightens the darkness surrounding the education of deaf children is that of another priest, a Frenchman named Charles Michel de l'Epée. His interest in the education of deaf people arose from a chance visit to a parishioner. The lady was not at home when he arrived, but her twin daughters indicated that he might wait for her in the parlor. Perhaps, trying to strike up a conversation, Epée was unable to get any vocal response from either of the girls. Upon returning home, the mother quickly, and gladly, dispelled the mystery: both girls were deaf. Seeing his curiosity and having no one else to turn to for help, the mother, who was very poor, implored Epée to undertake her daughters' education. He did, and he changed the historical course of deaf education.[38]

Epée's classical education was coupled with an inventive turn of mind. He questioned the established wisdom that said deaf children could not be taught and concluded that "the natural language of the deaf is the language of sign; nature and their different wants are their only tutors in it; and they have no other language as long as they have no other instructors."[39]

But Epée did not know sign language. What was he to do—create one? A common myth holds that he did just that. One author declared:

> Abbe de l'Epee, "Father of the Deaf," devoted his life to their needs, but only accidentally hit upon the idea for an alphabet and sign language. . . .
> He created a language of signs and spent his life teaching his deaf pupils

how to express ideas through this medium. When he died in 1789 his work
was continued by the Abbé Sicard, who improved his ideas and developed
new signs to perfect the language of symbols." [40]

To the contrary deaf people were not waiting, without a language, for
someone to come along and invent a sign language for them. The truth be
known, Epée studied the signs already being used by deaf Parisians. That
was his genius, recognizing that deaf people were communicating without
speech. He gathered a group of deaf people together, including his two
young charges. With their assistance Epée developed a signed version of
spoken French. He called the way he signed Methodical Signs, which
some scholars today refer to as Manual French.[41]

His insight into communication enabled him to see that a thought can
be represented by an arbitrary sign as readily as by a spoken word, but he
failed to see that the deaf Parisians had more than signs, they had a language. Missing that point, Epée imposed French grammar on the selected
group of signs. Even if he had realized that French Sign Language had a
distinct grammar, he might not have changed his approach. We are all
vigorous proponents of our own language, of its beauty, its expressiveness,
its inherent correctness. Such an attitude merely reflects the human condition, and we have no reason to doubt that it afflicted Epée.

Whatever one may think of Epée's educational strategy, a review of the
historical record will show that he astonished his countrymen and many
learned people throughout Europe by the performance of his deaf students. Epée held demonstrations for educators and government officials
from foreign countries. His pupils showed they had learned French, and
the Abbé would expound on the likelihood that they could learn any other
language by applying his instructional techniques. History records that
the demonstrations stirred great excitement.

Epée's fame spread to other nations in Europe, and they sent scholars
to learn his methods. In turn, some of Epée's disciples traveled to other
lands where they established schools. They opened schools in Holland,
Poland, Sweden, and Ireland, to name a few, but not England or Scotland.
That detour around Britain is another story, and it will give us the solution
to a seeming paradox (that deaf persons from the United States find it
easier to communicate with deaf French people than with deaf English
persons). But let us trace the French lineage a bit further before we look at
some other countries and eventually at our own.

Epée was well along in years when he began his work with deaf pupils.

Abbé de l'Epée

Lane (1984), a psycholinguistic researcher, pays tribute to the Abbé de l'Epée as follows.

> Why do we revere him? Because he did two things that are terribly important: first, because he was a priest, and because he was concerned with the poor, he saw that he would have to bring the deaf together to educate them. . . . And as a by-product, he created the deaf community. He created the essential circumstances in which a language could develop. Not because he understood this necessity, but for an adventitious reason. . . . If Epée's first accomplishment was the formation of a deaf community, his second was to call attention to that community. . . . He held public demonstrations in which the deaf transcribed the signs that he dictated into French, Italian, Spanish, and, of course, Latin, the language of the church. These demonstrations brought about a tremendous flurry of efforts in behalf of the deaf. This was a time when mental retardation was believed untreatable; when deafness and the ignorance of the deaf were considered similarly invincible; and here was a man who taught the deaf to converse in the tongues of the world, or so it would appear to the casual observer. The casual observer included kings and princes and emissaries from throughout the world.

We must, however, make a clarification to Lane's assessment of Epée's influence. Deaf communities have always existed. French Sign Language was available for Epée to learn because it had evolved within the Deaf communities in Paris and elsewhere in France. If Epée brought deaf people together, he did not create a Deaf community, he merely created the opportunity for an expansion of an already existing Deaf community. In much the same way, a technology company that hires one hundred deaf people to work in a large new plant in a remote area has not created the Deaf community.

Soon it was necessary to find a successor. Among his teachers at the Institut National de Sourds-Muets (National Institute for Deaf-Mutes) was Roche-Ambroise Cucurron Sicard. Sicard had come to the school from Bordeaux, and he quickly earned the reputation of a brilliant teacher. His most adept pupil was a deaf shepherd named Jean Massieu. Sicard wrote that, as he taught Massieu the formal signs developed by Epée, Massieu taught Sicard French Sign Language. Sicard carried Epée's procedures a critical step further, from learning a sign system designed to represent the grammar of spoken French to learning sign language, the lexicon and grammar of the Deaf community.

All of this revolution in the education of deaf children was taking place amidst a political revolt. The French National Assembly had declared Epée's school a national institution in 1782. Sicard, however, soon fell from grace. About 1796, during the Reign of Terror, he was seized by the mob and dragged before a tribunal. Sicard had little defense against the charge that he was a counterrevolutionary. He was jailed to await the guillotine. Then appeared Massieu with a plea in the form of a touching petition. The following translation preserves the eloquence of Massieu, who was deaf from birth and did not receive formal education until he was twelve years old.

> Mr. President, the deaf and dumb have had their instructor, guardian angel, and their father taken from them. He has been locked in prison like a thief, a criminal, but he has killed no one, he has stolen nothing. He is not a bad citizen. His whole time is spent in instructing us, in teaching us to love virtue and our country. He is good, just, and pure. We ask for his freedom. Restore him to his children for we are his. He loves us like a father. He has taught us all we know. Without him we would be like animals. Since he has been taken away we are sad and distressed. Return him to us and you will make us happy.[42]

Upon hearing the petition read by the clerk, the National Assembly rose to its collective feet and cheered. The vote to release Sicard was pro forma. Unlike a stage play, however, the story does not end there. In those chaotic days the order of the highest legislative body was ignored. Sicard was saved from beheading, but his discharge from prison occurred a week and a number of misadventures later. He did at last appear before a revolutionary committee that recognized him as a teacher of deaf students and arranged for his safe return to the school and his grateful students. The experience understandably scarred Sicard, so when Napoleon returned from Elba, Sicard took his two best pupils on a tour outside France. He was in London when a young clergyman from Connecticut came to hear his lecture. The meeting forged the French connection in the education of deaf children in the United States.

Thomas Hopkins Gallaudet, the Connecticut clergyman, had sailed to Europe at the request of Mason Fitch Cogswell, a successful Hartford physician who had a young deaf daughter, Alice. Untrained as a teacher,

Gallaudet had nevertheless made some progress instructing Alice. Her father was determined to open a school for deaf children, and he sent Gallaudet to England because that was the natural place from which to borrow culture. Furthermore, a Scotsman named Braidwood had established a school for deaf children in Edinburgh, and it was his reputation that provided the specific attraction. The Braidwood method followed the tradition that depended on teaching speech and speechreading. When Gallaudet arrived to learn the procedures, Braidwood proved ungenerous; he refused to permit Gallaudet to observe his methods unless Gallaudet agreed to sign on as a teacher for three years or to enter into a partnership with Braidwood to open a similar school in the United States. Disappointed, Gallaudet was in London contemplating his return to Hartford empty-handed when he saw an advertisement for a lecture by Sicard.

Unlike Braidwood, Sicard was generous. He invited Gallaudet to join him in Paris, where, because Napoleon had been defeated and the monarchy restored, Sicard would return to reopen his school. Gallaudet had read about Sicard's methods, so when it was indicated that Sicard would not charge for instructing him, Gallaudet accepted the invitation. In doing so, he allied the United States with France and Ireland, which also adopted the use of sign language for instructional purposes—in contradistinction to England and Scotland, which chose Braidwood's oral method.

Gallaudet remained in Paris about five months. When he prepared to return to America, he invited Laurent Clerc, one of Sicard's best teachers, to emigrate to Connecticut. Sicard approved of the plan, insisting only that Gallaudet give Clerc a written contract for his projected services.

Clerc brought to America the teaching methods of Sicard and the visible evidence of their success, as well as the notion that signed communication should have a prominent role in the education of deaf children.[43] Clerc himself was deaf. His remarkable development as a scholar undoubtedly had a strong positive effect on the New Englanders who met or heard about him. The visit by Clerc and Gallaudet to the Connecticut legislature resulted in that body's enactment of the first public support for special education in the United States—a grant to the Hartford school of five thousand dollars. Added to private donations, that sum enabled Gallaudet in 1817 to open a school in Hartford. It survives to this day and is now called the American School for the Deaf.

Clerc and Gallaudet's place in the history of deaf education has been unwittingly associated with the introduction of sign language to the United States. History is very generous in rewarding those whose work has been documented in print. Sign language, lacking a written component, may have disinclined deaf people from recording their place in history. Like those cultures that rely on oral history, deaf people passed on their legacies, folklores, and culture from one generation to another through sign language. Thus, the sign language that Clerc and Gallaudet brought did not fill a vacuum. Deaf people in the United States already used ASL. Deaf immigrants from European countries brought their native signs. These collided with each other and possibly with the signs of native Americans, resulting in early versions of ASL.

Martha's Vineyard

One such version was found on Martha's Vineyard, an island off the coast of Massachusetts. Martha's Vineyard was settled about 1640 by a small group of English immigrants, who intermarried with the native Wampanoag Indians. The birthrates over the next hundred and fifty years were unusually high, with families often having up to twenty children. Many of the numerous offspring were deaf. In fact, so many were deaf that deafness itself was not thought noteworthy. Nora Groce studied the island population and reported:

> Vineyarders themselves, used to a sizable deaf population, saw nothing unusual in this, and many assumed that all communities had a similar number of deaf members. Almost nothing exists in the written records to indicate who was or was not deaf, and indeed, only a passing reference made by an older islander directed my attention to the fact that there had been any deaf there at all.[44]

With as many as one in twenty-five persons deaf, how did the islanders adjust? The answer is beautifully summed up by one eighty-year-old resident interviewed by Groce: "Oh, there was no problem at all. You see, everyone here spoke sign language."

A complete reconstruction of the sign language used on Martha's Vineyard is being attempted and, while this may never be fully accomplished, the reconstruction so far makes it clear that it was unlike French Sign Language or mainland ASL. It appears that the sign language of Martha's Vineyard, like the culture of the inhabitants of the island, had developed in isolation and created unique elements. This phenomenon was repeated in countless other communities all over the country where deaf people congregated. Clearly, deaf people in the United States were using sign language long before the importation of French Sign Language.

That deaf people in the United States signed before the school at Hartford was founded does not reduce that school's impact on the further development of sign language. The school created an environment where sign language was used for social as well as educational purposes. It promoted the hiring of deaf teachers fluent in the use of ASL. It exposed new generations of deaf children to sign language and Deaf culture. All of these factors contributed to the standardizing of ASL, promoting its use and popularizing the education of deaf children. Before Hartford only sporadic attempts had been made to open schools for deaf children. After Hartford was established, schools quickly sprang up in the neighboring states: in New York in 1820, in Massachusetts in 1821, in Pennsylvania in 1822, and in Ohio and Kentucky in 1823. Today, the education of deaf children is mandated by federal law and extends throughout the United States, in public and private schools, benefiting more than sixty thousand deaf students.[45]

Shortly after the Hartford school was founded, Gallaudet left in a dispute with the trustees. Clerc, however, remained for more than forty years. He not only instructed deaf students, he was also responsible for teaching sign language to new teachers and to those from other institutions who desired to learn it. His influence and, through him, the influence of Epée and Sicard on the development of ASL must have been great. To some extent, the reverse must also have been true: Clerc learned ASL from the deaf people he met here. Thus, the ASL of today has demonstrable French origins, but the prevailing structure is probably more of a local outgrowth than an import from Paris. Clerc early abandoned the methodical approach of Epée for the grammar of ASL. His decision to concentrate on educational use of ASL predates today's recognition by deaf educators that their strength as teachers lies in their instructional use of sign language. As will be shown later, the use of sign language in schools has faced many roadblocks, but ASL's place in the Deaf community has remained constant.[46]

Gallaudet University

No history of sign language is complete without reference to Gallaudet University, still the only liberal arts university for deaf students in the world. The founder of the university was Edward Miner Gallaudet, the son of Thomas Hopkins Gallaudet and a deaf mother, Sophia Fowler. Edward came to Washington, D.C., at twenty years of age to head a school for deaf children established by a politician turned philanthropist, Amos Kendall. In May 1857 Kendall brought Edward Gallaudet and his mother to Washington. Edward's mother was essential to the arrangement, because Kendall did not feel it proper to entrust the living arrangements of the deaf students of both sexes to a young unmarried man. Sophia Fowler Gallaudet had been a student at the American School for the Deaf; she married Thomas upon her graduation. Sophia Fowler Gallaudet has received little credit from historians for her probable role in starting the Kendall School and inspiring her son to struggle for an institution of higher learning for deaf persons, as well as adding her much-needed skills in ASL and knowledge of Deaf culture to her son's first educational effort. Without her, in effect, that early elementary school might not have survived nor, consequently, would its role as the seed bed for the university have been fulfilled.

Amos Kendall

A chance encounter with a man who was putting deaf children on display to raise money for a school marked Amos Kendall's introduction to the education of deaf children. According to Kendall,

> An adventurer brought to this city (in 1856) five partially educated deaf mute children whom he had picked up in the state of New York, and commenced exhibiting them to our citizens in their houses and places of business. He professed a desire to set up an institution for the education of unfortunates of that class in the District of Columbia, raised considerable sums of money and gathered a school of about sixteen pupils.
>   Apparently to give respectability and permanence to his school, he sought and obtained the consent of some of our leading citizens, to become its trustees. It soon appeared, however, that he had no idea of accountability to them, and only wanted their names to aid him in collecting money to be used at his discretion. On being informed by the trustees that such an irresponsible system was inadmissible [*sic*] he repudiated them altogether. In the meantime the impression had gone abroad that he mistreated the children, and it led to an investigation in court, ending in the children being taken from him and restored to their parents, except the five from abroad, who having no parents or none who seemed to care what became of them, were bound to me by the orphans court and formed the nucleus of our institution.[47]

In 1864, with the United States still torn by civil strife, Edward Miner Gallaudet prevailed on Congress to charter the National Deaf Mute College, a name later changed to Gallaudet College in honor of Thomas Hopkins Gallaudet.[48] President Abraham Lincoln signed the act on 8 April 1864. From that date to this, Gallaudet University has been the bastion of ASL in the United States. Edward Miner Gallaudet believed that the accomplishments of the college and of its graduates clearly proved the worth of sign language in the education of deaf students. He remained president of the college until March 1910, a distinguished career of fifty-three years' duration. (For further discussion about Gallaudet University see chapter 7.)

1880: Sign Language's Nemesis

The use of sign language in deaf education has been challenged throughout its history. For some educators, such as Bonet in the sixteenth century, signs and the fingerspelled alphabet were coupled with the teaching of speech and speechreading. Since the seventeenth century and until the second half of the twentieth century, Germany and England had strong oral education programs, where speech was the major means of communication. Proponents of the oral approach also accepted the educability of deaf children and quarreled with advocates of sign language on how best to proceed with this education. The Abbé de l'Epée was involved in long debates by mail with the German educator Samuel Heinecke on the educational roles of sign and speech.[49] Wherever deaf children were educated, the issue was joined: speech versus sign. The opposition came to a head at the International Congress held in Milan, Italy, in 1880. That gathering saw the culmination of many earlier attacks on signed communication. The meetings were attended by the leading educators of the day. They passed a resolution that affirmed "the incontestable superiority of articulation in restoring the deaf-mute to Society and giving him a fuller knowledge of language."[50] After the vote favoring the oral approach, a delegate rose and proclaimed, *"Vive la parole!"*

Following the Milan congress, teaching speech became the educational goal, not only in Europe, but in the United States as well. Teaching language became of secondary importance to teaching speech, a distinction not then acknowledged. American schools that had formerly used ASL bowed to the wisdom from Milan, and sign language faded as a leading instructional tool. At the turn of the century, at another congress—this time in Paris—Edward Miner Gallaudet again sought a compromise, as he had in Milan. He proposed that instructional methods be tailored to suit the deaf person's needs and abilities, thus supporting both oral and sign language approaches. His efforts to resolve the conflict failed by a vote of seven for and one hundred against.

Deaf people in the United States quickly responded to the challenge from Milan. In August 1880 the National Association of the Deaf (NAD) came into being. The deaf leaders from the Deaf community who called that first meeting had in mind the continuing use of ASL in instruction and, equally important, the maintaining of positions for deaf teachers in schools for deaf children. If speech became the principal goal, it was felt, then deaf teachers' jobs would be in jeopardy. And the decline in the number of deaf teachers after 1900 proved that prediction sadly correct.

The NAD stands as its own affirmation of ASL. It is an organization of deaf people, not just for deaf people. In its more than one-hundred-year existence, the NAD has fought for the rights of deaf people, not only in education but in all aspects of life. That it has remained viable for so long testifies to its success in achieving its objectives. Among these are the defense of ASL and the encouragement of its development as the principal language of communication within the Deaf community in the United States.[51]

The opposition to sign language that the NAD faced was centered around the unproved supposition that if severely and profoundly deaf children learn to communicate in sign, they will not learn to speak because signing is easy for them to learn and speech is difficult. But research shows that what sign language seems to have done for deaf children is to aid their acquisition of language skills, spoken and signed.[52]

In summary, the educational use of sign language has always faced opposition. The Milan agreement merely tilted the arguments in favor of speech as a primary goal for deaf children. Time has not done away with these arguments. The unfortunate aspect is that the deaf child becomes a pawn in the hands of "experts" on both sides.

1960: The Return of Sign Language

From 1880 to 1960 the use of sign language in schools was in general suppressed. To appreciate that suppression from the educator's side, consider the opening remarks of the keynote speaker at a symposium on British Sign Language held in England in April 1980: "We are now at last—

Schools for Deaf Children and the Deaf Community

It is illuminating to correlate the emergence of organizations of Deaf people with the establishment of their schools. In the United States there is no record of any organization of deaf adults before 1817. The New England Association of the Deaf was founded in 1837, twenty years after the first permanent school for deaf students opened in Hartford, Connecticut. The U.S. Congress chartered the National Deaf Mute College (later renamed Gallaudet College and later still Gallaudet University) in 1864. Springing up in the same vicinity just sixteen years later was the National Association of the Deaf.

These two instances illustrate the general pattern of the emergence of organizations of deaf people. A school for deaf children is erected. Deaf children are drawn to it from all over a state or region,[53] as are deaf people seeking positions as teachers, residential staff, kitchen staff, and the like. The presence of a growing number of deaf persons leads to the call for some sort of mechanism to organize gatherings and exchange information. Lack of equal rights in the nineteenth century and most of the twentieth century increased the urgency for these organizations. Every group has its budding leaders and, for starters, why not use school facilities as a home base for meetings, sports, and other social gatherings? Add a name and a slate of officers, and there you have it: a new homestead for the Deaf community. Once established, Deaf organizations attract more deaf people to the area seeking employment so that they might enjoy the company of their own kind.

or perhaps once again—at a point of history in Britain when it is reasonably safe to discuss the use of sign language with most educators."[54] The choice of the phrase "reasonably safe to discuss" conveys the chill on positions contrary to the established one, especially disturbing in a twentieth-century democracy like Great Britain. But the advocates of oral approaches were neither more nor less devoted to the education of deaf children than those who approved of the use of sign. Their influence came from the use of speech as the foundation of their educational approach, which appealed more to the majority culture. Even schools that used sign language emphasized their efforts to teach deaf students to speak and speechread. For many years deaf children and their parents were made to feel that using sign language was a bad thing. Yet appreciating ASL as a true language and not simply a system for rendering English in signs is a critical step for deaf people in developing pride in who they are and the language they use. Until this step is taken, the "stigma of the deaf person is intimately related to his or her language," and the "deaf person can sometimes pass until he starts to sign." [55]

The change in attitude toward sign language began in 1960. That is the year William Stokoe published *Sign Language Structure*, a monograph presenting the then-novel thesis that sign language was indeed a language, not a coding system for the manual representation of a spoken language. In 1964 Stokoe and his associates released the now-classic *Dictionary of American Sign Language*. That second work hammered into place the position of ASL, a place secure from logical lexical assault. The impact of those two works on the Deaf community was substantial. They generated an entirely new approach to studying sign language. The improved status of ASL reflected favorably on the self-image of the Deaf community: its sign language had equal status with spoken languages; what its members preferred was legitimate; hence, they themselves were legitimized. William Stokoe's work made significant contributions to the linguistic uniqueness of sign language. But initially, deaf people did not see it that way.

Reflecting on his earlier experiences, Stokoe confided to his colleagues how his research was received at Gallaudet University, where he was a professor of English when he published his seminal works.

This, of course, was only the comedy's first act curtain. Publication in 1960 [of *Sign Language Structure*, Occasional Paper 8] brought a curious local reaction. With the exception of Dean Detmold and one or two close colleagues, the entire Gallaudet College faculty rudely attacked me, linguistics, and the study of signing as a language. My function was to teach English, they told me in a meeting to which I had been invited to talk about the occasional paper. If the reception of the first linguistic study of a Sign Language of the deaf community was chilly at home, it was cryogenic in a large part of special education—at that time a closed corporation as hostile to Sign Language as [it was] ignorant of linguistics. Even the general public joined in the outcry. One instance: When the National Science Foundation first granted support for research in Sign Language two letters attacking the foundation, the grant, and the research purpose appeared in the *Washington Post*. Both letter writers, descendants of A. G. Bell, based their objec-

The Father of Sign Language Research

In a tribute to William Stokoe, the first person to do a linguistic analysis of sign language, Gilbert Eastman (1980, 32), a deaf playwright, wrote the following.

> Dr. Stokoe taught me to be aware of Sign Language and to appreciate its beauty. I developed basic Sign Language courses, wrote plays, and went all over the country to conduct workshops on Visual-Gestural Communication and to give speeches about my work. But it was Bill Stokoe who helped me to develop pride in my language and my activities, and it was he who encouraged me to tell the truth. Dr. Stokoe is not a fluent signer, yet he has never stopped learning our Sign Language. Dr. Stokoe was the first linguistic researcher in ASL, and he became an internationally known advocate of deaf people and Sign Language. We should all honor him as the Father of Sign Language linguistics.

tions on the claim that grandfather had proved once for all that Sign Language is useless and pernicious in the education of the deaf.[56]

Linguists, however, respected what Stokoe had done—not all of them, to be sure, but in sufficient numbers to encourage him to continue.

At the one-hundredth anniversary of the NAD's founding, the Deaf community officially made amends for its earlier opposition. Stokoe was given a tribute most fitting for his accomplishments and most suited to his personality: his students and friends secretly prepared a *Festschrift*, a collection of essays published in his honor, *Sign Language and the Deaf Community*. The essays all begin with sketches by the authors recounting their experiences with this great teacher and researcher. Truly, a fitting tribute to a linguistic pioneer.

Notes

1. Reconstructing unrecorded historical events is prone to leading to a bevy of divergent thinking and lively debates. But the theories that arise from these deliberations are worth noting not only for their insights as to how our ancient forebears might have communicated, but also because the inferences embedded in them reveal much about the people making them. Not too long ago, origins of language focused solely on spoken languages. Today, gestures as a precursor to spoken languages are gaining support. For discussions about the origins of lan-

guage and the role of gestures see Caselli 1990; Hewes 1974a; Stokoe 1987, 1991; Volterra 1983; Volterra, Beronesi, and Massoni 1990; Volterra and Caselli 1985; and Wescott 1974.

2. Hewes 1974b, 14, reasoned that "the onset of serious manual gesture communication would have had to wait until our ancestors were mostly bipedal." That point explains why some researchers interested in animal communication prefer chimpanzees to gorillas, since the latter tend to keep their hands in contact with the ground to balance themselves when in motion. For a detailed treatment of early hominid anatomy in relation to language, see Hill 1974.

3. Additional references may be found in the bibliography appended to Wescott 1974.

4. DeFrancis 1989.

5. Fouts and Mellgren 1976, 342. In Van Cantfort and Rimpau 1982 the authors came to the same general conclusion from their positions as comparative psychologists. They urged greater rigor in the design and analysis of animal communication studies.

6. Terrace 1979.

7. Gaustad 1981.

8. Terrace 1982, 179–80.

9. Gaustad 1982, 181.

10. M. Muller 1861. *Lectures on the Science of Language*. Cited in Bonvillian 1982.

11. Bonvillian 1982, 13.

12. Hill 1977, 48.

13. Gould 1975, 692.

14. Sarles 1976, 167. Commenting on another controversial experiment in animal communication, a linguist writes, "A further telling, if oblique, bit of evidence comes from Gill and Rumbaugh (1974), who report that it took Lana 1,600 trials to learn the names for banana and M&M, but that the next five items were acquired in less than five trials each—two of them in two only. This stunning and instantaneous increment is inexplicable in terms of Lana's having 'learned how to learn' in the course of those 1,600 trials; learning curves just don't jump like that. It is much more plausible to suppose that for a long time Lana simply couldn't figure out what her trainers were trying to do, and then suddenly it clicked: 'My God, they're feeding me concept names—why couldn't they have *told* me, the dummies?' The concepts had been there all the while, and only the link between them and these mysterious new things that people were doing to her needed to be forged." (Bickerton 1981, 236).

15. Refer to the discussion of children's acquisition of sign language in chapter 2. Bonvillian, Orlansky, Novack, and Folven 1983; Newport and Meier 1986; and Schlesinger and Meadow 1972 reported on extensive data on young deaf children's communication behavior. See also Siple and Akamatsu 1991, a study of language acquisition in a fraternal set of twins where one child was deaf and the other was hearing.

16. Brown 1973, 97.

17. Shore et al. 1990, 82.

18. Woodward 1987, 383.
19. Volterra and Erting 1990.
20. Caselli and Volterra 1990.
21. Kushel 1973.
22. Hewes 1974a, 28.
23. Kinsbourne 1981.
24. Lambert 1981, 19.
25. Bellugi et al. 1990, 297.
26. *Ibid.*, 298.
27. Poizner, Klima, and Bellugi 1987.
28. Bellugi et al., 298.
29. Hewes 1977, 97.
30. In Bender 1981, the author translates Aristotle's comment: "Those who become deaf from birth also become altogether speechless. Voice is certainly not lacking, but there is no speech," 20. She notes that later translations, glossing the Greek *eneos* (speechless) as "dumb or stupid," altered the remark to read, "Those who are born deaf all become senseless and incapable of reason," 21. Thus, the overwhelming authority of Aristotle may have been skewed by his translators, with disastrous consequences for generations of deaf people.
31. Hodgson 1954, 72–73.
32. Romeo 1978, 356.
33. Flint 1979, 22, and Silverman 1978, 423.
34. Barakat 1975.
35. All of the Cistercian monk signs mentioned here were taken from Gryski 1990.
36. Chaves and Soler 1975. Much of the history of Ponce de León noted in these pages was drawn from this source.
37. Some historians now offer Manuel Ramírez de Carrión, not Bonet, as the successor to Ponce de León. Chaves and Soler 1975 characterize Carrión as "the first one to make a living in this profession." He hid his methods of instructing deaf children so assiduously that little is directly known of what he did; but apparently he did enjoy some success, and "his method was incorporated definitely in the history of western culture only when Juan Pablo Bonet, observing the progress of Don Luis [a deaf child of nobility], and snatching information where he could [,] put the method down in writing and published it in 1620." (Chaves and Soler 1975, 244).
38. Pertinent references to the Abbé will be found in Bender 1981; Flint 1979; Lane 1976, 1977, 1984; and Silverman 1978.
39. Cited by Lane 1976, 79.
40. Neal 1960, 16–17.
41. Lane 1984.
42. Lane 1977, 4. For a slightly different version see Bender 1981, 78.
43. We may never know the signing characteristics used by Clerc because of his use of French Sign Language and his association with educators who used methodical signs. Possibly, Clerc, like most deaf people today, drew on a range of

language skills depending on the context of the communication situation he was in.

44. Groce 1980, 12. Currently, anthropologists are investigating the use of sign language in a village in Bali where it is used by both deaf and hearing individuals.

45. Like the size of the deaf population, the number of deaf schoolchildren depends on the definition used. This estimate is actually the count of students with hearing impairments issued by the U.S. Department of Education for the 1992– 93 school year.

46. Lane 1980 has compiled a detailed, step-by-step account of attempts to suppress sign in France and in the United States. It is a dismal record, occasionally lightened by brave attempts to promote the use of sign in contradiction to prevailing sentiments. He expresses some bitterness of his own in a sardonic "Acknowledgments" that he has appended to that account: "I want to thank the individuals and federal agencies, notably the National Library of Medicine and the National Endowment for the Humanities, who, by maintaining that the deaf have neither a community nor a language but only a handicap and gestures, have redoubled my efforts to trace the social history of the American Sign Language of the Deaf." (Lane 1980, 159).

47. Atwood 1964. The quotation and much of the factual material about Gallaudet University appear in its official history, prepared by then-Chairman of the Board Albert W. Atwood on the occasion of the college's one hundredth anniversary.

48. Gallaudet College attained accreditation as a university in 1986, which led to its name being changed to Gallaudet University.

49. Garnett 1968. The author has brought together and translated the correspondence between Heinecke and Epée. The letters provide a fascinating account of two brilliant, opposing intellects. Let us not mistake, however, the intentions of either of them. They were both sincere in trying to provide deaf children with the best possible education.

50. Cited by Pahz and Pahz 1978, 30.

51. The National Association of the Deaf and other organizations founded by deaf people are discussed in chapter 7.

52. Dee, Rapin, and Ruben 1982. The authors followed eleven deaf children about two years of age for twelve to eighteen months after their parents began to sign to them. Instead of impeding speech development of these young children, sign appeared to facilitate it. Furthermore, instead of finding the children's language development delayed (which is usual for congenitally deaf children of hearing parents) the investigators found the children's language at or close to the norms for their years. The latter finding is consistent with the belief that the more language one knows, the easier it is to acquire more language.

53. Not every state or province has had or now has a school for deaf children. Those that did not would send their deaf children elsewhere while picking up the tab for transportation, accommodations, meals, and tuition. These other schools were not necessarily the nearest ones available. Prior to the establishment of the

Alberta School for the Deaf in Edmonton in 1955 deaf children in Alberta would take a train to Montreal, some three thousand miles away, to attend the Montreal School for the Deaf. This was the case even though Jericho Hill School for the Deaf in Vancouver and the Manitoba School for the Deaf in Winnipeg were closer.

54. Conrad 1981, 13.

55. The quotation is in Kannapell 1975. Her personal reminiscences may be found in Kannapell 1980, 106–107. A sample: To succeed "in a hearing world, I must talk well or at least write English well. I know that I was an 'oral failure' in the eyes of those people. I did not feel good about my speech and my English skills, but I tried hard to communicate with hearing people on their terms. I limited my facial expressions and body movements, was worried about using correct English, tried to use my voice, and was anxious to end conversations with them. Hearing people in general were always interested in how well I talked or heard or wrote English. They didn't seem to be interested in making friends with me. The teachers always corrected the errors I made in writing or talking. . . . They never sat down for a moment to chat with me or other students as friends.".

56. Stokoe 1980, 266–67.

2
The Structure of Sign Language

The generic term describing the use of hands to systematically convey thoughts and feelings is *signed communication*. Sign language is one kind of signed communication. Fingerspelling, or the act of representing each letter of the alphabet by the shape of the fingers, is another. Most, if not all, sign languages of the world include fingerspelling, a topic that will be taken up in chapter 3. In schools signed codes for spoken languages exist, and they too fall under the rubric of signed communication; we cover them in chapter 4. In this chapter we focus on American Sign Language (ASL).

ASL is the most extensively researched sign language in the world, which is why we will use it as our example of sign language vocabularies and grammars. What researchers have learned about ASL's lexicon and syntax has played a major role in bilingual programs for deaf children, and a continuing flow of new information about ASL will further influence its use in education. An examination of selected ASL structures will reveal its beauty and the ingenuity with which it and other sign languages resolve problems all languages face.

What Is a Sign?

The basic semantic unit in speech is the word; the basic semantic unit in sign languages is the sign. Saying that the sign is the manual equivalent of the word, however, is not accurate. Signs may represent more general concepts, with the refined nature of the concept derived from context and nonmanual signals. The fact that investigators of sign language often treat signs as words is their interpretation; it is not inherent in sign languages as there are no words in them. Perhaps there is no immediately satisfactory alternative, but we should remind ourselves of this ethnocentricity during our concentration on sign languages and, in particular, on ASL.

A sign is a hand-movement configuration that conveys meaning. It is made up of different handshapes in various locations relative to the signer's body and cast into a wide assortment of movements. As each of these parameters changes, the meaning of the sign changes. The production of a sign can be analyzed into four basic parts: (a) the shape of the hands, (b) the orientation of the hands relative to the body and each other, (c) the movements of the hands, and (d) the location of the hands relative to the signer's body.[1] In addition to the physical production of a sign, context and information from nonmanual signals determine a sign's meaning. Among nonmanual signals are facial expression and body posture, both of which will also be discussed.

Characteristics of Handshapes

We begin with handshapes, most of which also serve as letters in the American Manual Alphabet. If you already know that alphabet, you will recognize the references by letters and numbers to handshapes in descriptions of the figures that follow. If you are not, you can refer to figures 3.1 and 3.4 in chapter 3.

A change in location, movement, or orientation while keeping the handshapes the same creates a different sign. Figures 2.1 and 2.2 demonstrate how altering the movement changes the sign. Both hands have the same shape, the H hand.[2] Figure 2.1 shows the sign NAME. The orientation of

Figure 2.1. NAME   Figure 2.2. EGG

both hands is symmetrical, with the outstretched fingers of the right hand diagonally across the outstretched fingers of the left hand, with palms facing each other. The location is the front of the body, a little above the waist. The movement is a gentle striking movement of the right hand on the left hand. Changing the movement to parting the two hands in a rapid downward-outward direction, while keeping handshape, orientation, and location the same, gives a completely different concept—the sign EGG (Figure 2.2).

Two different concepts whose signs differ only in the movement of the hand are THINK and PENNY. In each the handshape is that for signing the number 1. Both signs have the same location, about the forehead. To sign THINK, the index finger moves toward and then touches the side of the forehead (Figure 2.3). Starting with the index finger on the forehead, as in the sign THINK, and then moving the pointing hand (a closed fist with the index finger extended) out from the head produces CENT or PENNY (Figure 2.4). Using the 1 handshape but changing the location indicates YOU by pointing at the person addressed or ME by pointing the finger at the signer's chest. The same handshape sweeping a 60- to 90-degree arc to the signer's side means THEY. The 1 handshape can also be used to point out other directions—for example, UP and DOWN, both signified as one would expect by pointing upward or downward.

In ASL some handshapes have added connotations. The indexing function of the pointing hand has already been illustrated. Bent fingers often have negative connotations. The X hand (one hooked finger) or a bent V hand is associated with harsh, negative ideas. Signs made with the one-

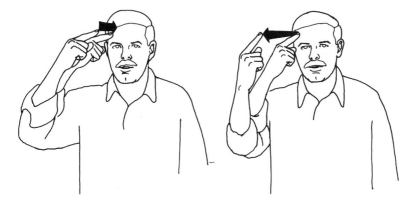

Figure 2.3. THINK   Figure 2.4. PENNY

Figure 2.5. WITCH   Figure 2.6. SUSPECT

finger X handshape and having negative connotations are WITCH (Figure 2.5) and SUSPECT (Figure 2.6). STEAL (Figure 2.7) and STRICT (Figure 2.8) are signed with the bent V hand.

The conceptual connections between certain handshapes and some cognitive-emotional categories also occur between speech sounds and cognitive-emotional concepts in spoken languages. Think about the sound *gr* in English. By itself it is an expression favored by cartoonists to signify anger: "Gr-r-r!" Its sound initiates dour words, like *gray, grief, grime, grubby,* and *grueling.*[3] These associations may be onomatopoeic, as in *buzz* and *hum,* or may have other roots. To say that such imitative speech sounds occur in English does not demean the language. The coincidence

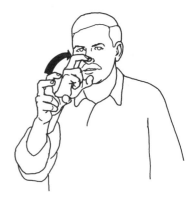

Figure 2.7. STEAL   Figure 2.8. STRICT

of affect and sound provides clues about origins to students of the language. The same holds true for handshapes and meanings in ASL. Their occurrences are noteworthy, though not definitive.

Characteristics of Orientation

The orientation of the hands—that is, the direction in which the palms face—is another important feature of a sign. In ASL, changes in orientation commonly inflect verbs by indicating subject and object. Such changes are often accompanied by a change in the direction of movement. The phrase ME-ASK-YOU (Figure 2.9) starts with the 1 handshape held in front of the body with the palm facing forward. As the hand moves ahead to complete the phrase, the index finger bends. If the palm faces you as it moves towards your body while the index finger bends, you have signed YOU-ASK-ME. Among the many other verbs that share this feature are BOTHER, BLAME, APPROACH, PICK-ON, PITY, SUMMON, HATE, and TEASE.[4]

Students learning to sign are prone to making orientation errors. Part of the problem might be their reliance on textbooks to learn ASL. Some learners find two-dimensional drawings and photographs difficult to emulate. Others find it hard to copy their instructor's signs when facing him or her. An instructor who senses this difficulty can have the students alongside her or him, facing in the same direction, so they can properly orient their signs.

ME-ASK-YOU

Figure 2.9. ME-ASK-YOU is an example of how meaning is incorporated into the orientation of the signs.

Figure 2.10. KNOW   Figure 2.11. LOVE

Characteristics of Location

The location of a sign relative to the signer's body does seem to have some regularly observed semantic relations. Cognitive signs in one way or another touch the forehead. Figure 2.10 shows the sign KNOW, which is made with an open B handshape directed toward the forehead. Signs near the heart or abdomen tend to connote emotions. The sign LOVE is made with crossed fists over the heart (Figure 2.11). To sign HATE, the middle fingers flick the thumbs as the hands execute a general throw-away movement from the chest (Figure 2.12); ANGER is signed by both hands making

Figure 2.12. HATE

Figure 2.13. ANGER

a clutching movement around the beltline, then moving sharply upward (Figure 2.13).[5]

TABOOS   ASL has some location taboos. Signs are almost never made below the waist. To do so would involve considerable effort, and the signs might be difficult to see. The nose is now freely used as a location in ASL, whereas formerly it was an area reserved for slang and obscene signs. While many ASL signs located at the nose are pejorative, Chinese Sign Language does not have similar associations. But in Chinese Sign Language, signs about the midsection have sexual-eliminative connotations. We will see in chapter 3 that this grafting of cultural implications onto signs occurs even in fingerspelled alphabets. Certain handshapes are forbidden in polite use in some cultures' sign languages and not in others.

INITIAL VERSUS FINAL   Sometimes students become confused with the starting and ending positions of a movement. Reversing the direction in which it is made can cost a sign its meaning, or it could give it an entirely different meaning. The signs JOIN and QUIT (Figure 2.14) are examples of signs that are structurally the same but whose movements are the reverse of each other. Other structurally similar signs that differ only in their starting and ending positions are OPEN/CLOSE, WHAT/ONCE, and FEEL/DISAPPOINTED.[6]

TURN-TAKING   Speakers drop their voices to signal they are through speaking. For signers the location of the hands plays a similar role in turn-

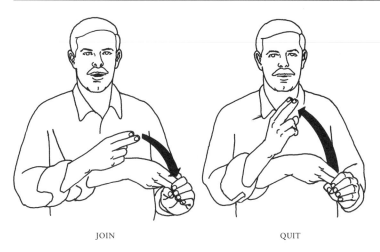

JOIN   QUIT

Figure 2.14. JOIN and QUIT are examples of signs that have the same handshape, location, and orientation, but differ in movement.

taking. While the hands are up, the signers intend to continue signing. When they drop their hands to their sides or move them to an at-rest position at the waist, they invite others to reply.

Characteristics of Movement

Movement of the hands makes up the fourth structural component of signs, no less important than the other three to conveying a sign's meaning. Movements can be classified under five broad aspects: type, direction, repetition, vigor, and extent.

TYPE A sign's movements may be linear, jagged, smoothly undulating, supinating, pronating, wriggling, pinching, and so on. Almost every type of movement that can be made with the hand occurs in sign language. When the two hands form a sign, they may brush, strike, clasp, circle each other, converge, or diverge. Portraying some of these qualities in drawings or still photographs is exceedingly difficult, if it is possible at all. That is one reason why ASL cannot be learned from books alone.

DIRECTION The direction the hands move often replaces the function served by word order in English. Directional verbs such as HELP, SEND, INSULT, ADVISE, and PAY illustrate this characteristic. Figure 2.15 shows how the sign HELP can be used to create the phrase I [WILL] HELP YOU.

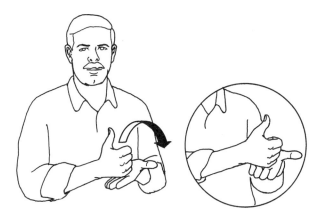

Figure 2.15. ME-HELP-YOU ("I will help you") is an example of directionality in ASL.

The HELP sign begins in front of the signer and moves slightly upward and outward toward the person being addressed. Reversing this movement gives the phrase YOU [WILL] HELP ME.

REPETITION   In some signs, repeating the movement pluralizes; thus, repeating the sign YEAR signifies "years." Repeating parts of a sign indicates plurality in other instances. The sign TEACHER has two parts: the sign TEACH and the sign for AGENT which when added to a sign indicates a person who performs an act, in this instance someone who teaches. To sign TEACHERS, only the AGENT portion of the sign is repeated. Repeating a verb sign can also change it to a participle: signed once, TEACH; signed twice, TEACHING.

VIGOR   The force with which one makes a sign, the emphasis one places on it, and the tension of the body that accompanies it all contribute to its meaning. A vigorous movement accompanied by appropriate facial expressions can change a sign from MEAN to VICIOUS. As with vocal inflections, the energy and speed with which a sign is made alters its meaning. Repeating the sign ASK in an intense manner results in INTERROGATE. Making the sign RUDE in a slow manner signifies VERY RUDE. Similarly, one can add sarcasm, irony, a reverse twist, and so on, to what is being signed by the manner of execution.

EXTENT   Figure 2.16 shows the signs SMALL, BIG, and ENORMOUS, the difference between them being the distance between the signer's hands.

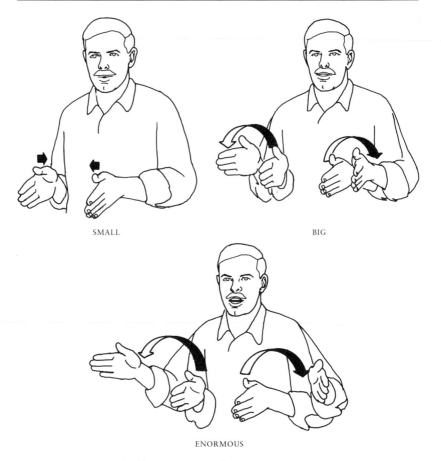

Figure 2.16.   An example of how movement affects sign meaning.

The extent of the movement with which a sign is made sharpens its meaning. The reader can consider the possibilities for increasingly finer shades of meaning as the size of movements are varied, along with their other four components.

Handedness

The configuration of the hands during the production of a two-handed ASL sign is rule governed. ASL imposes conditions of symmetry and dominance on two-handed signs. The symmetry condition states that if both hands move independently during the formation of a sign they will have

Figure 2.17. FALL-IN-LOVE

the same shape and the same movement (although the movement may be simultaneous or alternating) and the orientation of the hands also will be symmetrical or identical.[7] The sign EGG illustrates the symmetry principle.

ASL respects handedness. The dominant hand—right for the majority of people—is the active hand. When the left and right handshapes are the same, either the nondominant hand "echoes" (repeats) the movement of the dominant hand, or the nondominant hand does not move. So, in Figure 2.1, the right hand strikes the left hand, which remains still. If a person is left-handed then the movements are reversed: the left hand does the striking. In the sign EGG (Figure 2.2) both hands make the same movement in opposite directions. If the left and right handshapes are different, then the nondominant hand will remain stationery while the right hand moves. The sign FALL-IN-LOVE obeys this rule (Figure 2.17).

Left-handed people are accustomed to living in a right-handed world, so they usually adjust easily to learning signs from a person of the contralateral persuasion. However, if you are right-handed and learning signs from a left-handed teacher, you may have a period of confusion. We urge that you constantly be aware of handedness when observing signers.

Principle of Least Effort

For the most part signs are produced in a manner that optimizes efficiency or reduces efforts to make them. This leads to a Principle of Least Effort that states:

> When the same effect can be produced by two or more groups of movements, the one requiring the least energy will prevail.

Typically, signs that come in contact with the body are made with the palms facing the body or in a relaxed position. The sign ENJOY is made with an open hand moving in a circular movement, palm against the chest. Try making this sign with the back of the hand moving in a circle against the chest. It is awkward, and you will feel a strain in your wrist and forearm. The concept of least effort should be familiar from your experience with spoken languages. Take the pronunciation of *Barbara*; its spelling indicates three syllables, Bar-bar-a. But the repetitive bar-bar is difficult to pronounce, so the name is usually rendered Bar-bra. It sounds similar, but the second articulation takes less energy.

One test of this principle has been made by studying movies of signers made early in this century and comparing their signs to ones now in use.[8] The anticipated tendencies toward muscularly simplified signs emerges clearly. Comparing entries from earlier sign dictionaries to present-day ones also confirms the principle. Yet another illustration is noted in two-hand signs made above the shoulder. Over time these have tended to be made with just one hand, as in DEER, DEVIL, COW, and HORSE.[9]

Combining Elements

The differences in signs—in the handshape, orientation, location, and movement—can be small or large. As with distinctions in speech, the signer becomes attuned to subtle variations and quickly detects relatively minute differences in each aspect.

The potential number of signs that can be achieved by varying these four major aspects is huge. This structural richness is often overlooked due in part to the difficulties in portraying signs in print. While a sign's features can be elucidated by drawings or photographs supplemented by verbal explanations, nuances are often lost. Those nuances are vital to meaning, and they are especially difficult to show when they involve not one but a sequence of signs.

As with a spoken word, the articulation of a sign varies with what precedes and what succeeds it. The boundaries of the signs shown in these pages will shift somewhat when put into context. Consider the phrases "hate to dream" and "hate eggs," which in ASL consist of two signs for each, respectively: DREAM HATE and EGG HATE (Figures 2.18 and 2.19). In the former phrase the sign HATE will likely be made in a position level with the head. In the latter phrase the sign HATE will likely be formed in the

Figure 2.18. DREAM-HATE ("hate to dream")

same position where the hands are at the end of making the sign EGG (about waist level). Thus the signs one learns in isolation from other signs tend to be modified when they are used consecutively. (For more about learning to sign see chapter 5.)

Much of ASL's poetry comes from the way signs interdigitate. A smoothly flowing transition from sign to sign delights the eye, as do well-

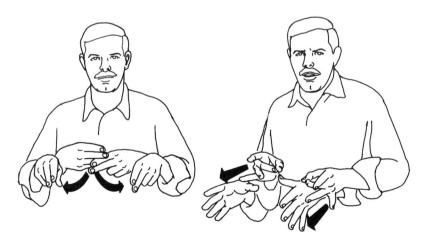

Figure 2.19. EGG-HATE ("hate eggs")

executed ballet steps. When done fluently, signing seduces the viewer as singing does the listener. Unfortunately, the limits of print frustrate attempts to portray ASL's spatial-sequential beauty.

Variations, Accents, and Eccentricities

Those who share a common language often differ in their expressions of it. What is true for speaking is also true for signing.

Idiosyncrasies

Every person signs in a way that is slightly different from everyone else. Some of the variation is due to the person's physique: longer or shorter hands and arms, and greater or lesser finger dexterity. Where the person learned to sign and at what age are also factors determining how signs will be executed. These idiosyncrasies should be expected. Students studying sign language must seek the regularities underlying individual differences in the production of signs. If they attempt to learn from sign lexicons, they will be frustrated when they see signs in continuous discourse.

Slips of the Fingers

Would you like to read the bird? Huh? Slips of the hand are common in ASL just like slips of the tongue are in spoken languages.[10] The sign BIRD is the same as the sign NEWSPAPER in all respects *except* location. BIRD is made with a closed fist with the extended thumb and forefinger tapping each other in front of the mouth. NEWSPAPER has the same handshape, orientation, and movement as BIRD but is done in the open palm of the nondominant hand (Figures 2.20 and 2.21).

Regional Variations in Signs

Before radio and television became widely used in North America, differences in English pronunciation were much greater than they are at present. The ubiquity of telecommunications has spread Standard American English into every nook and cranny of the nation, substantially reducing variations in spoken English. ASL has not had this wide exposure. In fact, the teaching of ASL is a relatively new phenomenon. Until recently, ASL was passed from person to person, a means of transmission not conducive

Figure 2.20. BIRD

to linguistic integrity. Furthermore, no writing system for sign language has found much acceptance, so the available sign language dictionaries have contained descriptions in English by observers who were often hearing and did not use ASL as a primary means of communication.

A misconception spread by older sign glossaries is that there is one and only one sign for a given spoken word, and, conversely, there is one and only one gloss for each sign. We recognize that there is no one way to execute a particular sign, any more than there is necessarily only one correct sign for a particular concept.[11]

> Almost all that has been put into print about American sign language gives, intentionally or not, the impression that a sign must be made precisely so,

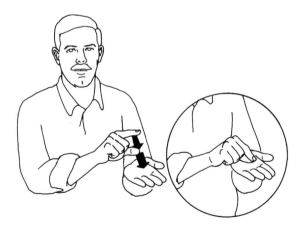

Figure 2.21. NEWSPAPER

will always be seen made that way, and admits of no variation. Nothing could be further from the truth. Individual, local, regional, and other differences operate at all levels in all languages.[12]

The persistence of ASL dialects, then, reflects the neglect it has had over the past two centuries. It receives little national exposure on television, a great homogenizer of language. Lacking an accepted written form, it suffers the irregularities that are inevitable when languages are passed from person to person. Perhaps one day, a cable station will broadcast programs and movies in ASL, and the regional distinctions in ASL will be reduced.

Nonmanual Signals

A major hurdle for many individuals learning ASL is that the hands do not say it all. Nonmanual signals from the face and body modify the intended meaning of a signed message. Raised eyebrows, puffed cheeks, dropping shoulders, and eyes glancing to the side are all linguistic signals. These nonmanual features of ASL may act as signs themselves (without accompanying hand movements) or as syntactic elements; that is, as the formal components that alter the meaning of a sign string.

In English the same set of words can be a statement or a question depending on the word order: *Are you the one? You are the one!* In addition, with the appropriate intonation and stress, *You are the one* can be made into a question, *You are the one?* ASL, too, has rules for changing a group of signs' interpretations.

The importance of nonmanual signals in ASL must not be confused with the facial expressions and body postures that accompany speech. True, there are similarities, but a nonmanual signal in ASL "has grammatical function that distinguishes it from the random and optional affective role such behaviors play in spoken languages."[13]

Eyes and Eyebrows

The way the eyes are used—the direction of gaze, for instance, or squinting—has considerable meaning in a sign phrase. Signers regularly establish the persons about whom they are speaking by assigning each a specific location in the signing space relative to the signer and initially glancing and/or pointing at those spots when naming the individuals. As a signer continues to talk about these people, he or she indicates them by looking at that location. Alternatively, pointing a finger at a particular location can accomplish the same purpose. Referring to people in this manner serves the purpose of pronouns in English.

Eye contact is another important element in sign language. Because deaf people cannot communicate unless they are looking at the message source, the persons to whom they sign must keep their eyes on the signer, even if they are normally hearing. Looking away interrupts the signer, especially if the averted gaze accompanies the initiation of signs. Thus, eye contact during signed conversations is a part of Deaf culture. Contrary to cultures in which looking directly at another person is considered impolite, deaf people must maintain eye contact to be polite.

Another function of the eyes is to emphasize a point. This might be done by looking away from the person addressed until one is ready to make a particular sign, and then fixing one's gaze while simultaneously making that sign. In this case the signer has broken eye contact, which is not only acceptable, it is meaningful: it serves to emphasize what is being signed. Closing the eyes has the same effect: signing LOVE and at the same time narrowing one's eyes signifies "to love very much."

In addition to eye gaze the eyebrows play a role in ASL. They add a question mark, going up at the appropriate point. They rise sympathetically, or they contract with anger. They may also contract to add emphasis to what is signed. Raising the eyebrows may also indicate surprise, while drawing them down in a frowning expression indicates negation or suspicion. As with the other elements of sign we have presented, the eyebrows add one element to the composite facial expression.

Facial Expressions

Reading facial expressions forms a part of understanding ASL. A frown while signing does not necessarily mean something unpleasant. A pinched face may serve as an adverb, adding *very* to the adjective being signed. It may provide emphasis, as in changing the sign for HALT to mean "stop immediately!" Also, protruding the tongue can change the meaning of a sign. This signals the difference between the signs LATE and NOT YET (see Figure 2.22). This aspect of ASL is critical to its appreciation. Facial expressions provide punctuation, indicating a question, for example. Of course, the preceding discussions of eyes and eyebrows are aspects of

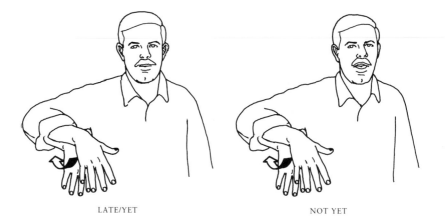

LATE/YET   NOT YET

Figure 2.22. Facial expression adds important grammatical information to a sign.

facial expression. Thus, facial expressions greatly enhance the meaning of signed communications, broadening and sharpening them.

This aspect of ASL puts nonnative signers at a disadvantage. Without specific instruction they may overlook the facial expressions accompanying signs or, worse, may misinterpret their meaning. Facial expressions also fulfill the same role as vocal intonation. Deaf people regard people who remain expressionless while signing the same as listeners regard people who speak in a monotone. Hence, facial expressions in ASL are analogous to vocal inflections in speech—and more.

Posture

The signer's body adds further meaning to a signed message. As noted, one asks a question in ASL by, among other aspects of signing, leaning forward. This expectant posture signals the desire for a response. By the same token, the signer's leaning backward suggests aversion or negation. To indicate a change of subject, one can turn to the right or left. A signer might say, while turning to the left, [HE] OFFERED ME $500 and, turning to the right, [SHE] COUNTEROFFERED $600. The signer's changes in posture make clear who is doing what; HE and SHE need not be signed. Just as not accompanying signs with relevant facial expressions would be boring at best and, more probably, noncommunicative, remaining rigidly upright throughout a signed conversation would be like speaking in a monotone and would fail to communicate fully.

Figure 2.23. NOW

Putting Them All Together

Of necessity we have discussed aspects of sign one at a time. But their real impact emerges most forcefully when various aspects are put together. Take the possibilities that can be derived from the single sign NOW (Figure 2.23). Asked with a questioning look, it can be translated as "Do you want it done at this time?" In addition to the facial expression—arched eyebrows and direct eye contact—the hands hold the sign for a longer period than would be true if the sign NOW was intended as an answer or command. If the signer leans forward with a slight thrust of the head toward the person being addressed, the question could be changed to "You mean right now?" Or if the question is one of incredulity ("Do you really mean now?"), the signer would add a look of incredulity and make the sign more slowly than for a simple response. To indicate a direct order, the signer assumes a more commanding expression and makes the sign NOW with a firm, downward stroke close to the chest, along with pursed lips, knit brow, and slightly narrowed eyes. Signed thus the message is, "Do it at once!"

Summary

To grasp fully the intent of a signed message, then, the receiver must attend to the handshapes, orientation, movement, and location of the sign, as well as and the accompanying facial expressions and body postures. In addition, as is true for all communications, spoken and signed, the context in which communication takes place adds further clues to the correct interpretation of the message being conveyed. These characteristics all interact and contribute to understanding what is being signed in ASL.

The Origin of a Sign

In chapter 1 we took up the history of sign languages. Here we ask different kinds of historical questions, questions about etymology: Where and when did a particular sign originate? How was its hand-movement configuration determined? These are intriguing questions, and the absence of accurate information encourages myths. Nature abhors a vacuum, and some people cannot tolerate an unsolved mystery. The truth, of course, is that for many if not most signs there are no written records to search through for sign origins. Their origins are shrouded in unrecorded darkness. Yet, when students take sign language classes, they often are given a derivation for the signs. One dictionary of signs provides an "origin" for almost every sign. The compiler of the dictionary does not reveal the sources of these etymologies; they are presented without explanation or apology and they are usually iconic.[14]

Even native signers may be incorrect when they make statements about a sign's origin, but the practice is harmless if it is not taken seriously. Etymologies (explanations of sign or word origins) can serve as memory aids and, as such, may be helpful. They can be counterproductive if they encourage the beginner to search out iconic elements in every sign and thus become confused and fail to generalize the interpretation of the sign when it is appropriate to do so. Take the sign KIND, made by holding the left hand, palm facing in, in front of the chest and circling it with the open right hand. One suggested origin is "as if winding a bandage around the arm."[15] To a present-day observer that may seem a fair description of what the movements resemble, but it can hardly be accepted as the origin. No record supporting that gloss has been found. Why bandage the arm and not the head? Why is the movement not symbolizing kneading bread? Such speculations may interfere with the student's appreciation of the sign's fuller meanings, which include "gracious," "gentle," and "good-hearted." How do these latter concepts relate to bandaging? Not too well.

Finding the origins of words in any language presents many difficulties, too. Eric Partridge sagely notes: "That etymology is a science, no one will deny; that it is also an art, far too many deny."[16] To say that one has found the origin of a word when its Latin root has been established only postpones the question of linguistic beginnings. From whence came the Latin? In the same lecture from which the above quotation was taken, Partridge concluded most aptly:

> Etymology is a perilous subject: for, reach one horizon, you find another equally distant, if not still more remote. One clue leads to another, which yields another, which yields to another, which ad-infinitums from days to months to years; and often one has to retrace one's steps.[17]

Since spoken languages that have been recorded for millennia present such difficulties, it is easy to understand why sign languages that have been only crudely recorded for a fraction of the time should present so many more problems to the etymologist.

The Grammar of ASL

American Sign Language, like all languages, is rule governed. Specific rules dictate how signs and nonmanual fieatures can be combined in order to produce meaningful communication. These rules allow signers to convey tense, plurals, compounds, negation, and different types of sentences (declarative, interrogative, etc.).

The Use of Space in ASL

The length of the signer's arms determines the boundaries of the visual space, or the signing frame. The signer can use the space to convey different meanings. For example, a private message may be signed within a small frame. Conversely, a signer addressing an audience would make use of the maximum frame size. In addition the space can be used to indicate the relative size of the object being described (see Figure 2.16).

Classifiers

Classifiers are ASL signs that represent specific locations and/or movements of a person or thing. The signer uses the classifier to indicate the action of the person or thing being described. For example, a teenager describing how his car hit a tree would first sign or spell CAR and thereafter would use the classifier handshape VEHICLE to show the movement of the car leading up to the accident (see Figure 2.24). The classifier VEHICLE can be used to mean "car," "bus," "truck," "boat," or any type of convey-

VEHICLE-HIT-TREE

Figure 2.24. An example of a classifier used to show movement—"The car hit the tree."

ance.[18] It can be moved in any direction to indicate the action of the vehicle being discussed. Classifiers also represent the size, shape, and other characteristics of a person or thing.

Pronouns

Signers use the space around them to indicate specific persons and objects. Once the persons or objects have been named, the signer assigns them a specific location, for example, to the signer's left or right. The signer then uses the pointing handshape to refer to the person or object named. This is the equivalent of using pronouns in English. The area directly in front of the signer is the common place for indicating YOU and ME. Pointing to the space to the left or right of the signer can be used to indicate HE, SHE, or IT. Context usually makes the gesture's meaning apparent.[19] Subsequently, by gazing at a position or by pointing to it, the signer indicates that the utterance refers to that person or object—a previously established but arbitrary reference point in space.[20]

The sign space is used to indicate subject-object relations. The direction of signs indicates the direction of the action. I GIVE YOU and YOU GIVE ME can be distinguished by the direction in which GIVE is signed. For the former sentence the sign GIVE originates by the signer's chest and moves out toward the person to whom the signer is talking. This single handshape and movement conveys the entire phrase I GIVE YOU. The pronouns are incorporated into the sign GIVE. If the signer wishes to express YOU GIVE HIM, the direction of GIVE is from the space directly in front of the signer [YOU] to the side where the third person has been established. This highly efficient method serves the function of pronominalization.[21]

Tense

How does the signer indicate the time at which an action is occurring, was occurring, or will occur? In ASL space again serves a grammatical function. The space in front of the signer is the future; immediately in front of or alongside the signer is the present; behind the signer is the past. These relations form a time line. The signer indicates the future by a forward movement of the hand. The present is the signer, indicated by signs like NOW (see Figure 2.23). The farther forward the movement, the more distant the future.

The past is indicated by a movement of the dominant hand toward the signer's back. Distant past is shown by accompanying the backward hand movement with an appropriate facial expression or by wiggling the fingers as the hand moves back. Figure 2.25 shows the general sign for PAST or AGO and the sign LONG-AGO. In LONG-AGO the distant past is shown by the open mouth, the arc of the sign, and the wiggling of the fingers.

The verbs in ASL do not generally inflect to indicate tense. GO, WENT, and WILL GO are all made with the same sign. To mark time, the signer

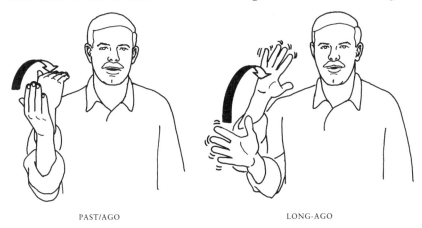

PAST/AGO   LONG-AGO

Figure 2.25. In ASL the past is indicated by moving the hand toward the signer's back and adding the appropriate facial expression.

Figure 2.26. FLY-BY-PLANE signed with a small arc indicates a short plane trip.

provides a signal at the outset of the communication. Thereafter, tenses are indicated only when the time reference changes. This arrangement makes attention and memory demands on the receiver that are not made by English, which constantly marks each verb's tense.

Time can also be indicated by the FINISH sign, indicating completion of an action. Depending on context, the sign phrase EAT FINISH [ME] can be translated into English as "I ate," "I have eaten," or "I finished eating." Likewise, modals can be used to indicate time. The ASL phrase 5:00 WE EAT WILL should be translated, "We will eat at 5:00."

The duration of an activity or condition can be shown without adding adverbial phrases as English requires. Signing FLY-BY-PLANE with a very slow, prolonged movement would tell the observer that the flight had been a long one. Signed briefly in an arc shape with a puffed cheek could indicate a flight across the Atlantic on the Concorde (Figure 2.26). A short hop within a state can be shown by signing FLY-BY-PLANE with a brief movement and a visible "pop" or "pah" made with the mouth.

Compounds

Many languages have the ability to create new vocabulary by combining existing linguistic elements. Compounding is an efficient method for enlarging the vocabulary of a language.[22] Compounds are formed when two distinct words or signs are combined to create a word or sign with an entirely different meaning. Examples in English include *homework* and *handbook*. Examples in ASL include MOTHER‾FATHER ("parents"), MAN‾MARRY ("husband"), and GIRL‾SAME ("sister").

Expressing Number

As explained previously, the plural form in ASL can be expressed by repetition of the sign. Making the sign MAN twice results in MEN. Another way to differentiate between singular and plural is by the extent of the sign. The signs for third person singular are made by pointing to a single spot. Sweeping the pointing finger will signify third person plural. Another means of indicating the plural form is to combine the noun with the sign MANY. In this use the MANY sign should be considered a quantifier that is not necessarily translated as "many" but serves to convert a singular noun to the plural form. Thus, the sign phrase MANY PLANE is correctly rendered as "planes."

Negation and Assertion

ASL has a number of ways of asserting and negating statements, as does every other language. Stating something is true, of course, is easy to conceive, but ASL offers several opportunities for distinctions that are contained within the sign. Signers can express thoughts varying from simple acquiescence to vigorous assertion by the way in which they make the sign and the accompanying facial expressions and body posture. A head nodding forward and backward is one universally understood affirmative response. ASL also uses signs, such as YES, OK, SURE, and TRUE, and modals such as WILL, CAN, and SHALL for positive assertion.

For negation all that is required to deny a statement is to make it with a headshake from side to side. Shake your head while signing I HELP YOU and it means you will not help. Figure 2.27 shows a sign for rejection. Although glossed as REFUSE or WON'T, it has a more general sense of negation. It can be combined with other signs to indicate their obverse. For example, a signer could first sign a rhetorical question such as *Will I go for a swim?* then answer this question with the WON'T sign. ASL also has the signs NOT, CAN'T, NO, NEVER, NONE, and DON'T. Any of these signs when placed at the end of an ASL utterance negates the expressed thought.

Figure 2.27. REFUSE

Questions

We have already pointed out how eyebrows, facial expression, and posture signal questions. In English we usually indicate a question by the initial interrogative: what, where, why, how, and so on, or by intonations. In ASL the question word may appear at the beginning or the end of a query. Figure 2.28 shows an example of the question word at the end of the question. The signs are GIRL THERE LIVE WHERE and they translate as "Where does that girl live?" It should be noted that the determiner *that* is not signed when it is indicated by the signer's gaze.

Another feature of ASL is that some question words have a more general meaning. When read as signed the sequence SCHOOL WHERE, made with the eyes gazing toward the person being addressed and with the signer's facial expression and posture indicating a question, asks, "Where do you go to school?" Again, note that the interrogative appears at the end of the utterance.

Conditional Statements

Contingency statements are typically made in ASL, as in English, with the conditional first, followed by the consequent. This order is represented in Figure 2.29. Though there is only one sign, RAIN, the facial expression and posture of the signer convey tension, saying in effect that something more is coming. Following this with the sign STAY and the signer's raised eye-

GIRL   THERE   LIVE   WHERE

Figure 2.28. GIRL THERE LIVE WHERE is translated as "Where does that girl live?"

RAIN   STAY

Figure 2.29. RAIN STAY is an example of a conditional statement—"If it rains, will you stay?"

brows indicates that a question is being asked. Together the two signs ask, "If it rains, will you stay?" The two-sign sentence translates into a six-word spoken utterance. The compactness comes from the combining of linguistic information provided by the signs, the syntax or ordering of the signs, and the nonmanual signals.

Sign Order

ASL has a variety of rules governing word order.[23] These include subject-verb-object (SVO) constructions, as in ME-GIVE-YOU; or SOV sentences, such as MAN BOOK READ (for "the man reads the book"); and even OSV sentences, such as CAR DOG JUMP-ON-IT (for "the dog jumped on the car"). The sentence construction chosen will depend on several linguistic features. SOV constructions occur only with inflected verbs. In sentences that contain classifiers that indicate location, the OSV order is common. (See preceding sections for example.)

The statement "I like my coffee black" (Figure 2.30), if read in the order signed, says COFFEE BLACK LIKE ME. Such a construction confuses and even discourages beginning ASL learners. But these reactions can be avoided by emphasizing that all languages have their own syntax, and transliteration of grammatically correct sentences in one language into a second language often renders sentences incomprehensible in the second language.

In the past some authors have advanced the idea that presumed syntax

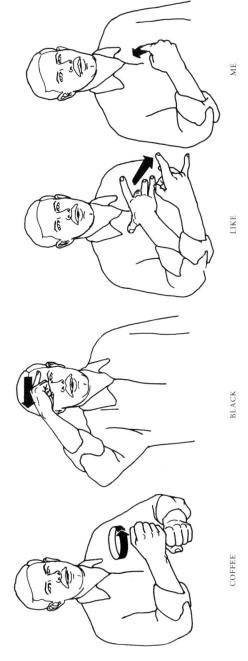

COFFEE   BLACK   LIKE   ME

Figure 2.30. COFFEE BLACK LIKE ME ("I like my coffee black") is an example of object-verb-subject word order.

rules in ASL are merely conveniences and that these patterns are not essential to meaning.[24] Carol Padden has replied with an impressive analysis of ASL sentence patterns that leaves no doubt of their syntactic necessity.[25] Implicit in her presentation is that the tendency to seek English-like rules for ASL is at the heart of misconceptions about its grammar.

Conclusions about ASL Grammar

The preceding samples of ASL grammar are intended to make the case for its unique characteristics and for the flexibility that operating in a spatial medium provides. ASL is an interactive language dependent on the location of the signer and the receiver, their eye contact, the use of the signing space, and the linguistic signals sent forth by the body and facial expressions. These features and others, like sign order, make up the articulation dynamics of ASL. Students striving to attain fluency in ASL must break from the auditory-sequential mindset on which speech thrives and develop a visual-spatial one that makes simultaneous expression of two or more thoughts possible.

In the preceding sections we have endeavored to illustrate ASL grammar without a complete accounting for its subtleties but with sufficient examples to make clear that it is a language distinct from English or any other spoken language.[26] We have emphasized that an adequate description of ASL requires that attention be directed beyond its hand signs to grammatical elements conveyed by facial expressions, body posture, and the ordering of signs.

Although ASL is independent of English, it does share characteristics with it, such as a common alphabet. Over time ASL may undergo further changes affected by the English language just as English gestures have borrowed—and will probably continue to borrow—from ASL signs.[27]

A prevalent form of signing in the American Deaf community that is neither ASL nor a signed code for English is Pidgin Sign English (PSE). It uses ASL signs in a word order resembling, but not exactly following, English grammar. In the United States and Canada this type of signing occurs largely when deaf people sign to nondeaf people. Because PSE arises when users of ASL interact with those accustomed to English, some linguists refer to it as *contact signing,* rather than PSE. Other linguists caution that it may in fact be a variation of ASL. Some researchers have categorized various forms of PSE by their resemblance to spoken English.[28] They devised a continuum with ASL at one end and English at the other. The closer signing resembled English word order, the closer to English it was placed on the continuum. Falling in between these poles were the forms of signing covered by the terms contact signing or PSE.

New thoughts about what constitutes ASL challenge the continuum thesis. From the first research on ASL in the late 1950s until now, linguists have seldom assumed that all of what a deaf person signs is ASL. Instead, when a deaf person's signing used a grammatical pattern similar to English, they argued it was not true ASL, where "true ASL" was defined as something different from English. One deaf teacher has noted that

> An unfortunate side to the otherwise marvelous wealth of new information about ASL was that the focus of the linguistic analysis was unbalanced. All the linguistic data being collected helped create a lopsided picture of ASL. Such an impression contributed further to the polarization between what linguists describe as ASL and what some deaf people see as their way of signing. Linguists have been putting aside aspects of ASL that appear to be English-influenced.[29]

Today it is generally agreed that there is a wide range of syntactic variation within ASL, just as there are numerous differences in signs for the same concept. Signing that was previously classified as being English-like is now being examined as another ASL grammatical construction. Broadening the breadth of ASL's linguistic structures makes it possible that today's contact signing will one day be recognized as a part of ASL. These continuing developments in the understanding of ASL call for more research to present the full picture of what it is.

Already, some deaf individuals are suggesting that the term ASL be used in a generic sense to encompass all types of signing used by deaf individuals. The rationale for this position is that "ASL is all-inclusive and adaptable, depending on the person one comes in contact with and also on the subject one wishes to communicate."[30] Put another way, the need to communicate supercedes a requirement that one adhere to a single type of signing. The options for communicating in a visual-spatial medium are great indeed.

We know that sign languages and spoken languages are distinct and function in different communication fields. But they are not completely without influence on each other. They do come together and when two groups of people with different linguistic backgrounds interact, some variations emerge in one or both of their languages. This phenomenon is readily apparent in the interactions of deaf and hearing people. Hearing people tend to use the word order of a spoken language to structure their signing behavior. When communicating with nondeaf people, some deaf people will consciously use a spoken language grammar to structure their presentation of signs. How much of an influence a sign language or a spoken language has on the resulting communication is dependent on many factors, including the degree of fluency in signing, the desire to use a sign language or a spoken language, and the willingness of the deaf person to use sign language with a nondeaf person.[31]

What has been said about the unique characteristics of ASL finds counterparts in the sign languages of Great Britain, Denmark, France, Ireland, Sweden, Thailand, and other nations whose sign languages have been subjected to linguistic analysis.[32] What emerges from these studies is that all sign languages face the same basic communication concerns—transmitting the concepts of time, number, gender, and so forth—and they use different strategies to solve them. They all have grammars, but the grammars are not the same for all.

Notes

1. William Stokoe, who provided the first linguistic analysis of ASL, has given labels to three characteristics of a sign: *dez* (the handshape), *sig* (the motion made with the hands), and *tab* (the position of the hands relative to the rest of the body).

2. For further details see Fischer and Siple 1990, Klima and Bellugi 1979, Lucas 1990, Sandler 1990, Stokoe 1978, and Wilbur 1979.

3. However, the connection between an initial sound and the meaning of the full word is not consistent in English; for example, *graceful* and *gracious* also begin with g-r.

4. Baker and Cokely 1980. The authors provide an extensive listing of inflectional verbs.

5. As with handshapes, the identification of location with particular meanings has numerous exceptions. Nonetheless, the underlying idea can be helpful in learning to sign and in appreciating the structure of sign languages.

6. Thus far, we have concentrated on the manual production of signs and have not taken into consideration nonmanual signals. Yet, for example, the sign DIS-APPOINTED will differ with respect to location (and movement) as well as with respect to body posture (the shoulders drop) and facial expressions that depict the various contexts associated with the concept *disappoint* , such as self-expression (e.g., I am very disappointed; I might be disappointed); inquiring about it (e.g., Are you disappointed?); and commenting on it (e.g., You will be disappointed).

7. Battison 1978.

8. Frishberg 1976.

9. Woodward and DeSantis 1977.

10. Bellugi, Klima, and Siple 1975. The authors discovered similar patterns of error in the sign production of deaf native ASL signers and the speech production of native English speakers in a short-term memory experiment. Hearing subjects made phonological encoding errors in confusing words, such as *vote/boat* and *tea/tree*. Deaf subjects made phonological errors that were related to handshape (WEEK/NICE), location (BIRD/NEWSPAPER), and movement (VOTE/TEA).

11. For an extended discussion of regional variations in signs, see Shroyer and Shroyer 1984. For instance, they illustrate twenty variations of the sign CHEAT, although even that lengthy list is incomplete.

12. Stokoe, Casterline, and Croneberg 1965, xxxi.

13. Sandler 1989, 198.

14. Riekehof 1978.

15. *Ibid.*, 73.

16. Cited in Crystal 1980, 81.

17. Crystal 1980, 100.

18. Baker and Cokely 1980.

19. *Ibid.*, 287.

20. Lillo-Martin and Klima 1990.

21. Stokoe 1972. The author recognized that "sign language, unlike English, often contains the subject or object reference, or more rarely both, implicitly in verb signs," 71. See Baker and Cokely 1980; Humphries and Padden 1992, and Wilbur 1979 for more about the pronominalization principle.

22. Dyer 1976.

23. For an analysis of the controversies over the ordering of signs, see Wilbur 1979 and Liddell 1980.

24. Crystal and Craig 1978.

25. Padden 1981.

26. This sentence should not be read as denying any similarities between ASL and English. In Stokoe, Casterline, and Croneberg 1965 the authors have pointed out, "One way in which sign language does resemble English syntax is in the use of auxiliary verbs," 283. That there are differences in syntax—some very large differences—remains, however, the point. ASL is a language distinct from English.

27. A Deaf baseball player, "Dummy" Hoy, at the end of the nineteenth century taught umpires to adopt the convention of calling balls with the left hand and strikes with the right hand. The same may be true of the hand signals used to indicate "safe" and "out." Another sign that has gained rapid acceptance by the hearing public is I-LOVE-YOU. It was used in 1976 by Jimmy Carter during his presidential campaign and is now freely used by politicians both as a way of garnering votes and as a token of appreciation to supporters.

28. Bornstein and Hamilton 1972; Stokoe, Casterline, and Croneberg 1965; Wilbur 1979.

29. Kuntze 1990, 76.

30. Bragg 1990, 9–10.

31. Deaf people often do not use ASL when signing to outsiders, partly because they do not believe the nondeaf person will understand it and partly because using ASL with another person indicates acceptance of that person as an insider

in the Deaf community. Thus, using ASL is a means of identifying with Deaf culture. With the rapid proliferation of ASL courses throughout the nation and with the livelihood of an increasing number of deaf instructors dependent on this proliferation, this attitude toward the use of ASL with nondeaf people may be challenged.

32. Brito 1990, Corraza 1990, Deuchar 1981, Hanson 1980, Jepson 1991, Serpell and Mbewe 1990, Smith 1990, Veinberg 1993, and Yau 1990.

3
Let Your Fingers Do the Talking

*U*sing the manual alphabet, a person can fingerspell any English word, no matter how long or complicated. The manual alphabet, then, is a way of coding a spoken language. For each letter of the English alphabet there is a corresponding hand configuration in the American Manual Alphabet. The twenty-six letters shown in Figure 3.1 appear static, but readers of the manual alphabet interpret both the handshapes and the motions the hands make in assuming those handshapes, something that is difficult to convey in drawings. Notice that two of the letters are literally drawn: *j*, with the little finger, and *z*, with the index finger.

Some Historical Notes about Fingerspelling

Fingerspelling is not a recent invention. Systematic use of the hands for communication has been attributed to the ancient Egyptians, Hebrews, Greeks, and Romans.[1] By this we do not mean the use of gestures or hand signals, like the Romans' thumbs-up or thumbs-down to show pleasure or displeasure with gladiators in the Coliseum. Rather, we mean the use of the hands for systematic, detailed communication. One early writer on this subject has interpreted the handshapes of various pre-Hellenic statues as indicating letters of the Greek alphabet or of its precursor.[2] If such interpretations seem fanciful, consider that the great sculptor Daniel Chester French may have used letters of the manual alphabet in his famous statue of Abraham Lincoln. If you examine Lincoln's hands closely, you will see that his right hand resembles the shape of an *A* and his left that of an *L*.[3] French had received great accolades for his sculpture of Thomas Hopkins Gallaudet teaching the letter *A* to Alice Cogswell, so he had some familiarity with the manual alphabet. Centuries from now the historian who guesses that Lincoln's hand positions illustrate letters of an ancient sign

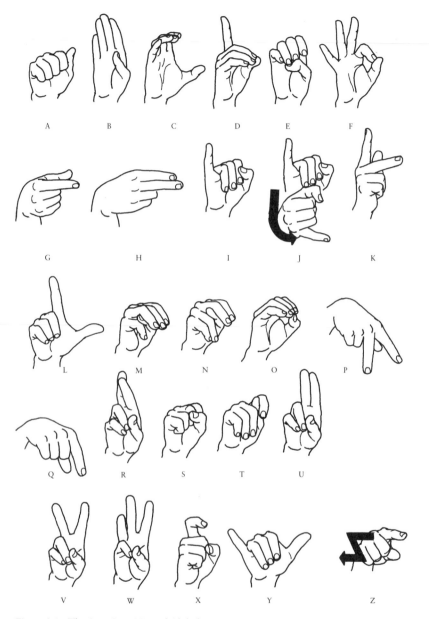

Figure 3.1. The American Manual Alphabet

language may be correct. Might not the guesses about ancient Greek sculpture also be on target?

At any rate, unequivocal evidence of the use of sign communication can be found in the writings of the seventeenth-century historian, the Venerable Bede.[4] He describes three different systems known to himself. From that day to this, evidence abounds of the uses of manual alphabets. Monks in the Middle Ages learned these alphabets for communication after taking vows of silence, and they may also have used them to keep their exchanges confidential.

Incidentally, some of the ancient alphabets would appear remote from today's fingerspelling of the modern alphabet. In an earlier form of the Italian Sign Language alphabet, letters were indicated by pointing to parts of the body. For example, the vowels were signaled by touching the tips of the fingers (A—thumb, E—ring finger, and so on). The English two-handed alphabet still uses the fingertips for the vowels, with the consonants now made by the right hand in the palm of the left hand. Other variations use parts of the left hand for every letter of the alphabet.

The identity of the first person to use fingerspelling to teach deaf students is not known. Credit usually goes to the Spanish priest Juan Pablo Bonet because he wrote the first book on educating deaf children, *Reducción de las Letras y arte para Enseñar a Hablar los Mudos*. The book contains a diagram of a one-handed alphabet. The Abbé de l'Epée adapted it to the French language, and thence it came to the United States with Laurent Clerc and Thomas Hopkins Gallaudet. Did Bonet invent the alphabet he used? He makes no such claim; instead, he discusses options other than the one-handed alphabet including one that uses the Latin names of body parts: *a—auris* (ears), *b—barba* (beard or chin), *c—caput* (head). The profusion of alphabets already known suggests that Bonet adapted an existing one-handed alphabet to his purposes rather than inventing one (see chapter 1, especially the section on Pedro Ponce de León). This makes sense; it is reasonable to suppose that deaf people have long used their hands to signify letters of the alphabet. That they did not document their signing does not detract from this supposition.

By publishing a manual alphabet, Bonet did exert an influence on the fingerspelling handshapes adopted by sign languages around the world. Many are similar to the one depicted in Bonet's drawings, even though some are based on different orthographic systems. Fingerspelling for Hebrew and Japanese, for example, share similarities with Bonet's system.

Why the English chose the two-handed, as opposed to the one-handed, manual alphabet as the vehicle for instructing deaf children is not clear. In 1644 the English physician John Bulwer published a monograph describing a communication method used by a deaf man and his wife; it was a two-handed alphabet. Bulwer's later book, printed in 1648, describes six other manual alphabets, so the English had ample choices. Scottish educator and philosopher George Dalgarno wrote *Ars Signorum, Vulgo Character Universalis philosophica et Lingua* in 1661. In that treatise a two-handed alphabet appears in which the right index finger points out vowels and the right thumb indicates consonants. Dalgarno went so far as to suggest that a glove with the locations of the letters printed on it be used to teach the alphabet.[5] This concept of a glove to facilitate fingerspelling predates by almost three centuries Dexter, a computerized glove that can fingerspell in response to typed input. This electronic device is designed for communication between deaf-blind persons and those who do not sign.

Later publications in England also feature two-handed alphabets. A booklet that appeared in 1698, *Digiti Lingua*, offered "the most compendious, copious, facile and secret way of silent Converse ever yet discovered Shewing how any two persons may be capable in half an hour's time, to discourse together by their Fingers only, as well in the dark as the light." Since the anonymous author identified himself or herself as "a person who has conversed no other wise in above nine Years," it is not unreasonable to suggest that the book was written by a deaf person. The alphabet recommended therein closely resembles the one in use in England today.

Spelling in the Air

Seeing the letters of a manual alphabet in their static position on the page can lead to a serious misunderstanding: that you always read the letters one at a time. In practice that is not the case. You usually do not listen for the separate phonemes of a spoken word; for example, what you hear is not "k/æ /t" but "cat." By the same token, you see word or thought units when observing fingerspelling. Your memory would be overloaded if you actually saw fingerspelling as a series of discrete letters. Imagine trying to follow a conversation that went along these lines:

"p-l-e-a-s-e-p-a-s-s-t-h-e-s-u-g-a-r-a-n-d-c-r-e-a-m!"

When fingerspelling several words consecutively, an experienced fingerspeller will insert pauses between each word. The pauses are minute, just as they are in speech, but they are essential to comprehension of any transmission of more than one or two words. The experienced fingerspeller also groups the letters into meaningful units or patterns. These units become recognizable as such and facilitate the speed with which fingerspelling can be read. An example of such a unit is /t-i-o-n/ as in *translation*. When fingerspelled rapidly, each letter is not clearly discernible, but the whole will usually be read correctly in context.

When fingerspelling, the first and last letters are held slightly longer than the interior letters in a word. This aids readers substantially since it cues them as to when a word begins and ends. It is essential to adopt a consistent rate of fingerspelling in order for readers to identify pauses and to differentiate the first and last letters. If the fingerspeller has a jerky style, reading becomes difficult, similar to unrhythmic speech. By the same token each deaf person has a unique fingerspelling style. Most will vary the speed with which they fingerspell a word to blend in with the point they are making. Emphasis, feelings, and sarcasm can all be incorporated into fingerspelling.

For most ASL letters the fingerspeller's palm faces the reader with a slight angle. The arm must not move about wildly, forcing the reader to search for the next letter. Movement is confined to the hand and wrist and does not involve the arm. Whatever the means used to stabilize the hand, the experienced fingerspeller confines the hand to a relatively narrow space. Unlike print, the letters do not move from space to space but remain in one place. There are exceptions to that rule. Some deaf persons will indicate a capital letter by moving the hand horizontally a very short distance as they form it. When a word ends in a double letter, it is not unusual to drag the last letter to the side. Abbreviations are commonly made by making a small circle with the hand while maintaining the shape of the letter.

Spelling can be done with either hand. Most people spell with their dominant hand, occasionally shifting to the other hand for variety or to relieve fatigue if they are fingerspelling for an extended period of time. To emphasize a point, one can also spell the same letters with both hands, but this only retains its effectiveness if used sparingly.

The fingerspeller must not forget other aspects of sign language. Fingerspelling, like signing, must be accompanied by facial expressions and body posture appropriate to the message being conveyed. These added cues affect the meaning of the words spelled much as vocal inflections affect speech. If a question is being spelled, the facial expression and body posture should be those used to signify questions. Other expressions and postures can be used to add adjectival and adverbial meanings rather than spelling them.[6]

Individual Differences

Individual variations in handshapes are to be expected. As in speech, the way a person makes each letter will differ somewhat, depending on the size of the hand, dexterity, and how fingerspelling was learned. Slight style variations may befuddle the student, a situation that parallels that of speech, where a difference in accent can make comprehension a problem. But with experience students correctly identify letters despite moderate departures in shape from the first-learned forms.

When to Fingerspell

Before continuing to discuss fingerspelling, a caution about when to fingerspell is in order. Deaf people usually limit fingerspelling to proper names. Even then, as you will read in chapter 7, they assign name signs to persons, objects, and events that will be referred to frequently. Though fingerspelled words are broken into units to facilitate their being grasped, reading several quickly becomes tedious. So, while it is an invaluable tool, fingerspelling is used sparingly. (For an exception to the foregoing, see the discussion of the Rochester Method, which appears below.)

Learning to Fingerspell

Some teachers of sign language believe that fingerspelling should only be taught after a basic sign vocabulary has been mastered. Some even suggest that fingerspelling not be given any instructional time, but that students learn the letters as they learn the signs. Since the signs incorporate many of the handshapes of the manual alphabet, such a procedure may not be unreasonable. As many college-level sign instructors will attest, however, each year more students attending beginner's classes have had some exposure to fingerspelling. They might have learned it as Boy Scouts or Girl Scouts. Others might have learned it from deaf classmates or in high-school sign classes. Those instructors who advocate introducing fingerspelling early in the course argue that conversations between deaf and hearing individuals will occur more readily if the hearing person can at least fingerspell.[7] Obviously, the matter must be resolved by each instructor with respect to the students in a particular setting.

Memorizing the twenty-six hand shapes of the manual alphabet usually takes about half an hour. Learning to use them, however, takes much longer. Like any physical activity, fingerspelling requires extensive practice to develop proficiency. One way to practice is to spell in front of a mirror. That way you can observe how your spelling looks to others while getting some practice in reading fingerspelling. You will still need an instructor to provide corrective feedback, though, because practicing errors can be worse than no practice at all.

Reading Fingerspelling

Most students find they rapidly develop spelling ability, but not reading ability. Indeed, some people claim they cannot learn to read fingerspelling fluently, regardless of the time invested. They may be correct. Just as with learning Morse code, sending (spelling) comes rapidly; receiving (reading), slowly. In part the difficulty can be overcome by concentrating on seeing ever-larger letter groups. As with learning to read print, you move from plateaus marked by seeing letters, then groups of letters, then words, and ultimately phrases. The assistance of an instructor will reduce learning time, and specific exercises can be helpful.[8]

In reading fingerspelling, as in listening to speech, the reader gains fluency by seeing patterns and filling in movements that are a blend of letters. If you look at someone spelling the word *cup*, you are not likely to see the letter *u* when it is quickly produced. The slight increase in time between *c* and *p* is the cue for the letter *u* . If you spell *cap* you can see how *u* and *a* are distinguished. When all else fails, context supplies the answer. Most people prefer their coffee in a cup, rather than a cap, and they hardly ever try to put a cup on their heads.

Another factor is the skill of the person whose fingerspelling you are trying to read. Realizing that someone may be spelling awkwardly will reduce the embarrassment of asking the speller to repeat, and repeat, and repeat until you correctly grasp the fingerspelled words. Bluffing will add little to improving reading ability. Guessing, on the other hand, is important to move you along, provided that you evaluate your guesses as you make them.

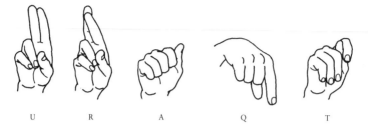

Figure 3.2. U-R-A-Q-T ("You are a cutie.")

Make It Short

To indicate single letters, as in abbreviations, fingerspellers commonly draw a small circle with their hand as they form the isolated letter. Figure 3.2 shows five letters that illustrate an amusing game. Say the letters aloud to form a sentence. Many deaf students enjoy these letter-word games, which depend on the way the letters sound and on what the sounds indicate as words. That is why you will see some deaf students spell, as they part, "C-U!"

Another example of word play results from the simultaneous production of the hand shapes I-L-Y while moving the hand in a small circle (see Figure 3.3). The original meaning of this combination was "I love you," and it has become popular among deaf and hearing people. Many politicians can be seen using this sign at political rallies. Over the years the meaning has changed to "I like you," which extends its applicability to more situations.

Figure 3.3. This sign for *I love you* is a result of simultaneously signing the letters I-L-Y.

Counting on the Fingers

Using the fingers to indicate numbers seems simple enough if one does not go over five with one hand or ten with both. The one-handed manual alphabet is not at all limited as to how high a number you can express; you can signify millions, billions, and beyond. For the sake of clarity and to allow for an infinitely large number, fingerspelling adopts a slightly different set of conventions than you might guess.

ONE TO TEN. Fingerspelling uses the shapes shown in Figure 3.4 for the first ten digits. Notice that 3 is not made in the popular manner; if it were, it would be confused with 6. A brief inspection of the chart will illuminate the logic of the system. For the first five digits, you hold up the requisite number of fingers with the palm of your hand facing you. After that, you turn the palm of your hand outward and indicate the numbers 6, 7, 8, and 9 by touching with the thumb, in turn, the little finger, ring finger, middle finger, and index finger. The number 10 is signed by holding up the thumb and giving it a slight shake.

ELEVEN AND BEYOND. The numbers 11 to 15 are made with the palm of the hand facing the body and 16 to 19 with the palm facing the audience. The number 11 is made by flicking the index finger from under the thumb. The number 12 is made by flicking both the index and middle fingers. For 13 the thumb is extended and the index and middle fingers

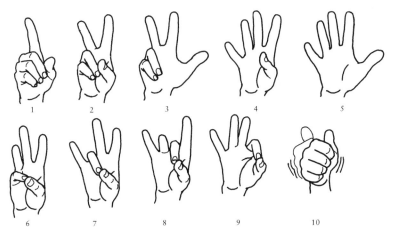

Figure 3.4. American Manual Numbers 1-10

wiggle up and down. The number 14 is formed by extending all fingers except the thumb and wiggling them up and down. The number 15 is the same as 14 except that the thumb is extended. Numbers 16 through 19 begin with the sign for 10—the extended thumb—followed immediately by the number 6, 7, 8, or 9. The logic continues with some variations for the remaining numbers up to 100—a highly consistent system, hence easily learned.

What about hundreds? Fingerspelling borrows the Latin letters C for hundred and M for thousand. Drawing the hand back when forming the letter C and then signing 35 produces 135. Following a 2 with an M into the center of the nondominant hand's palm is the sign for 2,000. From there it is easy to follow the logic to 1,000,000 (M repeated in the opposing palm) and beyond.

There are minor variations in the way the numbers are signed in the United States and Canada, just as there are regional variations in other signs.[9] Furthermore, like the letters of the alphabet, other countries have their own signs for fingerspelling numbers. To illustrate the point, Figure 3.5 shows the numbers 6 through 9 as made in Brazil and New Zealand.

Fingerspelling Conventions

A number of linguistic conventions have been incorporated into finger-spelling that allow for smoother transmission and easier comprehension of numbers. The ordinal numbers *first, second, third,* through *ninth* are made by first forming the number and then twisting the hand inward while pulling it slightly upward.

For signing sums of money, you form the numbers, palm away from body, and then twist the hand in a down and outward motion. For indicating cents, you touch the forehead with the index finger followed by the numbers indicating the amount.

Time is indicated by touching the wrist of the passive hand with the dominant index finger and then holding up the signs for the number of the hour and minutes. The sign in Figure 3.6 signifies seven o'clock.

To sign age, the convention is similar to that for time. First sign AGE and then, as the hand moves away from the body, sign the appropriate number of years. There are other fingerspelling conventions for phone numbers, addresses, and so on. They deepen an appreciation for the clever ways in which sign languages use the visual-spatial medium.

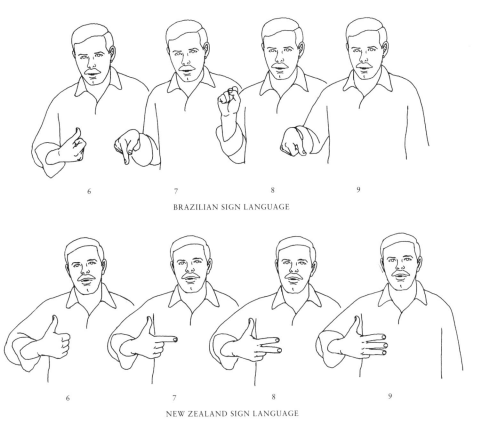

6   7   8   9

BRAZILIAN SIGN LANGUAGE

6   7   8   9

NEW ZEALAND SIGN LANGUAGE

Figure 3.5. Manual numbers, like manual alphabets, differ among sign languages.

7:00 (TIME + 7)

Figure 3.6. Time is indicated by first signing TIME and then the numbers for the hour and minutes.

Keeping Secrets

Manual alphabets have been used for centuries by religious orders whose members have taken vows of silence.[10] Youngsters who have learned fingerspelling from Boy Scout and Girl Scout manuals or from deaf persons delight in using it in situations where speaking is forbidden. They can fingerspell to each other across a playground or during a class. Discreetly passing messages in full view of others has great appeal, but the fingerspeller who desires confidentiality must be sure that possible viewers do not know the alphabet being used. Fingerspelling is legible at a considerable distance.

Obviously, one way to keep fingerspelling confidential is to keep it out of sight of all but the intended receiver. Such fingerspelling is very difficult to understand if the context is not known. The clandestine pair can also switch to the British two-handed alphabet (described later in this chapter), with the sender using the receiver's hand as the passive hand. Since the experienced receiver can then read the letters by touch, the hands can be completely out of sight. A deaf couple known by one of the authors has such conversations in crowds; to the casual observer, they appear to be merely holding hands.

Lexical Borrowing

Research by Robbin Battison has shown that fingerspelling has had a considerable influence on ASL's vocabulary.[11] He researched lexical borrowings—the linguistic term for influences of one language on another—and has found several instances in which the present-day form of a sign is a reduced form of a fingerspelled word. Several commonly fingerspelled words have been modified in such a way that they now resemble a sign. Some common two-letter words—*if, oh, OK, or*—have become highly stylized when signed, but their fingerspelled beginnings remain identifiable. Another example is the sign for *job*. The original J-O-B now looks like J-B, with a twist of the forearm as it moves from the *j* to the *b*. As shown in Figure 3.7, the sign now has only a faint resemblance to its fingerspelling origin.

The changes from fingerspelled words to signs sometimes involve more than a reduction in the fingerspelling to a simplified version of hand movements. Some lexical borrowings have taken on altered meanings. One popular sign expression is made by repeating the letters *d-o*, palm ori-

Figure 3.7. The sign J-B ("job") is an example of lexical borrowing.

ented toward the signer, with a questioning look on the face. In ASL it means, "What do we do now?" In a group of teenagers sitting around with time heavy on their hands, someone may suddenly sign it to stir the group to action.

In the United States and Canada fingerspelling and ASL are for all practical purposes inseparable. Very few deaf people use only fingerspelling or signing. The combination of fingerspelling and signing provides fascinating variations that are not all they appear to be on the surface. Uncovering their full meaning requires careful study. One researcher found that his informants occasionally were unaware of the genesis of some signs recently derived from fingerspelling. They offered plausible but inaccurate explanations of how the signs evolved. He illustrated the point with the borrowed sign for *bread* (Figure 3.8). It looks like the numbers 5 and 8, repeated two or more times. When asked how the sign came about, some younger informants said they thought it came from the pinching motion one would make to test a bread's freshness. Their resort to an iconic explanation does not fit the etymology.[12] Careful analysis indicates that the sign comes from dropping R-E-A out of the fingerspelled B-R-E-A-D. The anecdote offers a caution to those who attempt to guess the origins of signs. They typically seek concrete explanations that, aside from being incorrect, overemphasize the iconic nature of ASL.[13]

Legibility

How far can fingerspelling be projected? Research shows that fingerspelling is legible at a distance of up to three hundred feet. It can be read easily

Figure 3.8. This sign for *bread* is another example of lexical borrowing. The letters R-E-A have been dropped, resulting in B-D.

up to a distance of seventy-five feet by persons familiar with it.[14] Obviously, much shouting can be avoided by the use of fingerspelling. At the greater distances the spelling pace needs to be slowed to maintain comprehension. For hearing people the great distance over which fingerspelling can be accurately read recommends its use in noisy situations or where sender and receiver are separated by distances that would fatigue the vocal chords. By comparison, however, the legibility of sign over distances is much greater than that of fingerspelling.

Readers should not be fooled into believing that by fingerspelling they will make themselves understood by any deaf person who knows ASL. Many deaf people are bilingual in ASL and English, with English being their second language. As with other bilingual individuals, their fluency in English ranges widely. Although deaf people who can sign can also fingerspell, some comprehend fingerspelled English phrases without difficulty, while others do not. It is not that they cannot read the letters, but that they may not recognize the words. Knowledge of the language being fingerspelled is the limiting factor for comprehension.

Manual alphabets have some distinct advantages over signs. They are potentially more private than signs. Conversations can go completely unnoticed by others when one spells into the hand of the other person. It can be used in the dark, so it offers a vehicle for use with deaf-blind persons. Some read the one-handed alphabet by placing their hands over the speller's hand; some use the two-handed alphabet in which the spellers replace their passive hands with the deaf-blind person's hand.[15]

Fingerspelling around the World

Like sign languages, fingerspelling alphabets are not universal. Every sign language has its own alphabet, although some countries' alphabets appear to have common origins. Simon Carmel, a deaf anthropologist, has collated a number of manual alphabets from around the world.[16] Alphabets from several countries are found in Appendix B. Readers can readily see similarities and differences between the world's manual alphabets. Japanese Sign Language and ASL have similar handshapes despite the dissimilarity between Japanese and English orthography. Note that some alphabets are one-handed, like ASL, and others are two-handed, with a few combining one- and two-handed signs. Some, like the Argentine alphabet, also use parts of the body to signify particular letters, much as was the case with early alphabets used by silent orders of monks.

Manual alphabets are modeled on the spoken language's alphabets. If the spoken language has complex speech sounds, then the corresponding fingerspelling alphabet likely will be complex. Such is the case with the Thai manual alphabet, which strives to represent all of that tonal language's phonological intricacies.

> The Thai hand alphabet was based on the American one, using the American handshapes for Thai letters with the same sounds as much as possible. It uses two hands. The right hand is for the 44 consonants and 7 of the vowels. The left palm is for other vowels and four marks of tone. The index finger of the right hand has to point at the position required on the left palm. To mark a tone, point at the tip of one of the four fingers. Twenty-one distinctive vowels are formed by these combinations.[17]

Learning a country's alphabet, of course, is not the same as learning the country's language, signed or spoken. To fingerspell and comprehend German fingerspelling, you must know how to read and write the German language. Knowledge of its manual alphabet will assist in correctly fingerspelling German words, but it will not reveal their meanings.

As it turns out, the handshapes of the German manual alphabet closely resemble the ASL handshapes. In Ireland deaf people use a one-handed alphabet very much like our own. In fact, the Irish and American alphabets have the same country of origin, France. The French manual alphabet in turn was influenced by Spain's. The Russian manual alphabet shares some similarities to that of the French, but it is expanded to represent the additional letters in the Cyrillic alphabet. The same cannot be said about

Figure 3.9. In an older version of the Italian Manual Alphabet, some letters were made by the index finger pointing to different parts of the body.

fingerspelling in England, where deaf people use a two-handed alphabet. Australia, New Zealand, Scotland, and Yugoslavia also have two-handed alphabets. Among countries using one-handed spelling, the major differences from the ASL alphabet occur in countries that have larger or smaller alphabets for their spoken languages, such as Poland, Russia, the Philippines, Japan, and Thailand.

Countries may also have more than one fingerspelling alphabet. That is the case in Argentina, where one of the alphabets touches the body for some of its letters, as described above, and the other does not. An earlier version of the Italian manual alphabet also pointed to parts of the body to indicate different letters. Figure 3.9 shows some of these letters fingerspelling the name *Ruzio*.[18] As illustrated, fingerspelling a name in the old alphabet often involved touching half a dozen parts of the body. Some manual alphabets must be accompanied by mouthing of the corresponding speech sounds, a condition that does not apply to the American Manual Alphabet.[19]

In recent years, countries without a written alphabet, like Thailand and China, have developed fingerspelling that reproduces their spoken languages. In Taiwan and Hong Kong, deaf signers literally "trace ideographs in the air."[20]

International Manual Alphabet

The World Federation of the Deaf (WFD) has adopted an International Manual Alphabet (IMA) for use at its meetings. Except for the letters *f* and *t*, IMA is the same as the American manual alphabet (see Figure 3.10). The principal reason that IMA has a different handshape for the letter *t* is that the American configuration is an obscene gesture in many

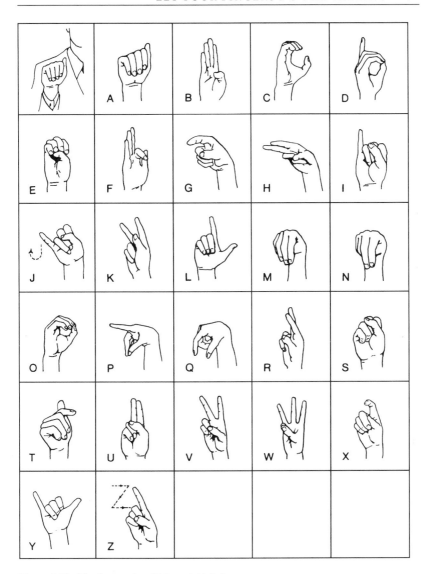

Figure 3.10. The International Manual Alphabet

Reprinted by permission of the publisher from S. J. Carmel (ed.), *International Hand Alphabet Charts* (1982): 87. n.p.: Simon J. Carmel.

European countries. Its meaning is the equivalent of a raised middle finger in North American culture. By the same token ASL does not use the extended middle finger, a shape that signifies the letter *a* in the Portuguese manual alphabet. There are other taboos in handshapes and movements that the WFD recognizes.

The fact that the fingerspelling alphabets of Austria, Brazil, Costa Rica, Denmark, Finland, Germany, Hong Kong, Ivory Coast, Liberia, Mexico, Nigeria, Singapore, Spain, Sweden, Taiwan, and perhaps a few more countries are similar to ASL may have contributed to the compromise reached by the WFD.

Uses of Fingerspelling

Fingerspelling's close mirroring of any spoken language may make it seem like the logical contender for first choice in manual communication. It is not, as discussed earlier ("When to Fingerspell"). There are the shortcuts mentioned above—abbreviations, conventions, and elisions—but despite these shortcuts, fingerspelling remains a tiresome way to carry on a conversation. People speak at an average rate of 250 words per minute. At that rate, intelligibility is not a problem. But fingerspelling at a rate greater than two hundred *letters* per minute (about fifty words) rapidly induces fatigue in the speller and cuts intelligibility sharply for the receiver. Nonetheless, communication solely by fingerspelling has been tried educationally (see "The Rochester Method" below).

A more subtle point sometimes goes unnoticed. English is a language that is spoken. It is adapted to the ear. To reproduce it manually does not necessarily make it more appealing for deaf people. ASL is a visually derived language—a language for the eye. Its syntactical differences from English may be related to fundamental distinctions in the operation of these two systems. As we have discussed in the first chapter, much more remains to be learned about how each of the two distance senses, vision and audition, works when the other is nonfunctional.

The Rochester Method

In 1878 Zenas Westervelt introduced the Rochester Method as a compromise between the two extremes warring over the education of deaf children—speech only versus speech and sign.[21] He was an advocate of oralism (the position that speech should be the basis of instructing deaf children), but he recognized the ambiguous nature of speechreading and sought to supplement it with fingerspelling. He was doubtless influenced by Alexander Graham Bell, already a proponent of oralism, who supported the use of fingerspelling. Bell advocated the following approach:

> Spoken language I would have used by the pupil from the commencement of his education to the end of it; but spoken language I would not have used as a means of communication with pupils in the earliest stages of education of the congenitally deaf, because it is not clear to the eye, and requires a knowledge of the language to unravel the ambiguities. In that case I would have the teacher use written language, and I do not think that the manual language differs from written language excepting in this, that it is better and more expeditious.[22]

Westervelt, as superintendent of the Rochester (New York) School for the Deaf, put this approach to a full test. He instigated simultaneous use of fingerspelling and speech, and this method of instruction remained in practice at his school until his death in 1912. Despite reports of its great success, the method faded after his demise. It has been revived from time to time, but its tediousness probably accounts for some of its unpopularity.[23] Today it has virtually no proponents. It is not even used at the school after which it was named.

Notes

1. Romeo 1978.
2. Kendon 1975.
3. In fairness, we must confess that the curator of the Daniel Chester French home-studio in Stockbridge, Massachusetts, disagrees with the "Lincoln's hand story." He regards it as an attractive myth and referred the first author to Packard 1965. Packard concluded that the *A* hand results from the model's holding a broomstick. About the *L* hand, Packard has no convincing explanation. That French was aware of the American manual alphabet is not disputed. There the argument must rest, since the only indisputable authority on the story's truth, French, is dead.
4. Romeo 1978.
5. Woll, Kyle, and Deuchar 1981.
6. For convenience in presentation we distinguish fingerspelling from signing in this text. However, students of sign language now regard the letters of the manual alphabet as signs and fingerspelling as a specialized form of signing.
7. Hoemann 1978 and Baker and Cokely 1980 recommend that fingerspelling be withheld until instruction in sign is well under way.
8. In Guillory 1966 the author has prepared a self-study guide to facilitate learning to read fingerspelling. The lessons advance from reading letters to seeing

syllables, then grasping whole words. It is probably more valuable when used with an instructor.

9. To complicate matters further, Canada is a bilingual country. As such, it has two deaf languages: ASL for English-speaking deaf citizens and Langue des Signe Quebecoise (LSQ) for the French-speaking deaf citizens. LSQ has its own vocabulary and grammar, aspects that distinguish it from ASL.

10. Abernathy 1959.

11. Battison 1978.

12. How did Battison (Battison 1978) discover a different origin of the sign, especially when some native deaf signers had a different explanation? His procedures are somewhat complex, but essentially they depend on asking informants for their independent judgments. These are then carefully analyzed until the consensus becomes clear. He also made use of historical accounts to buttress his interpretation. When a large group of signs is analyzed in this way, the results are impressive in the regularity with which patterns emerge. It is the systematic nature of the data that justifies their claim to validity—a claim that a single example could not make.

13. For a recent discussion of iconicity in ASL see Stokoe 1993.

14. Caccamise and Blasdell 1978. An interesting comparison is with speechreading. For persons with normal vision speechreading scores remain fairly constant up to a distance between twenty and twenty-four feet (Berger 1972). Thus, when distance is the governing parameter, fingerspelling is three or more times more legible than lip reading.

15. A thorough presentation of methods and devices used to communicate with deaf-blind persons will be found in Kates and Schein 1980.

16. Carmel 1982.

17. Carmel 1982, 74.

18. The illustrations were drawn from a reproduction of an earlier Italian fingerspelled alphabet in Carmel 1982.

19. In Padden and Humphries 1988, 120, the authors discuss the different ways in which deaf people in various parts of the world insure that the information they present is clearly received: "Italian deaf people also use a signed language, but they use mouthing and lip reading more prominently than do American deaf people. They mouth names of individuals, places, and other borrowed Italian vocabulary, whereas American deaf people either fingerspell English words or translate them into signs. American deaf people, according to the Italian counterparts, 'barely move their mouths' and 'fingerspell rapidly.' To represent Danish words, deaf people in Denmark use a manual system that disambiguates mouthed vowels and consonants. This system is used along with the signed language of the culture." We observed that New Zealand deaf people are also heavily reliant on mouthing words, but they supplement it by fingerspelling the first letter of the word using their two-handed alphabet.

20. Padden 1990, 192.

21. Scouten 1967.

22. Cited in Scouten 1967, 52–53.

23. Padden 1981.

4

The Many Faces of Signing

*A*merican Sign Language (ASL), like other sign languages, is a natural language; its origins were never recorded, but it is likely that no one person invented it. It developed over centuries, shaped by its numerous users in everyday situations. The fact that deaf people all over the world have created sign languages attests to their innate capacity for language and their need to communicate. In this chapter we will explore the multifaceted nature of sign language, including the international aspects of sign language, how researchers analyze it, and how children acquire it. We will then look at how the educational system in the United States has adapted ASL as a way to teach English.

International Signs

American Sign Language is not a universal language. A deaf person from the United States faces a whole new sign vocabulary and different grammatical structures when conversing with a deaf person from England, Australia, Brazil, or most other countries. There may be some similarities in signs, expressing some concepts, but there will be signs that, although looking alike, have different meanings. The ASL sign for *deaf* is the sign for a *hearing person* in New Zealand Sign Language. The ASL letter *t* has the same meaning in France as the raised middle finger does in the United States and Canada. The ASL sign for *thirsty* means *vice* in Argentine Sign Language. Still, because deaf people are adept at using gestures and their bodies for communicating, they more freely communicate with their deaf counterparts around the world than do most individuals reliant on speech.

The relative ease with which deaf people from different countries communicate led Margaret Mead to suggest that sign language should be adopted as an international language.[1] Dr. Mead was hardly naive about sign language; she knew that each country has its own signs and that signs vary among deaf persons in the same country. Nonetheless, she urged that sign be considered as a way around the attachment people have for their native tongues. She reasoned that all nations adopting one sign language would arouse fewer objections than choosing one spoken language over all others.

The potential correctness of Mead's suggestion is attested to by a recent creation—Gestuno. It is the product of a committee of deaf leaders brought together under the auspices of the World Federation of the Deaf (WFD). The WFD's Unification of Signs Commission, which assembled Gestuno, consisted of Josif Guejlman of Russia, Allan B. Hayhurst of Great Britain, Willard J. Madsen of the United States, Francesco Rubino of Italy, and, until his death, Ole M. Plum of Denmark. Perhaps because the committee's work was divided among only five persons, it accomplished the astonishing task of overcoming national linguistic prejudices and agreeing on a basic set of 1,470 signs in less than two years. The lack of funds from government or other sources and the great distances that separated committee members may also have contributed to the speed with which they worked. They took signs not only from their own countries' sign languages, but also from Finland and Sweden. They tended to select the most iconic among those they examined. For example, the Gestuno sign MONEY or BUDGET mimes a bag of money. The commission considered it more transparent than the corresponding ASL sign (see Figure 4.1).

What about syntax? The commission finessed this issue. As the chair

Figure 4.1. The Gestuno (left) and ASL (right) signs for *money*.

noted, "This use of signs in isolation presents both a problem and a challenge to newcomers to the situation."[2] True, but it seems to have been a
challenge eagerly met and a problem rapidly overcome, to judge from the
use of Gestuno at international meetings of the WFD, where it is one of
three official languages (French and English sign languages are the other
two). When using Gestuno, signers put the individual signs in the order
most congenial to themselves, allowing the viewers to make of them what
they will. In practice Gestuno is not as difficult to understand as the hap-
hazard grammar may make it seem, particularly for deaf persons, for
whom ambiguity in communication is part of their daily experiences.

Gestuno is mainly used at international meetings of deaf organizations,
such as those sponsored by the WFD or the CISS (Comité International
des Sports des Sourds—International Committee of Sports for the Deaf).
CISS sponsors the World Games for the Deaf (WGD) for both winter and
summer sports.[3] Gestuno, or International Sign Language as it is more
commonly referred to at international deaf sport events, is the only signing
permitted during meetings of the executive committee, though most delegates are not fluent in its use. Still, it facilitates communication and adds
a unique linguistic flavor to the WGD, and many deaf spectators are attracted to the games by its use.[4]

Outside of WFD and CISS meetings Gestuno is not widely used. Since
its *raison d'etre* was international communication, that is to be expected.
It is too early to decide whether it will eventually join Esperanto (an international spoken language) as a noble but failed experiment or whether it
will reach the hoped-for status of a truly international language. Even before the advent of Gestuno, deaf people were successfully communicating
with their foreign peers, by means of a combination of iconic signs and
pantomime. Cesare Magarotto, former executive director of the WFD,
has written: "Through the language of gestures, which they practice and
keep alive, deaf people are able to establish friendly relations across any
frontier."[5] He points out that the original fifty-four member countries of
the WFD arrived at a constitution expeditiously, despite the lack of a common language. Magarotto also notes that at the meeting convened in 1951
to adopt the WFD's constitution "no political issues, no partisan views,
no legal quibbles hampered their clear, precise argument."[6] Such
a harmonious meeting stands in contrast to the often discordant gatherings at the United Nations, and it must arouse the envy of all who have
observed U. N. delegates wrangling endlessly and fruitlessly over petty
details.

Gestuno is not a true language in the sense of national sign languages of the world; it arose from the choices of a committee, not naturally like the languages from which it drew most of its signs. But the group selecting the signs consisted of potential users, of deaf people accustomed to signing who would be dependent on their decisions in future international meetings. Perhaps these differences in origin explain why, unlike Manual Codes for English, Gestuno appears viable over the long run.

Methods of Investigation

By now the reader may be curious about how researchers investigate sign languages. What strategies and tactics do they employ to arrive at the conclusions they make about ancient communication (reviewed in chapter 1) and about present-day signing (discussed in chapters 2 and 3).

The discovery of unique conventions for expressing thoughts and feelings among deaf persons who signed opened ASL to different linguistic analyses than it previously had. Earlier catalogers of sign mistakenly used English grammar as a point of reference for ASL syntax. They also concentrated only on handshapes and movements, believing that a description of them would provide a complete account of the meaning in a signed message. Some observers complained that deaf signers were overly expressive, that they exaggerated their delivery. They did not realize that what they perceived to be "exaggerations" were the nonmanual equivalents of punctuation, inflection, adjectives and adverbs, juncture markers, and other linguistic features. What they regarded as superfluous is now recognized as essential to a full understanding of sign languages. These early researchers clucked their tongues at the delay a deaf person experienced in learning proper English, never entertaining the notion that they, the linguists, lacked competence in ASL.

Writing ASL

ASL lacks a widely accepted transcription system. This may be because it has only recently caught the interest of linguists. Or it may be that the logistics of coding a visual-gestural language are overwhelming and destined to result in something of little practical use. Earlier researchers relied on drawings or photographs, neither particularly good at depicting motion. Some tried verbal descriptions like the following description of two American Indian signs:

When the Mind Closes

The anthropologist, Garrick Mallery, expressed concern for the linguistic ethnocentricity of people. In his classic monograph on American Indian Sign Language, he wrote:

> It is necessary to take with caution any statement from a person who, having memorized or hashed up any number of signs, large or small, has decided in his conceit that those he uses are the only genuine Simon Pure, to be exclusively employed according to his direction, all others being counterfeits or blunders. His vocabulary has ceased to give the signs of any Indian or body of Indians whatever, but becomes his own, the proprietorship of which he fights for as if secured by letters-patent. When a sign is contributed by one of the present collaborators, which such a sign talker has not before seen or heard of, he will at once condemn it as bad, just as a United States Minister to Vienna, who had been nursed in the mongrel Dutch of Berks County, Pennsylvania, declared that the people of Germany spoke very bad German.[7]

GALLOP. Make sign for RIDE; then bring hands in front of center of body, hands held edgewise, left near the body, right in front of same; move the hands simultaneously up and down several times in vertical curves, to imitate action of horse.

RIDE. If animal is meant, make the sign for HORSE and then move hands forward in small curves. If riding a vehicle make the sign for same, and then make sign for SIT on left palm.[8]

As you can see, such descriptions tend to be long and often imprecise. The sign GALLOP is described in terms of the sign RIDE, which in turn requires the reader to know the sign for *horse* and signs for various vehicles, as appropriate. An example of a verbal description of an ASL sign can be equally difficult to grasp:

WIFE: Make the sign for *female* (thumb of dominant hand stroking the side of the face at the jaw line) followed in a single motion by the sign MARRY (hands clasped together in front of chest).

Several conventions have been created that use English words to indicate a sign with equivalent meaning. The idea seems reasonable only if you accept a one-word-one-sign correspondence. That way of looking at

ASL, however, leads to some of the errors made by people learning to sign; directed by their search for word equivalents, they overlook critical features of ASL, including nonmanual linguistic cues (discussed in chapter 2).

Photographs provide a better representation of signs, although they are still unsatisfactory because they do not depict movement clearly. Photographs might also suffer because they include too much detail. Drawings might be a better alternative. Supplemented by verbal descriptions and by arrows to indicate direction of movement, they can give a fairly accurate idea of the distinguishing features of a sign. They lack a third dimension and, if the sequence of movements is complicated, they can become so cluttered they are difficult to read. Sequences of drawings help, but they can be cumbersome. Making accurate sketches requires skills few people have, and there is the ever-present problem of finding competent artists, especially those familiar with sign.

Why not write sign? Researchers in the field could use a shorthand to record their observations of signers. The solution would be some written form, much more incisive than our alphabet system but similarly compact. Several systems have been created. In the first sign dictionary using linguistic principles, Stokoe and his colleagues developed a notational system that uses special symbols with which to write the description of a sign.[9] The British Sign Language Workshop has adapted it to British Sign Language, adding a fourth category: orientation, which expands the description of the hands' positions relative to each other.[10] Linguists in other countries have made similar adaptations of Stokoe's system, retaining its basic concepts and most of its symbols (see Appendix A for a reproduction of its symbols).

Another method developed for representing signs is the Sign Writer.[11] This system makes extensive use of the computer and relies on symbols to depict the various characteristics of a sign, including facial expressions

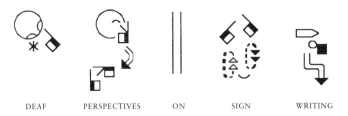

DEAF   PERSPECTIVES   ON   SIGN   WRITING

Figure 4.2. The sentence DEAF PERSPECTIVES ON SIGN WRITING written in Sign Writer.

such as raised eyebrows and the protrusion of the tongue. Figure 4.2 shows a sentence using the Sign Writer. The system, developed by Valerie J. Sutton, is now programmed for use on a personal computer. Sutton publishes a newsletter that includes many English sentences transcribed into Sign Writer. Again, like Stokoe's notations for signs, the Sign Writer has not caught on in the field of education. One reason for this might be ethnocentrism. The jump to an alternative symbol system to express language has to first overcome a resistance to anything that does not conform to the conventional alphabet. Like all other nonalphabetical notational systems, another of the Sign Writer's drawbacks is readability. How long would it take for someone to learn this system? Who would be motivated to do so? So far, the answers to these questions are not encouraging for its widespread use.

Other notational systems have been developed, again without much acceptance. Cohen, Namir, and Schlesinger (1977) have used the Eshkol-Wachmann Movement Notation System, created to record dance routines, to display Israeli Sign Language. Their book, translated into English, serves as a guide to the sign language used by Deaf Israelis as well as to the transcription system. George Sperling (1978) proposed that ideographs, like those used to write Japanese and Chinese, be composed for ASL. He has illustrated what such a system would look like but has not yet published this idea beyond the demonstration sample.

Modern technology, particularly the use of videos and films, compensates for the problems inherent in writing a sign language. The recordings can be viewed repeatedly by groups of qualified informants. In that way the reliability of interpretations can be determined, which is a scientific requirement. Researchers worry about the representativeness of their informants' language preferences—a concern that grows larger when a sign language is being studied because of the many variations of signed communication in active use. A sign language user in one part of the country may fail to understand a sign that is widely used in another part. Furthermore, using informants who communicate well in a spoken language, while often easing the researcher's task, may bias the findings if such informants' judgments about sign language grammar is contaminated by their knowledge of a spoken language. If signers of different ages, from different parts of the country, and with different school backgrounds all agree about a particular point, the researcher has strong evidence for the generality of that point. If they disagree, the researcher may have clues to a deeper understanding of the language by uncovering differences that relate to age, social class, and other factors. For reasons such as these, the modern linguist prefers to record material and present it to several informants rather than rely on one or two, as the earlier researchers did.

Because it is relatively inexpensive and flexible, requiring little technical background and minimal paraphernalia, video cameras have been widely used in recent studies of ASL. But whether on film or videotape, these permanent records also provide visual documentation of sign changes over time. Even though film and video images are two-dimensional representations of three-dimensional activities, they have been a major contributing factor in the development of a deeper appreciation of ASL. In the not-so-distant future, we could expect the development of computer programs that allow three-dimensional images to be projected on a monitor to provide the most accurate means for documenting ASL signs.

A Warning about Translation

Translations of any language always risk some loss of meaning or even misunderstanding, especially when a careless translator chooses the first meaning for a word or sign with multiple glosses. Kornei Chukovsky, a famous Russian translator complains:

> Translators often suffer from a peculiar anemia of the brain that causes their texts to waste away. What a calamity for a Hemingway, or a Kipling, or a Thomas Mann, or some other full-blooded author to fall into the hands of these anemic invalids! . . . I speak here about those translators whose vocabulary is wretchedly impoverished: a foreign word to them has only one lonely little meaning. . . . To them a horse is always a horse. Why not a steed, or a stallion, or a mount, or a jumper, or a trotter?[12]

ASL is no exception to this observation. Doing full justice to its semantics requires great care, a lot of time, and considerable empathy, as well as intimate knowledge of both languages and cultures. Good translations can be works of art in themselves.

Bilingual native users of any language can greatly contribute to an understanding of their native language and the translation process. Being able to converse with the investigators in their language, the natives can translate from and into the target language. The investigators may ask for an explanation of particular expressions (back translation) or ask how to express a concept (forward translation). Together, these two techniques

Who Does the Research?

Since studies were begun on matters relating to deaf people, nearly all researchers have been nondeaf. Research questions were typically framed from a pathological perspective that looked for deviations, as in "How does the language of deaf children differ from that of hearing children?" Now that deaf people are being viewed as a group with a unique culture and language, the pathological orientation to research with deaf people has fallen into disfavor. Deaf people are taking a stand on research and demanding that investigators include deaf people on their research teams. Roslyn Rosen, a deaf leader at Gallaudet University and the National Association of the Deaf, speaks out on this issue:

> The pathological paradigm was shifted with the advent of deaf researchers, scholars and practitioners in various human services disciplines in the 1970's. Deaf people, having intrinsic experiences, develop research questions, hypotheses and issues appropriate to deaf people. . . . Deaf researchers make sure that research projects are constructed according to deaf realities. Such research projects yield norms appropriate for deaf people. . . . research findings by or with deaf researchers tend to be more positive, human and cultural rather than negative and pathological.[13]

serve as a check, one on the other, and as a means of rapidly expanding knowledge of the grammar.[14]

Signed languages, like spoken languages, cannot be translated properly by exact equivalents—word to sign in this case. The purpose of translation is to convey meaning, not of the individual words or signs, but of the complete utterance. A simple matter such as plurality in ASL illustrates this point. To indicate the plural form in ASL a sign can be repeated. Seeing this repetition, a naive translator may incorrectly write "man, man," when the correct English equivalent is "men."

Compounding is another feature of ASL that could lead a translator astray. The ASL sign elements MAN-HOLD-BABY means "father"; translating the sign into its elements would be ridiculous. Similarly, translating the sign BELIEVE (Figure 4.3) as "mind-marry" would be a mistake even though BELIEVE is a compound of the two signs MIND and MARRY. In ASL that sign indicates the concept of belief. How it arrives at that is not a straight-

Figure 4.3. The sign BELIEVE is a compound formed from the signs MIND and MARRY.

forward matter. Neither is a strictly phonological analysis of English compounds. The word *mindless* in English can be shown to be made up of two separate words: *mind* and *less,* but interpreting it as "having less mind" would miss the definition—"heedless, inattentive, unintelligent."

Translators must be aware of differences in ASL and English syntax. The signs COFFEE BLACK LIKE ME are correctly translated into English as "I like my coffee black" (Figure 2.30 and the discussion about it in chapter 2). Another source of difficulty for translators is that ASL signs can be glossed in more than one way. If a deaf architect signs STRUCTURE (which may look like a pantomimed gesture for *house*), should it be translated as "building," "house," "structure," or what? The same sign made by a small child could, depending on context, be interpreted as "home." Obviously, the level of English vocabulary chosen to translate a sign should be consistent with the linguistic status of the signer.

Comparative Linguistics

Comparative linguistics is used to contrast and compare how languages have developed under various circumstances throughout the world. In this way we can gain insight into the paths that language development might have taken from earliest times until today. This is not simply etymology, but the broader investigation of how language problems are dealt with in different cultures. How does a particular language handle the concept of time? By what means does a speaker indicate that an action has taken place, is now occurring, or will take place later? Do all cultures have such concepts? How do the languages account for gender, age, and other human attributes?

Observations of similarities and differences in languages highlight universals when they occur and expose linguistic characteristics that are modality specific. As the previous chapters have illustrated, all languages must account for time, but how they convey that concept depends on the language and its modality. Above all, comparative linguistics supports the innate capacity of all persons for communication.

Studies of Language Acquisition

One popular approach has been to observe the acquisition of sign language by young deaf children.[15] Seeing how children acquire their first language provides insights into the syntactical structure of the language, insights not easily made from observations of adults only. Comparing language acquisition in deaf children with that in hearing children can lead to uncovering the relationship between visual-spatial and auditory-temporal languages. Such comparisons provide clues to the reasons spoken and signed languages diverge structurally. As one example:

> When hearing children acquiring a spoken language make the transition from prelinguistic gestural communication to language, a modality change occurs. Deaf children acquiring a sign language communicate prelinguistically and linguistically in the same visual-gestural modality. Thus, comparisons between hearing children acquiring spoken language and deaf children acquiring sign language may help to clarify the relationship between prelinguistic communication and language.[16]

From 1958 to 1964 a Dutch educator studied motion pictures of deaf schoolchildren in Holland and the United States while they were signing to each other.[17] He concluded that the Dutch and American children developed different sign languages that not only had specialized vocabularies, but also had syntactical rules differing from their native speech and sign languages. Because sign language was, and still is, rarely taught to deaf schoolchildren, even in schools that use signed communication in the classroom, the development of these new signs and deviant grammatical forms offered evidence of how languages create conventions and signs when established ones are unknown or inadequate.

Two linguists examined six deaf children ranging in age from seventeen to forty-nine months whose parents did not know or use ASL or any other form of signed communication.[18] The investigators found that these children developed a structured signed communication system without ever having seen one. Their results strongly support the notion that humans have a natural inclination for systematic communication in contrast to the idea that children learn their caretakers' language by imitation only. Studying the evidence, reviewers conclude that "there is a human biological capacity for language representing a set of internal norms for language" and, if "input in any language development situation is inaccessible or inadequate, for whatever reason, humans will construct their grammar on the basis of these internal norms."[19] In other words, people are predisposed to the learning of language in whatever form it might take.

These studies show how deaf children acquire sign language, but what about hearing children who have deaf parents? Do they acquire both sign and spoken language? And if so, which develops first? Several researchers have looked into this. One researcher studied several sets of deaf parents and their children.[20] The six children, some hearing, some deaf, were observed over the course of a year, and in that time all developed sign language skills.

In another study, two researchers observed a young hearing child with one deaf and one hearing parent to determine which language she acquired first.[21] At seven months the little girl demonstrated her first word—in sign. This contrasts with the emergence of hearing children's first spoken word, which usually occurs between ten and fourteen months of age.[22] Over the following year she alternated in her acquisition of speech and sign, suggesting that learning the one did not interfere with learning the other.

The data from this and other studies indicate that it is easier for children—whether hearing or deaf—to learn to communicate with their hands than it is to learn to speak. Children who are exposed to both signing and speaking in infancy develop sign language first. A major reason for the earlier emergence of signs is that children less than a year old have better neurological control of their hands than of their speech mechanisms. Consider the case of Davey, a hearing child of hearing parents who were fluent signers. The parents signed and spoke to Davey from infancy and as a result he acquired his first fifty signs at fifteen months of age and his first fifty spoken words at sixteen months of age.[23] A normal control group exposed only to speech attained the fifty-word average for male children at 22.1 months of age. In fact Davey had acquired a combined total of fifty spoken and signed words by fourteen months of age—an amazing eight months ahead of the control group.

These observations in natural environments of early language acquisition expose some of the linguistic treasures that may be buried under earlier prejudices against sign language. Clearly, sign holds primacy in early language development.

More Features of Sign Languages

How adequately can you communicate in a sign language? Can you swear in sign? Does a sign language have derogatory signs? Are sign languages up-to-date, with signs for the new drugs and technologies? Space flight? Medical terminology? The answer to all these questions is yes. ASL has a full range of blasphemies. There may not be a precise one-to-one relation between the swear words of English and the ASL versions, but there are ample signs to cover all pejoratives and cast every curse. As for technical terms, many have sign equivalents. *Signs for Computing Terminology* is a book that illustrates signs for words like *circuit, floppy disk,* and *computer terminal.*[24] It gives testimony that, as technologies demand new signs, ASL will accommodate them.

No aspect of sexual behavior is without a sign, whether male or female, homosexual or heterosexual. *Signs of Sexual Behavior*[25] and *Signs for Sexuality*[26] are two books where these signs have been collected. Distinguishing between various sexual signs is critical, as seen in a court case where a deaf man was asked if he wanted to rape the woman he was alleged to have attacked. The interpreter signed, "Did you want to *have intercourse with* the woman?" Obviously, his yes response could have resulted in his conviction—a conviction based on a misinterpretation.[27]

Knowledge of the range of sexual signs is useful. Sexual signs include names for body parts, very important to physicians examining deaf persons. Therapists working with emotionally disturbed deaf clients need to know them. Similarly, a dictionary of terms for drug use, including slang in vogue, is invaluable for counseling deaf teenagers.[28] Special collections of signs have been developed for teaching highly technical subjects, for use in medical emergency rooms, and for other specialized purposes.[29]

Where in the World?

There are about 450,000 words in use in the English language. No other language has a vocabulary anywhere near this size. But where did all of these words come from? As Robert Claiborne points out in *The Roots of English*: everywhere.

"Alcohol" and "alkali" are from Arabic; "amok," from Malay; "bizarre," from the mysterious Basque tongue of northern Spain. "Coach" comes from a Hungarian town; "parka," from the Samoyeds of the northern Urals; "skunk" and "chili" from the Native Americans; and "taboo" from Tahitian. "Okay" was brought into English by slaves from West Africa; "corral," by Mexican cattlemen—who learned it from Portuguese sailors, who learned it from the Hottentot herders of southern Africa.[30]

Sign languages also use signs that have their origins in another sign language. ASL was heavily influenced by French Sign Language. However, documenting the correspondences is made difficult by the lack of written records of sign.

The Expanding Vocabulary of Sign Language

Sign languages add signs just as spoken languages add words. New concepts call for distinctive ways to indicate them. In English we have such loan words as *blitzkrieg*, from the German, and *hara-kiri*, from the Japanese. For other examples, see "Where in the World."

ASL probably borrows from other sign languages, though the lack of written records makes this difficult to prove. If one finds, say, ASL and Portuguese Sign Language both using the same sign, how can one determine which borrowed from which? As for signs based on English words, ASL often uses a fingerspelled letter to sign a new word. For example, the letter Q signed in context stands for *Quaaludes*. Such instances affirm ASL's recognition of English, though it cannot directly borrow words. It also borrows words by modifying their fingerspelled form (see "Lexical Borrowing" in chapter 3 for examples).

Iconicity

How do you determine the extent to which signs are iconic (that is, to which they are attempts to picture the subject or action)? Pantomime uses actions to picture objects and activities not present. The mime conveys the presence of a wall by the way he reacts to a part of the space around him; or he may go through the motions of eating a meal, though no food or implements are there. When the signer expresses the thought, "I am going to the movies," does he pantomime the action, or does he use arbitrarily selected signs? The question has relevance to sign language's status as a language, since pantomime lacks the linguistic status accorded abstract symbols.

First of all, if signs are iconic, then uninformed observers should be able to recognize them. A number of studies have presented signs to persons who have never studied ASL and asked them to guess what they mean. The results have shown consistently that most signs are not transparent, that their meanings are not correctly identified by naive persons.[31]

Second, researchers find that signs for the same concepts are different in various sign languages.[32] For example, the sign DEAF in ASL is made by moving the index finger from mouth to ear or vice versa. In New Zealand Sign Language this same sign means "hearing," as in a person who can hear normally. Since the concepts are universally understood, the fact that their representations differ in various sign languages argues against the iconicity of sign.

A third strategy for studying iconicity turns to native signers for evidence. Deaf persons cannot read signs from another sign language on first contact, something you would expect them to be able to do for iconic signs. Along these same lines researchers have asked native signers for explanations of the signs they use. These attempts to uncover iconicity reveal conflicting rationales and post hoc explanations that do not accord with the established knowledge of a sign's origins, where such knowledge exists.[33]

An equally compelling argument against imposing an iconic explanation on most signs is that it cannot be invoked as a factor in young deaf children's acquisition of them. Take the sign MILK. For those who regard it as repeating the motions of milking a cow, the application of that iconic element is difficult to support in face of the obvious lack of experience with cows on the part of most young deaf children, who nevertheless do learn the sign quickly and easily. Most of these same children only know that milk comes from cartons bought in supermarkets, something not derivable from the sign.

Even if signs do contain some iconic elements, that feature does not detract from the arbitrariness of the signs. Of every sign that is supposedly iconic we could ask why has the particular aspect of an object or action been chosen to represent the whole? Those making that claim would need to show consistent reasons for the choices of elements in the signs on which they base their argument. So far, no such consistencies have been demonstrated. Furthermore, signs tend to become more and more arbitrary over time; they change in a direction away from the imputed iconicity as they pass from generation to generation.[34]

Some researchers have found that iconicity is sometimes used by deaf people for poetic or humorous purposes. This can be seen in a description of a poetic rendering of the sign SLOW (the right hand brushing along the left hand from fingertips to wrist).[35] A deaf actor took nearly twice as long to make that sign as any other sign in the poem he was reciting. It is the equivalent of a speaker drawing out the syllables of the word "slo-o-o-wly." The way the sign was made emphasized its meaning. Native and fluent ASL signers appear to make use of possibilities for being "picturesque," for spicing up their signs with paralinguistic features. Some iconic-seeming elements may actually have linguistic purposes as modifiers. They differ from pantomime in that they are conventionalized, regularly conveying meaning beyond the supposedly representational aspect. What at first appears to be iconic, then, may be a grammatical construction. That this confusion occurs is demonstrated by signs that are judged to be iconic in isolation but are not correctly identified when presented in complete expressions. The result is either mistaken attribution or total absence of transparency.[36]

The final word on iconicity rightly belongs to Stokoe, who argues that it is not a bad thing. After all, the function of a language is to communicate. If signs with greater iconic features aid communication, then iconic features should be looked upon as valuable. The genius of sign languages lies in their combining abstractness with iconicity in ways that facilitate communication.[37]

How Many Signs are in ASL?

Any discussion of a sign language's capacity to add signs usually prompts the question, "How many signs are there?" The answer can be no more precise than the answer to the same question about a spoken language. Using ASL as an example, we would first have to decide what would be counted as a sign. Do you count all versions of *to do* or only the infinitive form? Do you include all regional variations of a sign? There is a text on regional variations of a selected group of signs.[38] In this text, the word *candy* has fourteen variations. You can see that this decision alone would alter the total greatly. What about compounds? How that decision is made will grossly affect the answer.

You could count entries in the leading sign dictionaries. The most extensive contains 5,200 English words, for which there are 7,200 illustrations, according to the publisher.[39] Why nearly a fifth more drawings than words? Because ASL has more than one sign for a single English word, just as a single English word may have several glosses. But do entries in dictionaries represent the extent of ASL's sign field? Hardly.

The question about the number of signs can be approached in another way. In 1962 Dean George Detmold, who directed student dramas as well as heading the faculty of Gallaudet University, commissioned a tour de force to demonstrate that ASL had unlimited linguistic scope. He asked William Stokoe to translate into sign Act III of Bernard Shaw's *Man and Superman* (the play within a play called "Don Juan in Hell"). The act is almost wholly made up of speeches by the four characters: Don Juan, Donna Elvira, her father, and the Devil. Their discussions are largely of abstract subjects—love, hate, peace, and war. Here is a representative sample of one of the speeches:

> *Don Juan*: Pooh! why should I be civil to them or to you? In this Palace of Lies a truth or two will not hurt you. Your friends are all the dullest dogs I know. They are not beautiful: they are only decorated. They are not clean: they are only shaved and starched. They are not dignified: they are only fashionably dressed. They are not educated: they are only college passmen. They are not religious: they are only pewrenters. They are not moral: they are only conventional. They are not virtuous: they are only cowardly. They are not even vicious: they are only "frail." They are not artistic: they are only lascivious. They are not prosperous: they are only rich. They are not loyal, they are only servile; not dutiful, only sheepish; not public spirited, only patriotic; not courageous, only quarrelsome; not determined, only obstinate; not masterful, only domineering; not self-controlled, only obtuse; not self-respecting, only vain; not kind, only sentimental; not social, only gregarious; not considerate, only polite; not intelligent, only opinionated; not progressive, only factious; not imaginative, only superstitious; not just, only vindictive; not generous, only propitiatory; not disciplined, only cowed; and not truthful at all—liars every one of them, to the very backbone of their souls.[40]

That speech, like the rest of the dialogue, was successfully signed by a talented group of deaf college students. The production was so well received that the students were invited to repeat their performance on a local television station, which they did to considerable critical acclaim.[41] Incidentally, you will not find a sign for every word in Don Juan's eloquent peroration; *passmen*, for example, is not only not a term in ASL, it is also not used in American English. Of course, Stokoe found signs that were true to the playwright's intent. That problem usually arises in translating from one language to another. ASL is not limited in its ability to express concepts, whether technical or artistic or whatever. If there is any limitation, it exists only in the minds and hands of the translator.

Communication Methods in Education

Speechreading and Cued Speech

Speechreading (or lipreading) has frequently been proposed as a receptive alternative to manual communication. The deaf observer interprets changes in lip shapes and other clues on the speaker's face to decode what is spoken. Speechreading is a difficult skill to acquire, and excellent speech readers are few and far between. As every deaf person knows, even in the best of times, speechreading is a guessing game. In English sixteen different mouth movements are distinguishable. These sixteen represent the thirty-eight English phonemes.[42] Thus, the mouth movements for differing speech sounds may look the same, and the distinguishing features are

---

Guess What?

In spite of the facts, stories abound of expert speechreaders being brought into court to interpret videotaped dialogues. Most authors of spy thrillers cannot resist the temptation to include a fictional character who from several miles away speechreads through binoculars a madman's sinister plot. And it is true that when Queen Elizabeth attended a Maryland football game many years ago, *Life* magazine paid an expert speechreader to observe her and report her comments. (She made so few that the idea never received an adequate test, though it did arouse protests from those who felt the Queen's privacy had been violated.)

made by invisible articulators, such as the tongue and larynx. To clarify the point, look in the mirror as you say *bop, mop, pop.* Visually they are nearly identical. Or try to distinguish between *dime* and *time.* If one of those two words appears on a speaker's face, along with a questioning look, do you reach for your wallet or your watch?

In 1966 Orin Cornett conceived of a technique for improving speech-reading accuracy. He reasoned that deaf children, like everybody else, need a formal communication system at an early age. Sign language fulfills that need, but hearing parents (the majority of deaf children's parents) are usually slow to learn one. Even manual codes for English require time and effort to achieve a reasonable competence. For Cornett the obvious solution was to devise a simple technique to aid speechreading. It would focus on English, a language familiar to most North American parents of deaf children, and would be quickly mastered by them. The result of his reasoning was Cued Speech.[43] Cued Speech is *not* another form of sign language, nor is it a version of fingerspelling. It is a speechreading aid consisting of hand signals (cues) that indicate speech sounds. Cued Speech proponents prefer to associate it with oral education of deaf children.[44]

Cued Speech uses four hand positions to distinguish eleven English vowels, and eight handshapes to differentiate twenty-five consonants, plus movements for some diphthongs (Figure 4.4). The user of Cued Speech need only distinguish between three lip shapes—open, flattened-relaxed, and rounded. The hand position then identifies the intended phoneme among the look-alikes.

Teachers of deaf children have long used hand signals in teaching speech. A finger on the nose typically indicates nasality; on the throat it indicates voicing. Such simple signals contrast vividly with the numerous cues suggested by Cornett. This contrast is not unexpected as there is a major difference between the use of a few hand signals to cue speech characteristics (voiced, unvoiced) and their use to clarify an entire conversation. Simple as the system sounds, there is much for users to learn, and much to keep in mind besides communicating when using the system. Cornett recognizes these points and urges that his approach be learned by students who already have a strong language base and that it be used to clarify ambiguous words and statements. He refers to Cued Speech as a "back-up system." It has achieved a modest degree of success in a few programs scattered throughout the United States and Canada but has made no greater impact on the education of deaf children than was planned by its innovator.

Vowel Positions   Consonant Handshapes

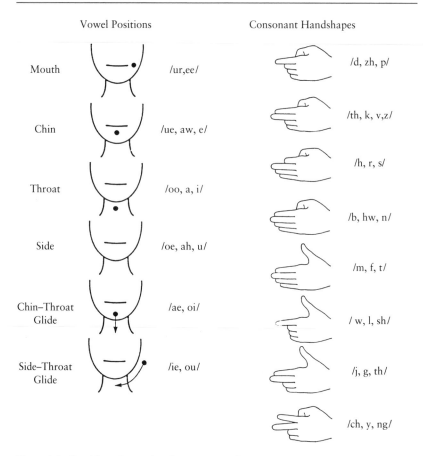

Figure 4.4. Cued Speech vowel and consonant codes.
Source: Cued Speech Office, Gallaudet University, Washington, D.C.

Historically, Cued Speech is the end of a line of compromises between strict oralism and supplemented oralism. Two French educators in the nineteenth century thought it likely that a system of hand signals to indicate which consonant was being spoken would improve the education of deaf children.[45] Their intention was to use speech in teaching deaf children, with the hand signals resolving the difficult-to-distinguish lip configurations. Because fewer hand shapes would be involved, they reasoned, the system would be easy to learn and fast to apply. In Denmark, Georg Forchhammer created a similar system that he named the Hand-Mund (Hand-Mouth) system.[46] It has been used in Danish schools for deaf children for most of this century. The system has not been adopted by other Scandinavian countries.

A Historical Recap of Sign Language Use in the Classroom

Between 1880 and the late 1960s a majority of educational programs for deaf children forbad sign language in the classroom. When many deaf students failed to reach satisfactory levels of educational achievement, some teachers hoped that by tapping into deaf adults' preferred form of communication, deaf students' instruction would become more effective. On the surface the notion appears reasonable: if signs are unrestricted in their capacity to convey thoughts, then why not use them to represent spoken languages? Deaf children have limited access to spoken English but have full access to signs. So all teachers need do is replace English words with ASL signs. If there is no sign for a particular word, create one or fingerspell it. The result will bear little resemblance to ASL. Instead, it will be a *manual code for English* (MCE).

The Abbé de l'Epée followed that line of reasoning in creating his Methodical System of French Signs and using it to set up the first school for deaf students in Paris in 1755.[47] In the eighteenth century his method swept across Europe, gaining broad acceptance for the then-new idea that deaf children could be educated.

Returning to the United States from France in 1816 Thomas Hopkins Gallaudet and the deaf teacher he recruited in Paris, Laurent Clerc, followed Epée's approach with the slight modification of using English syntax for ordering the signs. And why not? The method had received glowing reports of its successes in France and in several European countries. Historians now acknowledge that Clerc, who succeeded Gallaudet as the leader in education of American deaf children, changed his mind about Epée's method, choosing instead to use natural sign language (see "Laurent Clerc Reminisces"). For Clerc, the Methodical System opened the educational door, but once through that door natural sign language took over.

The evidence we have from the period 1817 up to 1880 suggests that deaf students were doing well in terms of educational achievement. The use of signs that stimulated the education of deaf children, however, rapidly faded after the Milan conference of 1880. With the occasional exception of the secondary level where a few deaf teachers were employed and allowed to sign, sign language was not used in deaf students' classes.

Halfway into the twentieth century, the instructional pendulum began to swing back. In England in 1955 Pierre Gorman took up the work of Sir Richard Paget, who conceived of "a new sign language."[48] Now known as the Paget-Gorman Systematic Sign Language, it is a code for English

Laurent Clerc Reminisces

Drawing from the annals of deaf education, Harlan Lane attempts to capture Laurent Clerc's eventual departure from using MCE in the classroom by putting himself in Clerc's shoes to reveal his thoughts.

I confess that I learned this system of methodical signing from Sicard just as Epée's pupils had from the master, and I espoused it for some years, even after coming to America with Gallaudet. Thus we would first express some thought in American (or French) Sign Language, for example, "Try to understand me," which requires two signs, appropriately placed and carried out, that we can label TRY and UNDERSTAND-ME. Then, using the same sign language, we would teach and explain the ten methodical signs so the student could express the thought in manual English. . . . It took the genius of Sicard's disciple and successor, Roch-Ambroise Bébian, to help us realize that all this was a needless encumbrance on our instruction, that the labor involved in teaching the ten methodical signs was the very labor required to teach the corresponding English sentence. There was no need for the intermediate step of manual English. And so increasingly we presented the idea in American Sign Language and then turned at once to the written language. By the 1830s methodical signs had disappeared on both sides of the Atlantic.[49]

similar to Epée's code for French. This approach was stimulated by deaf students' lack of academic achievement since the abolishment of signing in the classroom.[50]

In January 1969 deaf individuals, parents of deaf children, children of deaf parents, sign-language interpreters, teachers, and educational administrators met in California "to discuss appropriate, effective ways to represent English in a gestural mode."[51] Gerilee Gustason, one of the authors of *Signing Exact English,* said that the main concern of this group "was the consistent, logical, rational, and practical development of signs to represent as specifically as possible the basic essentials of the English language." Their goal was to develop "an easier, more successful way of developing mastery of English in a far greater number" of deaf students.[52] The participants later split and developed three competing systems: Seeing Essential English (SEE 1), Signing Exact English (SEE 2), and Linguistics of Visual English (LOVE). Of the three systems only SEE 2 remains widely used in American schools. Other similar systems include Signed English, Manual English, and Preferred Signs. Collectively, these various approaches have been called artificial or contrived signs, but most often in the literature they are referred to as Manual Codes for English (MCE), a usage we have adopted for this book.

A number of factors supported the use of MCE over ASL in American schools. Deaf adults' pride in ASL had barely surfaced in 1969, and research into its structure had barely begun. To hearing teachers unfamiliar with signing, ASL looked like a disorganized mishmash of gestures. They dismissed ASL as a "foreign" language that should have no place in the classroom. Still, they could not deny the communication effectiveness of sign. Having looked into the Deaf community and found a language they could not understand, the communication engineers reverted to MCE. After all, it looked to them like English. Indeed, it is English—on the hands.

Furthermore, teachers found MCE easier to learn than ASL, or at least that is what they thought. To learn ASL takes a lot of time and effort because both vocabulary and grammar must be learned, while on the surface it appears that MCE demands only that equivalent signs for spoken words be learned and not a new grammar. In reality signing MCE in the way it was meant to be signed requires a great deal of signing skill and the more fluent people are in signing ASL, the more likely they are to be able to sign MCE. But this fact did not deter the field from rushing ahead in support of MCE. Finally, for educational administrators confronting parents, being able to tell them that their children would be taught in English—though the English would be signed instead of spoken—had the advantage of lowering any resistance to the curriculum. The only advantage MCE could not claim over ASL was that its use had been demonstrated scientifically to be more advantageous to the deaf student.

Common Characteristics of MCE

We will not attempt to provide an in-depth description of the structure of the various MCE systems. Some have all but disappeared from the field, and those that are still around are often inconsistently used, even by many of their supporters. What we will do is outline what we believe are the critical elements that most share. The reader should be aware that some versions of MCE do not follow the examples below, and some add other principles.

PRINCIPLES OF SIGN SELECTION/FORMATION. The main source for MCE signs is ASL. In deciding whether or not to use an existing sign,

MCE applies various tests. One principle is the two-out-of-three rule. Each English word is characterized by its sound, spelling, and meaning. If a word matches any two of these characteristics, it must have the same sign, irrespective of whether or not an ASL sign is available for each of the words. Words that have multiple meanings, such as *run, board,* and *case,* are signed the same way even when their meanings differ. MCE uses the same sign for *fall* in each of the following sentences:

- You might *fall* on the ice.
- What is your *fall*-back position?
- *Fall* in line!
- I will see you in the *fall.*
- The deal will *fall* through without your support.

In ASL each concept associated with the word *fall* will be signed differently. Similarly, ASL uses different signs for *right* (the direction), *right* (correct), and *right* (entitlement), while most MCE systems require the same sign for all three.

A second principle is to avoid ambiguity. If a sentence uses the word *tree,* MCE adopts that ASL sign (Figure 4.5). To sign FOREST, ASL repeats the TREE sign, but MCE regards that solution as insufficiently definitive and modifies the existing sign by incorporating the fingerspelled first letter of the word into it. For FOREST, SEE 2 signs TREE with an F handshape, as shown in Figure 4.5.

Two rationales for using initialized signs are that (a) exposure to them helps deaf children learn the English words, thus aiding their print reading and speechreading, and (b) the initial letter provides greater specification

TREE   FOREST

Figure 4.5. MCE signs for TREE and FOREST

Figure 4.6. Three forms of the verb *to be* in MCE.

of the word designated by the sign. This reasoning makes clear MCE's basic purpose: to replicate English manually.

VERBS. If there is no acceptable ASL sign, MCE creates one. For example, ASL does not have signs for the various tenses of *to be*, so MCE adds them.[53] Figure 4.6 shows three forms of the copula *to be* used in all MCE systems. The handshapes distinguish *is, are,* and *were* by forming the initial letter of each word. In addition, the sign for *were* reverses the direction of signing *is* and *are* to show the past tense by taking advantage of ASL's time line (see chapter 2).

Another modification of verbs puts them in their participial mode. In ASL creating participles does not follow a single rule. In English the participle is usually made by adding *ing* (in the present tense) or *ed* or *en* (in the past tense). To indicate the present participle of any verb, MCE follows the verb sign with an -ING sign as in the sign DRIVING, which is signed DRIVE + ING (Figure 4.7).

MCE also has signs that correspond to English affixes or markers. SEE 1 has 127 such affixes, SEE 2 has 67, and Signed English has 14.[54] To use them, the MCE signer adds them to the verb sign as appropriate. For example, SEE 2 and Signed English both follow DEVELOP with a sign for -MENT to sign *development* (Figure 4.8). ASL distinguishes between the verbal and nominal forms of the concept by repeating it. Signed once, DE-VELOP is a verb; signed twice, it becomes the noun DEVELOPMENT.

PRONOUNS. MCE differentiates the seventeen pronouns of English with seventeen different signs. As discussed in chapter 2, ASL uses a much simpler strategy to accomplish the same purposes. Which strategy teachers

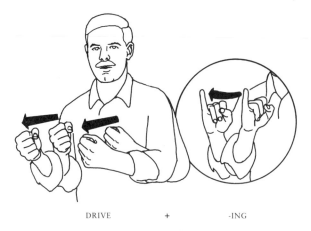

DRIVE   +   -ING

Figure 4.7. In MCE the progressive tense is signed by adding the *-ing* marker to the verb.

use depends in part on what they are trying to accomplish, as in providing a manual code for English, and in part the prevailing language of instruction in their classroom. However, there are social consequences of choosing MCE signs over ASL, as is true in how one speaks English (see chapter 7).

Signing MCE

When teachers first learn one of the MCE systems, they are often told to keep their signs close to their chests and within sight of their mouths, the

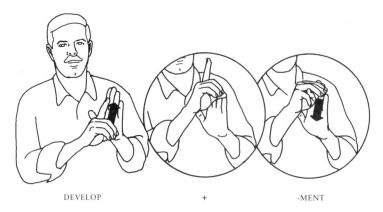

DEVELOP   +   -MENT

Figure 4.8. The SEE 2 and Signed English sign for *development* is made by combining DEVELOP and the *-ment* marker.

notion being that deaf students will be better able to read lips if they do not have to divert their gaze too far from the mouth of the speaker. This idea makes a lot of sense to naive signers and those who are not dependent on signing or speechreading for communication.[55] Yet observe any signed conversations with deaf people and see how they concentrate their gaze on the signer's face, not on the hands or lips. You will also notice how they freely use the space around them for signing.

Critique of MCE

Although MCE uses ASL signs, this does not mean that it is ASL. All creators of MCE systems take great pains to explain that the role of MCE is to provide a visual-gestural model of English. The creators of SEE 2 say that their system "is NOT a replacement for ASL and is meant for use by parents of young children and by teachers of English."[56] The creators of Signed English are just as careful in separating their system from ASL.

> Signed English is not a language. It is not a substitute for the American Sign Language. It was designed for a different purpose. The basic reason one uses ASL is to communicate with users of that language. Signed English resembles ASL primarily because the overwhelming majority of signs are taken directly from ASL. When a sign "enters" the Signed English system, it becomes the semantic equivalent of one given English word. Much of the time, the ASL sign and the sign word have the same meaning. Sometimes they do not. Moreover, sign order and structural characteristics differ as well between ASL and English.[57]

History shows that whenever MCE gains in popularity there follows a *decline* in its use. Laurent Clerc was no exception. Though Lane is only offering his interpretation of events from an era in which little was documented, his conjecture that Clerc abandoned MCE in favor of ASL nevertheless accords with the facts as we know them. And Clerc's reasoning seems applicable today (see "Laurent Clerc Reminisces"). Bernard Bragg, a deaf actor, has attempted to take the steam out of the ASL-vs.-MCE debate and shift attention to the effectiveness of a communication act.[58] He states that the separation of ASL and English-based signing and the disparaging of the latter are counterproductive to the total act of communicating as well as to the acquisition of English by deaf children. He advocates the use of the abbreviation "ASL" as a generic term that would embody all forms of signing. If ASL becomes the only label for signing, then it would reduce the amount of energy and effort expended on labeling, analyzing, and comparing different forms of signing. Leo Jacobs, a deaf educator, has expressed doubts about the value of MCE and calls for a full acceptance of ASL as the language of instruction. He recognizes that not all deaf people sign ASL in the same way and that any "deviation of ASL should be accepted as either useful teaching tools or comfortable adaptations to meet the needs of particular cultural groups."[59]

The proposals of Bragg and Jacobs do have support in the Deaf community and among teachers. And why shouldn't they? After all, the business of ASL is to communicate effectively and appropriately. ASL meets this objective. It is an eclectic language in that "it borrows and incorporates whatever is needed from various usages to complete the communicative act successfully when deaf people of different backgrounds or the deaf and hearing communities meet and need to communicate."[60] If ASL were the only label for signing, perhaps teachers, parents, and others would drop the debate about how to sign and get on with the business of communicating.

A look at media outlets in the Deaf community such as the *NAD Broadcaster* and *Silent News* reveals an ever-growing dissatisfaction with MCE in the Deaf community. The explosion of ASL courses and ASL's increasing exposure in the general media over the past few years have aroused support for ASL, rather than MCE. Nevertheless, MCE has contributed to the current ASL renaissance. When it was introduced, it did not represent a threat to the status quo of English as the primary language of the classroom. It provided a cushion for parents and teachers making the transition from a strictly oral approach to one that incorporated signs. Once MCE became accepted, teachers and parents became more willing to attend to what deaf people had to say about using ASL as an instructional language in schools.

Few teachers, however, have used an MCE system the way it was meant to be used.[61] From the outset the correct application of MCE faced an uphill battle in the schools as most teachers had to learn it on their own time and without role models to emulate. Variability in its implementation has confounded research on its effectiveness. What research has been conducted has been interpreted as demonstrating that MCE has met its goal, at least with some deaf children.[62] The positive evidence, however, has not slowed the decline in MCE's popularity after the initial enthusiasm that greeted its reappearance in the 1970s.

An important consideration in discussing reactions to MCE is that its creators neglected the physiology of seeing and hearing. First, adding suffixes burdens short-term memory by violating the recency effect: we remember best what we see last. MCE unwittingly places emphasis on the ending rather than the root of a word (sign). Vocally, this can be overcome by the way words are pronounced, with the emphasis on the root. Second, MCE ignores ASL's great economy by adding features that burden visual communication. Adding signs for pronouns that can be indicated with a glance or incorporated into the motion of a signed action verb is unduly laborious.

The choices and inventions of signs in MCE have sometimes provoked ridicule among deaf people. ASL's origins have deep iconic roots.[63] Signing RIGHT (the direction) to indicate entitlement and correctness seems ludicrous to ASL signers—and to us. English imposes no such rule, providing numerous synonyms for many of its concepts and permitting more than one gloss for a single word. It appears the creators of most MCEs have been more concerned with replicating speech than with communicating. Thus, the fading of MCE from educational use may be due in large part to its overinsistence on trying to copy too closely the speech act by using the hands. Whatever the reasons for its lessened popularity, none of the systems seems impervious to correction. It may be too early to close the book on MCE.

Deaf people have their own ways to present English structures using their knowledge of ASL. Marlon Kuntze, a deaf teacher, notes that the coexistence of English and ASL has led to the "gradual infiltration of English structures and their modification into what fits within the system of ASL."[64] This feeling has been echoed by others, as the following quote shows:

> MCE just may have worked itself out of the education system. After more than two decades in the trenches its support is quickly waning. This is not as tragic as some might expect. Presenting English in signs whether it be through signs, fingerspelling or a combination of both is part of the linguistic make-up of the deaf community. Deaf parents will resort to some form of community-based signed English from time to time with their deaf children. Perhaps, the demise of MCE would lead to a more natural and acceptable way of representing English in signs.[65]

Thus, there may be no need to create a sign system for expressing English in signs since a mechanism is already available to proficient ASL users. This view is shared by many deaf people and is the basis of ASL/English

If the Shoe Fits

The late deaf educator and rehabilitation expert Larry Stewart came to terms with the many communication options, including MCE, that deaf people face in their daily lives and he commented humorously:

> "Plain deaf folks have discovered a great truth. . . . [I]n the great trenches of life, where daily battles are fought and won or lost, linguistic theory—and all other academic theory for that matter—counts about as much in the great scheme of things as a flea on a leaf floating down the Mississippi River at spring flood. The reality is that most deaf folks have had to use whatever was at hand at the time, theory be damned, including SEE-1, SEE-2, SEE-Heinz 57, Siglish, the Rochester method, Cued Speech, gestures, flipped birdies, demonstrations, pointing, eye blinking, face twitching, head nodding, ear wiggling, and just about everything else that might possibly help to bridge the vast gulf that normally separates us deaf people from one another. In attempting to communicate with hearing, non-signing people, deaf people have had to resort to lip reading, writing, gestures, pointing, demonstrations, head nodding, smiling, frowning, more than one birdie, squinting, grimacing, scowling, and just plain gazing in stupefied resignation when all else failed." [66]

bilingual education programs at various school programs in the United States and Canada.

Notes

1. Mead 1976.
2. Madsen 1976a.
3. Stewart 1991. The author has written extensively on the role of sports in the Deaf community and the influence of ASL on the socialization of deaf athletes and spectators.
4. Stewart 1993b.
5. Unification of Signs Commission 1975, foreword.
6. *Ibid.*, 2.
7. Mallery 1881, 332
8. *Ibid.*
9. Stokoe, Casterline, and Croneberg 1965; see also Brien 1992.
10. Woll, Kyle, and Deuchar 1981.
11. Publications describing the Sign Writer can be obtained from The Deaf Action Committee for Sign Writing, P. O. Box 517, La Jolla, Calif., 92038-0517.

12. Quoted from *The art of translation: Kornei Chukovsky's A high art*, translated by Lauren G. Leighton, Leighton 1984, 81.

13. Rosen 1993, 3.

14. Stokoe 1972, 1978. The author has a fine methodological review. He is particularly well worth reading, since he was the first researcher of ASL. Some additional perspectives into the methods used by sign language researchers will be found in Fischer and Siple 1990; Hoemann 1978; Klima and Bellugi 1979; Lane and Grosjean 1980; Lucas 1990; Lucas and Valli 1989; Siple and Fischer 1991; and Wilbur 1979.

15. A sampling of cross-cultural investigations of sign languages has been conducted in Brazil (Pereira and De Lemos 1990); China (Klima and Bellugi 1979, Yau 1990, Youguang 1980); France (Sallagoity 1975, Woodward and DeSantis 1977); Grand Cayman, British West Indies (Washabaugh 1981); India (Jepson 1991); Providence Island, Colombia (Washabaugh 1980a, 1980b; Woodward 1979b); Scotland (Brennan and Colville 1979); Sweden (Ahlgren 1990); Taiwan (Smith 1990); and Yuendumu, Northern Territory, Australia (Kendon 1980).

16. Volterra and Erting 1990, 1. Their book provides a comprehensive overview of research on language acquisition in deaf and hearing children.

17. Tervoort 1975.

18. Goldin-Meadow and Feldman 1977.

19. Gee and Mounty 1991, 65.

20. Maestas y Moores 1980.

21. Prinz and Prinz 1979.

22. deVilliers and deVilliers 1978.

23. Holmes and Holmes 1980.

24. Jamison 1983.

25. Mikin and Rosen 1991.

26. Woodward 1979a

27. Woodward 1979b, 1–2.

28. Woodward 1980. This collection of drug-related signs ranges from AA (Alcoholics Anonymous) to *wack* (angel dust or PCP).

29. For example, Kannapell, Hamilton, and Bornstein 1979.

30. Claiborne 1989, 3.

31. Hoemann 1975, Klima and Bellugi 1979, and Wilbur 1979.

32. Signs for particular concepts differ substantially from language to language. For instance, in Klima and Bellugi 1979 the authors demonstrated as many differences between signs in ASL and Chinese Sign Language as between words in English and Chinese. In Battison and Jordan 1976 and Jordan and Battison 1976 the authors determined the ability of native signers from various countries to comprehend signs from other countries. Native users of ASL, Danish Sign Language, French Sign Language, Chinese (Hong Kong) Sign Language, Italian Sign Language, and Portuguese Sign Language viewed videotapes in their own and the other five languages. The researchers concluded that "deaf signers can understand their own sign language better than they can understand sign language foreign to them." Jordan and Battison 1976, 78.

33. Battison 1978, 177–178.

34. Frishberg 1975.

35. Klima and Bellugi 1979.

36. Hoemann 1978.

37. Stokoe 1993.

38. Shroyer and Shroyer 1984.

39. Sternberg 1981.

40. Shaw 1903, 97–98.

41. *Variety's* critic wrote, "There is much dramatic impact and force in the performance which are spoken with the fingers, hands, and arms. . . . The performers play the play. Their faces speak even if their lips do not, and there were no excessive dramatics or overdone acting. It was in fact, a remarkable professional job by college students" (cited by Tadie 1978, 308).

42. For an extensive treatment of all aspects of speechreading, see Berger 1972. The speechreader integrates the facial information with the context and knowledge about the speaker to make an intelligent attempt to determine what has just been said.

43. Cornett 1967.

44. Stewart and Lee 1987.

45. One was Friar Bernard of Saint Gabriel, the other a Monsieur Fourcade (Wilbur 1979).

46. Wilbur 1979.

47. The signs the Abbé de l'Epée incorporated into his system were largely provided by deaf users of French Sign Language, but the grammatical structure of French guided the sequence of sign production. This choice is not surprising, since Epée naturally thought like a person who had always heard, who grew up with and depended on the French language for communication. His ideas about language acquisition were based on that linguistic model. Living in the eighteenth century, how could he think otherwise? That he hit on using sign at all sets him apart, and above, teachers of his day. They viewed deaf people's sign language as signaling deprivation of the ultimate passport to societal acceptance: speech. Nonetheless, as noted in the preceding chapter, the Abbé de l'Epée validated his success in educating deaf children by their abilities to read and write French and not by their use of French Sign Language.

48. Paget 1951. The latest version, by Paget and Gorman, *A Systematic Sign Language*, was published by the Royal National Institute for the Deaf, 105 Gower Street, London WC1E 6AH, in 1968.

49. Lane 1984, 62–63.

50. Some might say that print would be an obvious solution. However, reading and writing had been a part of deaf education for years and, while some success may have been noted, there remained a missing link in deaf children's ability to understand English. Reading achievement for students graduating from schools for deaf students prior to 1980 averaged about fourth-grade levels.

51. Gustason, Pfetzing, and Zawolkow 1980, ix. Their book, *Signing Exact English*, is the most widely circulated MCE text and has been the primary source of sign vocabulary for many teachers of deaf students since its first edition was published in 1972.

52. Cited in Gustason et al. 1980, ix.

53. Many sign dictionaries show the index finger moving straight out from the lips as representing all forms of *to be*. Most linguists do not accept that sign as part of ASL, considering it a sign introduced by English speakers and not used by native signers (Stokoe, Casterline, and Croneberg 1965.)

54. Anthony 1971; Bornstein, Kannapell, and Saulnier 1973; Gustason, Pfetzing, and Zawolkow 1980.

55. Simultaneous communication (SimCom)—speaking and signing at the same time—has been used as the principal instructional mode at Gallaudet University since its inception as the Columbia Institution for the Instruction of the Deaf and Dumb and the Blind (ca. 1860). It has dominated the total communication programs in U. S. and Canadian schools since the late 1970s.

56. Gustason et al. 1980, xi.

57. Bornstein, Saulnier, and Hamilton 1980, 468. These words of caution, however, have sometimes been ignored by teachers who believe MCE can substitute for ASL rather than simply be an option for classroom communication.

58. Bragg 1990.

59. Jacobs 1990, 55.

60. Bragg 1990, 10.

61. For examples of how classroom teachers sign, see Kluwin 1981b, Luetke-Stahlman 1988a, Mayer and Lowenbraun 1990, Strong and Charlson 1987, and Woodward and Allen 1988.

62. Brasel and Quigley 1977; Gilman, Davis, and Raffin 1980; and Luetke-Stahlman 1988b illustrate different approaches to investigating the effects of MCE on deaf children's English skills.

63. See Stokoe 1993.

64. Kuntze 1990, 77.

65. D. Stewart 1993a, 335.

66. L. Stewart 1990, 118.

5
Learning to Sign

Does watching other people sign arouse your desire to learn how to sign? Many people find sign language fascinating and seek opportunities to learn it. When you see sign language courses on the screen as you scan computer listings of college courses, you might check your schedule to see if you can fit one in. Or if you hear about a course being offered at your church or local community center you might sign up for it. Then again, you may be wise to ease off a bit and explore your options: Where to take a sign language class and at what level of difficulty? Who is teaching it? What reasonable expectations should you have in how fast and how well you will learn sign language?

Let's examine these and some related questions. As in previous chapters we will often use ASL as our model for discussing how you can learn a sign language.

ASL Instruction

Until the second half of this century sign language was not taught in the United States. When the Metropolitan Washington (D. C.) Association of the Deaf set up its first classes for the public in 1964, it was one of the few places in the United States where ASL was taught.[1] Today, at some time during the year, in every large city and many smaller ones, you can take ASL courses. They are offered by universities, community colleges, high schools, voluntary agencies, and organizations of deaf persons. These courses will be offered to you, provided you are not deaf. That is not to say that deaf people will not be permitted to attend the classes, but rather that the classes are not intended for them.

Odd as it may seem, educators seldom offer ASL instruction to deaf students. Even schools for deaf students seldom have sign classes. These

ASL Goes to School

ASL is prominent in the Deaf community and has wide acceptance as the language of choice among high school and college students wanting to learn a second language. Few schools for deaf children openly endorse the use of ASL as a language of instruction, but at Gallaudet University instructors may use it if they wish. A deaf instructor at Gallaudet questions the absence of ASL in the education system:

> The idea of using ASL in the classroom is too dangerous for teachers, no matter whether ASL provides full access to curriculum content and no matter what the researchers are trying to say about the very rich linguistic structure of ASL as a language separate from English.[2]

Still, the number of ASL course offerings in American institutions of higher education leaves little doubt that ASL has come of age. It may not be everywhere that deaf students are taught, but doors are opening.

same schools may provide classes to persons with normal hearing—parents, incoming staff, members of the community. As for their deaf students, the schools seem to assume that it is sufficient to use sign in their classes. Compare their experience to normally hearing students who grow up in English-speaking homes, receive twelve years of instruction in English (their native language), and then must take at least one year of freshman English if they attend a university. Educators defend those extensive English studies by pointing out that it is the language on which students will depend for the rest of their lives. But isn't it the same for deaf students? Won't they depend on signed communication, at least in part, for the rest of their lives? More and more, deaf people are coming to see these practices as untenable, and they are demanding that deaf students be taught ASL as well as English.

Locating Sign Language Classes

Opportunities to learn sign language have grown, so you frequently have choices in location, sponsorship, instructor, and curriculum. As with any other course of study, we recommend classes taught by accredited institutions of education, such as high schools, technical institutes, community colleges, and universities. Adult continuing education courses are usually a good bet if you do not want a degree in some specialty or profession. Most such programs do not insist on prior academic credentials or specific course prerequisites.

Service organizations and Deaf clubs also have sign language classes. Some are excellent and some are suited only to learning a few basic signs or brushing up on skills you already have. Occasionally, parents of deaf children get together and hire a tutor to teach them to sign. It stands to reason, however, that institutions for which education is a full-time concern are more likely to do a better job than organizations and individuals for whom education is only an incidental undertaking. In the past the latter often initiated their sign programs because no sign language classes were offered in their region. Since sign language has become popular, classes are filled and often oversubscribed as soon as they are announced. The very popularity of sign language should make you wary of the instructional possibilities. Student demand may for a time outstrip the supply of quality instructors.[3]

Choosing Your Sign Language Instructors

Thomas Hopkins Gallaudet wrote in 1847 that "the language of signs is not to be learned from books. It must be learned, in a great degree, from the living, looking, acting models."[4] Well said, and as true today as it was 150 years ago. Finding good models, however, is no easy task because of the explosion in the number of sign classes and in part to the lack of university programs that prepare sign language instructors.

One reliable source of sign language teachers are Deaf adults (that is, people whose first language is ASL and whose cultural identity lies in the Deaf community). But fluency in sign language and familiarity with Deaf culture do not alone ensure that a person will be a good teacher. Knowledge and the ability to convey it do not necessarily go together.[5]

We realize you might not always have the freedom to select your teachers. When you do, there are ways of ascertaining an instructor's qualifications. One is to check with the National Association of the Deaf (NAD). It offers programs for present and prospective ASL teachers, conducts certification examinations, and maintains a register of those who have attained various levels of competence. NAD sponsors the Sign Instructors Guid-

When the French Teacher Has Just Learned to Parlez Vous!

Imagine having an instructor of Spanish or French who just learned the language a few weeks before trying to teach you. Not many years ago, the first author met a teacher from a nearby school district who had taken a summer class in sign at New York University. She excitedly told him that, on the strength of that six-week course, her superintendent had put her in charge of teaching sign to the remainder of her school's staff that fall. She expected the author to be as pleased and proud as she was. He wasn't. A similar incident occurred to the second author, who recalls seeing a newspaper advertisement listing, as the ASL instructor, one of his students. What appalled him was that she was still taking his beginner's course! Fortunately, these travesties are abating.

ance Network (SIGN). Membership in SIGN is an indication of an instructors willingness to take part in professional development activities.

Instructors might also be members of the ASL Teachers Association (ASLTA) and have an ASL Instructors Certificate. This certificate indicates that an instructor has attended one or more workshops on ASL instructional strategies and has taught ASL classes for a number of years. The certificate may be granted to individuals who are not formally trained as teachers, but many holders of ASL Instructors Certificates have, in fact, completed their college preparation as elementary or secondary teachers. ASLTA seeks to help its members exchange information about instructional methods and resource materials and improve their skills through professional development workshops and other forms of short-term training.[6]

Sign Language Curriculum

Initially, curricula for sign courses consisted of teaching vocabulary and little else. Students were generally taught to order their newly acquired signs in accordance with the grammar of a spoken language, if grammar was mentioned at all. The available textbooks reflected that approach, being largely collections of drawings illustrating signs with little or no concern with how they should be put together to form thought units. After some time an appreciation for sign language, and specifically of ASL as a language, stimulated a new breed of authors. Dennis Cokely and Charlotte Baker came out with a series of books that gave an in-depth description of ASL grammar.[7] They wrote an accompanying guide for teachers that helped raise instructional standards and encouraged consistency in the way ASL was taught. Three deaf authors—Tom Humphries, Carol Padden, and Terrence J. O'Rourke—followed shortly with a systematic treatment of ASL structures and vocabulary.[8] Accompanying these books were videotapes that provided students with opportunities to observe a variety of master signers. These seminal efforts turned the educational tide. Today, in addition to the books noted above, there are several well-thought-out ASL texts and instructional guides.[9]

Methods of Instruction

Language teachers have long known that a student's initial exposure to a language should be substantial. Berlitz has developed a technique called "Total Immersion," in which the student conducts all communication, for several hours at a time, solely in the language to be learned. The same principle is followed by the U.S. State Department in preparing diplomats for a foreign service assignment and by the Mormon Church in teaching new languages to its missionaries.

Research at New York University has found concentrated instruction to be the most effective method for beginners.[10] Students who spend eight hours a day in class for one week, with sign as the sole means of communication, quickly develop sufficient signing ability for simple, everyday discourse. A popular variation is the sign language retreat, at which students assemble in a remote location where not only their days but also their nights are occupied with ASL. Signs prevail at mealtimes, at coffee breaks, and in after-dinner games, as well as in the classroom. That regimen can be stressful, but almost every student who undergoes such an experience ends the retreat with at least minimum competence in sign.[11] The intensive approach builds strong motivation. Once students have an initial base in the vocabulary and grammar of ASL, they acquire new signs quickly, and their drive to learn more becomes self-renewing.[12]

Two specific ASL instructional strategies are the direct experience method (DEM) and the functional notation method (FN). Keith Cagle, a Deaf instructor who conducts ASLTA workshops, describes the two methods as follows: "DEM emphasizes the use of target language with no voice and lip movements allowed upon the introduction of new sign vocabulary. The environmental settings are also used to teach new signs. The FN approach involves the use of target language and is centered on the dialogue in daily functions."[13] Thus, some ASL instructional strategies are similar to the teaching of a spoken language in that there is an attempt to make the vocabulary and phrases to be learned of practical value to the students.

Whatever the instructional technique used, there is much to be said for sign language classes that meet a few hours per week, even though we jokingly refer to this strategy as the "slow-drip method." It is of greatest value to those who already have some knowledge of the sign language being studied. In such cases spaced instruction is an excellent way to sharpen and maintain skills and to expand vocabularies. We recommend both—begin with an intensive exposure to the language and follow it with a lengthy period of spaced instruction.[14]

Instructional Aids

The evolution of sign language instruction continues as new aids appear on the market. Interactive video disks, CD-ROM videos, and animated computer programs are three promising technologies that should improve students' acquisition of ASL. Michigan State University uses compact discs (CD-ROM system) accessed through a campus-wide computer network. The system allows students to practice some two hundred ASL phrases on their own time. Its greatest virtue—one shared with videotapes and films—is that it provides dynamic representations of signs. As hardly needs to be discussed, these are far superior to drawings in textbooks. The advantages of compact discs over videotapes and films include nearly instant random access, eliminating time wasted in rewinding and fast forwarding to find a particular sign, and greater durability.

As with all forms of video technologies used outside of the classroom, students find self-study less intimidating than practicing before a teacher or another student. They can repeat a bothersome sign again and again without concern that they will be boring someone else or making themselves look ridiculous. Granted, students miss objective feedback when studying on their own, but that deficit can be made up in the classroom.

Signing in a Vacuum

Can someone learn to sign alone? Is it possible to pick up a book and a few videos and learn sign language? You can learn to speak a spoken language and attain some degree of fluency just by listening to audiotapes. Perhaps one day advanced technology will allow you to videotape yourself and then have that videotape analyzed against a computerized model. With this type of feedback, perhaps, you could go it alone with some degree of confidence. For now, what we know is that learning sign language from a book alone is rarely successful. Sign language is a series of dynamic articulations of the hands, face, and body, which are very difficult to portray accurately on a two-dimensional surface. Support is needed to ensure that a learner is producing a sign correctly.

What about television and motion pictures? These can be much more helpful but, again, it is doubtful that one can learn from them alone, since they provide no feedback. You may watch a signer on the screen and believe that you are faithfully copying the motions. But you may not be, and so you spend much time practicing errors. Another subtle point is that you must mentally reverse the image on the screen, shifting from the viewer's orientation to the signer's. Some people do this easily, others do not. They can, however, be useful as supplements to classroom instruction and as refreshers once you have learned to sign.

Finally, in signing, feedback is critical not only because it helps in the production of signed sequences, but also for the emotional support it can provide. Both the instructor and classmates can provide the support most students need to sustain their progress during the early difficult days of language learning. Students especially need others for practice; a mirror offers insufficient feedback. Practicing errors must be avoided as signs are learned. Classmates aid each other in providing the hours of correct repetitions needed to shift a language from the conscious to the unconscious level of execution.

Psychologically, learning a sign language should be easier for a native English speaker than learning other languages because of retroactive inhibition—the conflict that occurs between old and new learning. It arises when the learner encounters words that sound (or appear) similar but have different meanings in the two languages. In French, for example, *tin* means "block of wood," not a metallic element. The German *Boot* means "boat," not a foot covering. Among the languages that share the twenty-six letters of our alphabet, such confusions are inevitable.

Another facilitating aspect of learning a sign language is its novelty.

Communicating with hands is different from speaking. Student and teacher can capitalize on the excitement that generates in order to maintain interest ahead of the frustrations that beset the journey to competence. Learning ASL may be easier for some people than learning another spoken language, but it still is not easy.

Second-language Learning

For most students the study of sign language will fall under the heading of second-language learning. Therefore, for the native English speaker learning sign language is like learning Greek. It is not code shifting, as in learning to write one's native language; it is learning a new language and a new code form.

What do students find easy or difficult about learning sign language? Such a question was addressed in interviews with twelve teachers and seventy-two students of ASL.[15] At the outset the investigators noted that hearing students face the change of acquiring a language in a visual-gestural medium, which challenges their traditional means of processing language presented in an aural-oral modality. Students also face the uneasiness of communicating with the body—something that is not as culturally ingrained in them as it is in the Deaf community. Investigations show that students and teachers feel that difficulty in learning ASL structures is directly related to the degree to which the structures differ from English. Gaining practice in ASL structures was also difficult as both Deaf teachers and Deaf adults in the community tended to code-switch to a more English-like form of ASL signing. Students also commented on the pros and cons of Deaf and hearing teachers. For some, Deaf teachers provided a more realistic picture of communicating in the Deaf community by exhibiting a variety of ASL structures, whereas hearing teachers tended to be less flexible. It was also noted that for some students explanations in English can be less frustrating than receiving the explanation in ASL and without speech. Educational interest in second-language learning is of fairly recent origin. The State Department's Foreign Language Institute, the Peace Corps' Action program, and the Mormon Church's Language Training Mission have taught foreign languages to thousands of native English speakers, but they have not published their methods or studied the factors that influence their results. Linguistic researchers, on the other hand, have undertaken a great deal of research, partly fueled by the acknowledged backwardness of the United States in the study of foreign languages.[16]

Some of the research has looked at the charge that bilingualism might be intellectually debilitating. To the contrary, studies from Canada, Israel, New York, Singapore, South Africa, and Switzerland suggest that bilingual persons have cognitive and linguistic advantages over those who are monolingual. In one Canadian study the children who were bilingual in English and French outperformed those with only French on verbal and nonverbal tests of intelligence, on academic achievement tests, and on tests of French language competence, in spite of the two groups' having been carefully equated on social class, intelligence, and language achievement. What is more, the bilingual students seemed more flexible and diversified in their thinking than the monolingual students. The findings in this and in other investigations apply only when both languages that are acquired are valued socially by the individuals who command them. When one of the languages is denigrated, the result can be a subtractive rather than an additive bilingualism; that is, if one of the languages is not respected, then it interferes with, or subtracts from, intellectual activity.[17] The latter qualification may account for the finding that among some groups, like Mexican-Americans in the Southwest, bilingual children often do less well in school than do their monolingual peers. In the Southwest Spanish has not been a highly regarded second language. Efforts are being made to alter that attitude; if they succeed, the region may be rewarded by gains not only in the Mexican-American children's self-esteem but also in their academic achievements. The application of this reasoning to deaf children is equally pertinent if a sign language is considered their first language and a spoken language their second. This is, in fact, the basis for some school programs adopting a bilingual-bicultural approach to educating deaf children.

This brings us to sign language learning from the student's perspective. For adults, the first difficulty arises if they approach second-language learning differently than children do. Adults tend to be more deductive, preferring to be given the grammatical rules and then trying to apply them. When they reach an impasse on how to express something in another language, adults search their memories looking for a clue. Children tend to operate inductively. At a similar impasse they simply express something. In that way they discover pronunciation rules and principles of grammar through experience.

Do the differences in approach mean adults learn less well than children? Not exactly, but they do have more barriers to surmount. Their standards are higher than children's and they have more distractions (work, family). So far, the ideal age for acquiring a second language appears to be adolescence, a conclusion that is apt to startle teenagers and their parents.[18] It should encourage adults who desire to learn a second language. The old adage that, in learning a language, younger is better does not hold up to close, systematic examination. The adolescent and the adult may both have an edge when mastery of a second language is the objective. Age is no excuse for avoiding sign language.

Or is it? Sign language is a language that requires manual dexterity. Sign language rules might be learned, but whether the hands will do what you want them to do is another matter. This is in contrast to an adult learning a second spoken language. The tongue and other articulators have had decades of practice wagging, flexing, and tossing about little puffs of air. Much like a fine-tuned engine being transferred to a new car body, there is no reason to suspect the engine will not run. The same is true with learning to speak a second language. The speech might be a little halting, but it is there. The transfer from speech to signs, however, is like asking the car engine to run a boat. It can be done, even done smoothly, but with difficulty. So too with the transfer from speech to signing. How are signs stressed? Emotions projected? Questions asked? Adapting to this change in the medium of a language can be accomplished. Even the challenge posed by dexterity considerations can be met.

Assessing Language-learning Capabilities

A first step toward meeting the challenge of learning sign language is attitudinal. Do you have the right attitude? Are you motivated to learn? Motivation plays an expectedly large role in language learning. Your teacher can aid you by making the classes interesting and by reinforcing your early approximations of signing correct sign language vocabulary and grammar. But you can help yourself by some introspection to determine your own reasons for wanting to learn sign language. What are your expectations? Proficiency in a month or two, or determination to attain fluency over the years? Learning sign language may cure your shyness in public; it may lead you to an exciting career; it may gain you new friends or a spouse. Then again, it may do none of these things. After all, sign language is simply a language and what it does for you will depend on how you use it.

Another variable that may affect your ability to learn sign language is empathy—understanding another person's feelings without feeling what that person feels. You may know, for example, why someone is angry without feeling angry yourself. Empathy requires sensitivity to aspects of another person's behavior. This is why a study of Deaf culture in sign language courses is important. This sensitivity in turn is a factor in acquiring a second language, or at least another spoken language.[19]

For years signing in public was certain to garner condescending stares. Not only did American society have cultural proscriptions against broad hand gestures in communication, but the very act of signing was taken to be an indication of deviancy—something not normal and unwanted. Deaf people were a stigmatized group. Their intimate association with signing focused unwanted sympathy and sometimes scorn upon them by the majority.

Today, some Deaf people have made their mark on society through appearances on television and movie screens. Linda Bove, as the deaf librarian on *Sesame Street*, and Marlee Matlin, winner of an Academy Award for her role in *Children of a Lesser God*, have done much to bring sign language to public attention in positive ways. Matlin especially has made it chic to know sign through her frequent appearances on television. This has increased public exposure to Deaf people and ASL and has decreased the stigma attached to signing. Equally important in achieving that positive change are the many normally hearing students who are finding out for themselves about ASL.

Notes

1. Madsen 1976b. For a brief account of the first classes funded by the federal government to teach sign language to the general public, see Schein 1981.

2. Valli 1990, 131

3. Opportunities to learn ASL have also grown in other countries. The British Deaf Association and the Royal National Institute for the Deaf sponsor British Sign Language classes throughout the British Isles (Brennan and Hayhurst 1980). Sign classes may be found in such cities as Edinburgh, Bristol, Leeds, and Newcastle, as well as in London. Many other countries throughout Europe have begun to expand the teaching of sign language beyond the realm of professionals interested in its educational use. In Africa and several countries in Asia and South and Central America, sign language instruction has become increasingly available.

4. Cited in Kanda and Fleischer 1988. Original citation: Gallaudet, T. 1847. The natural language of signs and its value and uses in the instruction of the deaf and dumb. *American Annals of the Deaf* 1:55–59, 79–93.

5. Kanda and Fleischer 1988, 193. The authors list competencies and behaviors of qualified ASL instructors: "Linguistic and cultural competence undergirded by interaction with members of the Deaf community and accompanied by proper attitudinal characteristics. . . . ASL teachers should be educated demonstrating knowledge and application of educational and pedagogical principles along with

formal study of the language being taught. . . . [They] should be able to integrate second language teaching theory and methodology in their classrooms. . . . [They] should be engaged in activities leading to personal and professional growth and development."

6. More information about ASLTA can be obtained by writing to ASL Instructors Certification, c/o Communication Access Program, NAD Home Office, 814 Thayer Avenue, Silver Spring, Md. 20910-4500. The Communications Access Program also has information about ASL instructors in various locations around the United States as well as a publication for selecting an ASL class.

7. Baker and Cokely 1980.

8. Humphries, Padden, and O'Rourke 1980.

9. Recent ASL curricular materials include Humphries and Padden 1992, and Lentz, Mikos, and Smith 1989.

10. Feldman 1978. The author has described the New York University experience with intensive sign-language instruction. Various linguistic researchers have acknowledged the potency of intensive or "total immersion" approaches to other foreign language learning (Diller 1981, Lambert 1981).

11. During the retreat, students agree not to talk except at specified "speech breaks"—a diversion found necessary to overcome occasionally drastic frustration among those accustomed all their lives to speaking.

12. ASL retreats are held in many states. Information about them can be obtained by contacting the NAD or schools and agencies serving deaf people.

13. Quoted in Johnston 1993.

influential of these—14. Students of psychology will recognize this prescription as the resolution to a long-running debate about the virtues of massed versus spaced instruction, a discussion of which can be found in any basic psychology textbook.

15. McKee and McKee 1992.

16. Winitz 1981.

17. Cummins 1986, 1989; Grosjean 1982; and Lambert 1981.

18. McLaughlin 1981. Another reviewer cites a study suggesting that "college students may be five times faster than nine-year-olds in learning foreign languages" (Diller 1981, 76).

19. Studies have found that individuals who score high on empathy scales score higher than others on the ability to speak a second language (Tayler et al. 1971). The data from that research coincide with the position that affective variables—empathy being among the most influential of these—play a sizable role in determining achievement in second-language acquisition (D. Brown 1973). Motivation, too, is another powerful emotion. With rare exceptions (and these exceptions are considered pathological), children display a strong desire to aquire their native language. That tendency probably plays a large part in their obvious ability to learn other languages (Diller 1981). Babies born in one culture and moved at infancy to another will learn the language of the second culture. Children raised in bilingual homes, provided the two languages are both socially acceptable, will learn both. What appears to be genetic in humans is the motivation to communicate and, hence, to acquire language.

6
Sign Language Economics

*L*ess than two decades ago, American Sign Language (ASL) had little commercial value. Now signing is a marketable skill. Many professional and business people regard it as an asset. The lawyer who can sign has great appeal to members of the Deaf community. The same holds true for physicians, accountants, and dentists. Tradespeople, such as barbers, hairdressers, and restaurateurs, can increase their commerce with deaf persons by learning to sign. Travel agencies have found it worthwhile to sponsor tours and cruises led by signing guides. Some airlines have tutored flight attendants in sign so they can communicate with deaf passengers. A department store has advertised a signing shoppers' aide for deaf customers. The list goes on and on, but the point remains: ASL has financial appeal.[1]

The potential for opening new markets and increasing sales to deaf customers by learning sign has brought many people to ASL classes. That interest has opened opportunities for teachers and publishers of sign language materials. Sign has proved useful in previously unexplored areas of therapy, the theater, television, and even the Navy. But the single largest area of application for sign is in interpreting.

Interpreting in Sign Language

Communication is vital to the delivery of many services. In recognition of its importance, the U. S. Congress mandated that rehabilitation clients be served in "their native language or preferred mode of communication." That phrase in the Rehabilitation Act Amendments of 1978 has been interpreted to mean that rehabilitation agencies must provide personnel who can sign to deaf clients. But what does the agency do if it has no one on staff who can sign? Does it place the deaf client "on hold" until a counselor completes a quick course in ASL? Or does it reject deaf clients alto-gether? Federal regulations in the United States exclude both options in favor of a third.

In the third option the agency employs a sign language interpreter to facilitate the communication between deaf clients and the professionals who are available to them. The same solution—use of an interpreter—covers most of the instances that require high levels of linguistic compe-tence in ASL and English. This solution finds legislative support in other federal laws, the most recent of which is the Americans with Disabilities Act of 1990 (ADA). Among its provisions ADA mandates that public fa-cilities "provide auxiliary aids and services to achieve effective communi-cation for people with hearing, speech, and vision disabilities." Auxiliary aids and services include "sign language interpreters; assistive listening de-vices; and telecommunication devices for people who are deaf."

Historical Perspective on Interpreting

Sign language interpreting as a means of earning a living is a logical idea that emerged as a profession in the United States only in 1964 and shortly thereafter in Canada. In that year a national conference officially recog-nized interpreting as a profession and led to the establishment of the Reg-istry of Interpreters for the Deaf (RID). In the years since 1964 great changes have occurred. Prior to 1964 interpreters only performed part-time, often providing their services as a favor to deaf friends and family members or as an obligation to their church. Today, they expect to be reimbursed, and they usually are. Before 1974 preparation to become an interpreter consisted of little more than some sign classes. Now univer-sities in Canada and the United States offer degrees in sign language interpreting.

Before the 1960s interpreting was usually a favor granted by a few hearing people who knew sign. At times a hearing child of deaf parents or a teacher of deaf students undertook interpreting assignments. Members of the clergy who had a deaf congregation and had learned to sign acted as interpreters. This "whoever's available" mentality was successfully challenged at the Ball State Workshop on Interpreting for the Deaf, held in June 1964. From then on interpreting was no longer viewed as a favor but rather as a deaf person's right.[2] Instead of engaging any person who could hear and knew some sign, deaf people began to assert that interpre-ters should be educated, that they should observe a code of ethics, and that they should be paid for their services. Quite a change from what one deaf leader at the Ball State workshop reported as the minimum requirements for interpreters: "They must be able to hear; they must be able to sign; they must be willing; and they must be available."³

The Registry of Interpreters for the Deaf came into being at the Ball State meeting. Establishing a professional organization before there was a profession was an inspired move. By its very existence RID forestalled questions that might have proved embarrassing and, worse, that might have impeded the growth of the interpreting movement. State officials, knowing little about the deaf population and less about interpreting, were easily convinced that everything was in order simply because there was a registry of interpreters. They did not inquire whether the persons listed on it were qualified or where they had obtained their education. (Does one ask such questions of the bar association or the medical society?) Furthermore, since RID existed, there must have been a demand for the service. Or else why have such an organization?

The fact was that no formal educational program for interpreters existed in 1964. There were only a few classes teaching some form of sign language. Ten years after an interpreter-training curriculum was first proposed at the Ball State meeting one was finally published.⁴

During its first year RID had fewer than three hundred members— barely averaging six per state—not very many for a national organization. Averages, of course, mean little to service provision. Most states had only one or two RID members, and some had none. Again, RID's presence implied that adequate numbers of interpreters were available or nearly so. In a way that was the case, because in those early years there was very little demand. Interpreting as a profession was such a novel concept that deaf people had to be educated to use interpreters. Most deaf adults had never hired one. For those who had done without them for most of their lives it took time to become accustomed to them. By holding annual meetings RID drew attention to the value of interpreters and to deaf persons' need for their services.

The biggest stimulus to interpreting in the United States came from the Rehabilitation Act of 1973. It contains Title V, "The Bill of Rights for the Handicapped," the fourth part of which consists of a single sentence: "No otherwise qualified handicapped individual in the United States . . . shall, solely by reason of handicap, be excluded from the participation in, be denied the benefit of, or be subjected to discrimination under any program or activity receiving Federal financial assistance." The brevity of that section increases its power. Because so much activity receives federal money, the scope of the coverage is enormous, and its example carries over to activities not specifically covered by the act. It does not define "participation," so deaf people and their advocates have taken that word to mean they have a right to communication in all federally funded meetings. In their view the absence of interpreters in such circumstances clearly indicates discrimination against deaf people. The probable impact of the act was immediately clear to a small group of educators and rehabilitators interested in the deaf population. In 1974 they formed the National Interpreter Training Consortium (NITC).[5] NITC sought support from the Rehabilitation Services Administration. After lengthy negotiations a five-year federal grant was awarded. It totaled $1.5 million, at a rate of about $300,000 per year—a bargain for the government.

When NITC came into existence in 1974, RID had five hundred members—a substantial, though insufficient increase, over its initial three hundred. Not that there were five hundred interpreters available for duty in the United States, because easily half were agency executives who, while able to interpret, could hardly be expected to take time away from their administrative duties; others were sympathetic to RID but could not sign well enough to provide effective service. Still others were deaf people who had joined RID as a gesture of support, not intending to be interpreters. Consider, then, the sorry state of affairs: less than five hundred interpreters to serve the 450,000 deaf people in the United States who depended on sign language for communication.

NITC responded to that situation in three ways. First, to upgrade the skills of those who were already trying to meet the demand for interpreters, it offered weekend and summer programs on the fine points of interpreting, as well as teaching the basics to those who needed them. (Remember, none had ever attended a formal program of preparation for interpreting. They knew sign, they could hear, and they were available—but lacked interpreter education.) Second, for those who had never interpreted NITC developed a three-month training program that prepared persons with basic signing ability to become interpreters. Though none of the NITC organizers were satisfied with such brief instruction, they realized the urgency of the situation. Third, NITC prepared teachers of interpreting, a completely new occupation.

NITC developed its own curriculum, one that it continued to revise and refine over the five years of its existence.[6] The entire NITC operation was of the bootstrap variety: it put together whatever personnel it could find, and that cadre in turn trained others. Equally important, NITC encouraged other institutions to establish interpreter training. The objective was to have at least one training program operating in every state.

Over its five years NITC had a major impact on the numbers of interpreters in North America. By 1980, when its federal grant expired, RID had certified more than three thousand interpreters. The increase of 2,500 interpreters from 1974 to 1980 cost U. S. taxpayers an average of about $600 per interpreter—a small price to pay for such an important advance in any social service.

The plan to develop training programs and personnel proved to be a substantial boon. In 1980 the U. S. Congress passed legislation to establish twelve training programs. The competition for the funding was open to any institution of higher education, and sixty-two applied initially. Though only twelve receive federal funds, fifty-three institutions now prepare interpreters in the United States and eight do so in Canada.[7] Quite an increase over the original six!

Educational Interpreting

In Canada and the United States the largest number of interpreters are employed by schools, from the elementary grades through university graduate schools. With the support of interpreters, education at all levels in all schools has been opened to deaf students. Since 1975 U. S. federal legislation has mandated integration of deaf students with their hearing peers in public schools.[8] A similar educational philosophy in Canada has spawned numerous opportunities for interpreters in North America. Interpreters make possible the educational integration of deaf and hearing students. As one authority has argued, however, interpreting is only one part of a successful program that seeks to simultaneously educate deaf and hearing students.[9] Nonetheless, from the standpoint of providing employment for persons fluent in ASL the present approach to educating deaf students provides a bonanza.

The Nature of Interpreting

What exactly is interpreting? It may seem a simple matter: putting the words of one language into those of another. Many factors, however, make the question a complex one. Beginning with the language factor,

The Bane of Translation

The famous Russian translator, Kornei Chukovsky, lamented the dryness with which most translators choose words, as follows:

> A boat is always a boat to them, never a ship, a craft, a canoe, or a scow. A castle is always a castle. Why not a keep, a palace, a mansion, a stronghold? Why is it that so many translators always write that a man is thin, not lean, spare, emaciated, frail, gaunt, or skinny? Why not a chill instead of a cold? Why not shanty or shack instead of hut? Why not chicanery or trickery instead of intrigue? Why is sad always sad, and never sorrow, melancholy, anguish, or grief? Many of these translators think that girls are only pretty, when in fact they are apt to be good-looking, cute, comely, attractive, not bad-looking.[10]

Sign-language interpreters, too, can fall into a linguistic rut.

interpreting experience quickly shows that learning ASL is different from learning to interpret. Knowledge of ASL is a prerequisite to interpreting, but knowing ASL does not qualify one to interpret. An interpreter must also be conversant with the ethics, professional responsibilities, economics, and technical aspects of interpreting. Even in ASL class students must learn something about Deaf culture; for interpreters, that knowledge must be comprehensive.

Interpreters should have a superior grasp of both languages with which they are dealing. Expressions in one language sometimes have no direct equivalent in another language. Take the French *faute de mieux*; an English dictionary translation hardly conveys the richness of that phrase. It means "for want of something better," but it means more than that. In French it carries a sense of resignation and a hint of contempt. The things one does *faute de mieux* are being downgraded. Such idioms are numerous in any language.

Even single words may have very different connotations than one might expect from their dictionary definitions. If you call for your steed rather than your horse, you are either being pompous or making a joke. Steed is not an English word found in daily discourse. What is more, the way something is said—the facial and bodily expressions that accompany it, as well as the vocal emphasis on it—adds to its meaning and may even express the opposite of what a word alone means. Does the speaker's tone

Finger and Tongue Twisters

Consider interpreting the following passage from a calculus lecture.

A digraph is called *unipathic* if, whenever *v* is reachable from *u*, there is exactly one path from *u* to *v*. Obviously, every path in a unipathic digraph is a geodesic.

Or restate the following sentence from a legal transcript in plain English, keeping in mind that a simultaneous interpreter has only seconds between an utterance and its rendering.

Plaintiff realleges all of the preceding allegations as are hereinafter set forth verbatim.

imply sarcasm? If so, the signed equivalent must convey that. Simply providing a sign-for-word or word-for-sign translation will often not represent the message accurately.

Regardless of the language involved, linguists insist that exceptional fluency is essential in the languages one translates from and into. That may seem to go without saying, but deaf persons frequently encounter interpreters who know very little ASL. Even more awkward is having an interpreter whose command of both English and ASL is limited. Think about your own ability to interpret for someone talking about cybernetics and the electronic information highway. Or the chemical content of a spew of volcanic fumes. Interpreters have been known to leave the scene in frustration when they cannot understand what the speaker is talking about.

The same holds true for countless ASL idioms. The idiom shown in Figure 6.1 is made up of three signs that are glossed literally as TRAIN GONE SORRY. While the correct meaning depends on the context, it typically means something like, "Too late, you missed what I said and I'm not repeating it."

Other factors contributing to the complexity of an interpreter's task relate to the environment.[11] Interpreters must be aware of, and try to exert some control over, their surroundings. For example, lighting critically affects a deaf person's ability to see, so the interpreter should not stand in front of a source of bright light. (If you do not immediately appreciate this point, stare at a window on a sunny day and notice how quickly your eyes fatigue.) Another visual factor is the clothing worn by interpreters; what

TRAIN   GONE   SORRY

Figure 6.1. TRAIN GONE SORRY is an ASL idiom.

they wear forms the backdrop against which their hands will be seen. Gaudy shirts and dresses make poor backgrounds, and glittering jewelry is distracting and should be avoided by interpreters.

Interpreters must also take steps to ensure that they hear the speaker correctly. But what if more than one person tries to speak at the same time? That happens often enough at conferences and meetings. And what about the speaker who mumbles or reads a list of names at a high rate of speed? Any of these circumstances can render the interpreter manually mute. These are some of the everyday difficulties facing interpreters, difficulties they must overcome to interpret accurately and effectively.

Sources of Interpreters

Interpreters come from all walks of life but at one time this was not the case at all. At the beginning of the century and until the 1960s interpreters

---

Watch Those Commas!

Vocabulary is not the only consideration in interpreting. Context, vocal emphasis, tonal quality, pace—all of these extralinguistic features can alter the words spoken. The story of the ancient Greek soldier who misunderstood the Delphic oracle illustrates the importance of extralinguistic features. The prophecy, as he heard it, was "Thou shalt go, thou shalt return, never by war shalt thou perish." Unfortunately, he misinterpreted the message. He died in battle without realizing he had misplaced a comma: "Thou shalt go, thou shalt return never, by war shalt thou perish." [12]

consisted largely of hearing children of deaf adults, teachers of deaf children, and members of the clergy. Hearing children of deaf adults typically became interpreters for their parents by default. They interpreted conversations between their parents and salespersons, bank managers, car dealers, doctors, and numerous other people. Interpreting was not something they were prepared to do; they just did it—and they did not always do it very well. It was after all a task for which they had no formal preparation. Some would be called upon as adults to interpret (usually voluntarily) for other deaf adults as well as their parents. Others lost interest in or resented being interpreters, or they pursued careers that did not allow time for even occasional interpreting. While children of deaf adults are still among the single largest group of those becoming professional interpreters, most now do so only after receiving a formal education.

Teachers are another group that has traditionally been called upon to interpret. Generally, they are not a good source. Teaching deaf children does not foster good interpreting skills, and conflicts have arisen between the authoritarian role of teacher and the passive role of interpreter. Being fully occupied in the classroom during the day, they often do not have the time or the energy to take on additional responsibilities in the evenings. The use of teachers also presents another drawback: they have already established a role vis-a-vis deaf people. It is an authoritarian role, suitable to the classroom but inappropriate to the nonintrusive functions of the interpreter. It is often difficult for teachers to switch from dominant to submissive relations with current and former students, although their greater awareness of the interpreter's role over the past two decades has made this switch easier.

The third major source of interpreters in the days before RID was the church. The Episcopal Church in 1850 was the first to assign a minister exclusively to a deaf congregation. He was one of Thomas Hopkins Gallaudet's sons; the other son, you will recall, founded what was to become Gallaudet University. Like teachers, religious workers face a role conflict when doing other than religious interpreting. They have been accustomed to donating their linguistic gifts, so the monetary demands of professional interpreting are foreign to them. Interpreting outside of church services, which typically follow a fixed pattern, is made difficult by the shifting nature of assignments, the speed and unpredictability of interchanges, and the variety of clients, from highly educated and highly verbal to illiterate and shy—all of whom must be served by the professional interpreter.

More and more, interpreters entering the field are coming from as di-

Teaching a Lesson

A few years ago a teacher was asked to appear in court to interpret at the trial of two minors—deaf boys from his class—who ducked under the turnstile in a New York subway station and were caught by a transit patrolman. Because the transit patrolman could not communicate with them, he took them to the station and booked them. At the juvenile court hearing the judge listened for a few minutes to the testimony, all dutifully interpreted by the teacher, and then started to dismiss the case. At that point the interpreter said to the judge, "Your Honor, I believe you are making a mistake. These are deaf youngsters and they need to be taught a lesson." He went on in that vein, no longer interpreting, urging that the boys be punished. The boys could only guess that their judge was not the man sitting on the bench but the teacher who was there to interpret for them—to help them. Such behavior violates the present RID Code of Ethics.

verse a set of backgrounds as candidates for the other professions. The prospective interpreters will, of course, have higher than usual interest in languages but will in most other respects be bright, energetic, and interested in working with people. (For further discussion of this point, see "Interpreting as a Career," below.)

Interpreter Ethics

Ethics are the hallmark of a profession. In pre-RID days no ethical considerations guided those who interpreted other than their personal values. One interpreter boasted to the first author about her experiences as a courtroom interpreter in the 1930s and '40s. "You don't know how often I would save a deaf man by telling the judge what he *should* have said rather than what he signed!" Although a deeply religious person, she saw no reason that would bar her interference in that person's life and felt no shame for corrupting the testimony of another person. Deaf people object to such parentalism.[13] They resent especially interpreters with a for-their-own-good attitude. The RID Code of Ethics requires interpreters to neither add nor subtract anything transmitted between parties. The interpreting task requires faithful rendering of what is said to deaf people and signed by them. Nothing more and nothing less—but what a challenge that is.[14]

Interpreters do not invent dialogue or tailor an expression to suit the occasion. If the speaker is foul-mouthed, the interpreter must be prepared to curse—in sign or speech. The interpreter is not an editor, a moralist, an adviser, or a pal. Interpreting is no longer a favor; it is a right. And enlightened deaf people are prepared to criticize interpreters, to discharge those who perform badly, and to seek out the well-trained, conscientious practitioners.

Ethical provisions warn interpreters against accepting assignments beyond their ability to fulfill them adequately. Interpreters must conduct themselves in a fashion that shows respect for those they serve and for their professional colleagues. Other articles of the ethical code deal with payment for services and proper conduct before, during, and after interpreting sessions. From the viewpoint of many deaf people the most important ethical restraint on interpreters is confidentiality. Deaf people often reveal intimate, potentially embarrassing, or possibly damaging information through interpreters who serve them in physicians' offices and during legal encounters. The fear that an interpreter might reveal details of such meetings weighs heavily, even though the RID Code of Ethics specifically and strongly forbids such revelations. Those who engage interpreters must be aware, however, that not all professional interpreters belong to RID or the Canadian equivalent, Association of Visual Language Interpreters of Canada (AVLIC), which has a similar ethical code.

Over the years RID's and AVLIC's codes have been revised to take up issues previously unanticipated, rewrite ambiguous sections, and eliminate unnecessary ones. The codes are likely to see further revisions that are not now foreseen. But as they stand, the RID and AVLIC codes do credit to the interpreting profession.

How to Work with Interpreters

Most hearing people feel awkward the first time they use an interpreter. This is not to say that they may not enjoy or appreciate the experience. It is simply that, well, what do you do? Do you talk to the interpreter or to the deaf person? How do you know the interpreter is signing what you want to say? Such questions are entirely expected and no apologies are needed for asking them.

You always face and talk directly to the deaf person or audience, as the case might be. You never say through the interpreter, "Ask her if she is coming." You do say to the deaf person, "Will you be coming?" No need to worry about the positioning of the interpreter as the interpreter and the deaf person will arrange that. For instance, when mediating between a deaf client and only one speaker, the interpreter always sits next to the speaker. The deaf person needs to see the speaker and the interpreter at the same time. The interpreter usually stands a little bit behind a public speaker, which enables a deaf audience to see the speaker and, simultaneously, the interpreter. Seeing the speaker's face, gestures, and posture aids deaf people because the interpreter may not always be able to convey the speaker's vigor, anger, humor, or other emotions. When able to see both interpreter and speaker, the deaf person can pick up these cues.

When interpreters were first beginning to be used on a large scale, their roles were largely undefined. Interpreters have been asked by deaf students to fetch coffee or pick up a book. Some teachers would not permit the interpreter to stand next to them while they lectured. Psychologists have asked interpreters to give tests; physicians have expected the interpreter to provide the deaf patient's medical history in that patient's absence; lawyers have called on interpreters to reveal the contents of confidential discussions. As ludicrous as some of these situations now sound, they did occur and sometimes still do. Hindsight is a great asset but situations had to play themselves out in real life before they could be professionally addressed. Today, these situations seldom arise as they are quickly resolved by informed deaf individuals and trained interpreters.

Different Shades of Interpreting

How does one interpret for a person who can neither see nor hear? One book lists seventy-six different techniques and pieces of equipment that can be used to communicate with deaf-blind people.[15] Among the techniques are the two-handed fingerspelled alphabets (see chapter 3). In one version the interpreter's right hand forms the letters on the deaf-blind person's left hand. That method is effective at fairly high speed when used by pairs who are familiar with it and who develop numerous short-cuts and abbreviations.

What about the deaf person who can see but does not know sign or fingerspelling? Some deaf persons prefer to speechread, even if they do know sign. In such cases an oral interpreter, a person who is skilled at repeating what the speaker is saying, can be employed. The oral interpreter is particularly valuable when visual conditions make direct speechreading of the speaker difficult or impossible. Teachers may turn to the blackboard and continue to speak as they write on it. Sometimes deaf persons must sit too far from the speaker to permit speechreading. Some speakers have moustaches or beards that obscure their mouths. In all such circumstances deaf persons who prefer speechreading need an oral interpreter who sits nearby, in their full view.

Interpreting Other Sign Languages

Up to now we have talked only about interpreting in ASL and English. But interpreters sometimes encounter other languages. Nowadays in New York there are frequent requests for interpreters who know Russian or Ukrainian Sign Language. Spanish is another popular language on both coasts, but in addition to different Spanish accents the sign languages of various Spanish-speaking countries—Argentina, Cuba, Mexico, and Puerto Rico, for example—are not the same. The interpreter needs to know both spoken Spanish and the deaf persons' sign languages.

Unusual Settings

Apart from language variations interpreters also get called on to interpret in a wide variety of situations, such as courtrooms, hospitals, banks, real

Signs in the Deep

During World War II a Gallaudet College professor was engaged by the U. S. Navy to teach frogmen to sign. These underwater demolition experts needed to communicate with each other when in proximity to the enemy. Using radio transmission was too dangerous, and speech was not possible underwater. The answer proved to be sign language. Of course, divers have long used hand signals to communicate, but their messages are usually simple commands or requests. The frogmen, to the contrary, needed to be able to communicate at length and with specificity—something that sign language enabled them to do.

estate agencies, car dealerships, and so on. Each setting entails mastery of a different vocabulary, signed and spoken, as well as dealing with circumstances imposed by the location and whatever protocol it sets for the interpreter's behavior.

Perhaps the most challenging assignments are stage productions. Although stage productions have long been interpreted, only recently have operas been among them. In 1981 New York City Opera offered signed productions of *Susannah* and *The Merry Widow*. Janacek's *Cunning Little Vixen*, Puccini's *La Fanciulla del West*, and others have since been added to the repertoire. Typically, at least two interpreters, and sometimes three, work the performances, one doing the female and one the male voices. The interpreters require extensive rehearsal to coordinate their signs with the music, making the transitions from one sign to the next blend smoothly as if being sung. The response from deaf people has been excellent. The hearing audiences have not complained, many feeling that the interpreters and the deaf members of the audience add to the performance's excitement.[16]

Interpreting plays typically takes one of two routes. One way has the interpreter off to the side and well lit. The other has interpreters on stage, moving with ("shadowing") the actors. Usually, not all performances of

---

When Sign Turns Sour

Hollywood has a Deaf Actors Guild (DAG), which is active in gaining more roles for deaf actors in movies, TV programs, and commercials. DAG opposes hearing actors portraying deaf characters. In 1993 the Deaf community's publications joined with DAG to mount a protest against the release of the movie *Calendar Girl*, because a normally hearing person plays the role of a deaf man. Why the movie's producers made that casting decision after auditioning several experienced deaf actors has not been explained to the Deaf community's satisfaction. An earlier protest over Amy Irving portraying a deaf teacher in the motion picture *Voices* did not prevent the movie's release, but it may have affected its earnings.

Both movies did poorly at the box office, so perhaps in time Hollywood will stop casting hearing persons as deaf characters.

the play are interpreted, as the potential deaf audience in most cities is small.

Another boon to the interpreting profession has been the interpreting of government proceedings. In North York, a suburb of Toronto, a Deaf activist, Gary Malkowski, was elected to the provincial Legislative Assembly in 1990. His presence brought sign language interpreting into the living rooms of every home in Ontario, as all parliamentary sessions were interpreted. Deaf Canadians can also follow televised sessions of the Canadian Parliament, most of which are signed. Signing for public meetings will likely become an increasingly frequent assignment for interpreters.

Interpreting as a Career

For most interpreters the work is hard. It combines considerable physical activity (often standing on one's feet and keeping one's arms in nearly constant motion for an hour or longer) and complete concentration. The combined physical and mental strain leads many interpreters who are working alone to request a rest period every forty-five minutes or so, depending on the nature of the interpreting task. Such breaks are also welcomed by the deaf audience, since watching the same interpreter carefully for long periods of time can be more fatiguing than listening is for the hearing audience. The reason lies in the differences between eyes and ears. When a deaf person blinks to relieve strain or turns away from the speaker the communication link is cut. But the ears never close, so one can drift away mentally and remain fairly certain of being able to detect changes in the flow of a speech in time to refocus attention. In some situations interpreters work in pairs to ensure that fatigue does not interfere with their performance. Recall also that continuous interpreting over long periods of time can lead to repetitive strain injury.

The physical strain of fingerspelling has associated it with repetitive strain injury (RSI). RSI encompasses injuries that occur when a physical task is performed repetitively without sufficient time for recovery. An example of RSI is carpal tunnel syndrome, a painful and sometimes disabling condition affecting the nerves and tendons of the hand. Sign language interpreters are at risk for this disorder, and some wear a specially designed glove that supports their hand and relieves stress.[17]

Outside the major cities the principal difficulty facing interpreters is keeping busy. But in metropolitan areas there is a great deal of interpreting to be done and few qualified to do it. One Midwest university uses a cadre of twenty full- and part-time interpreters to interpret for about twelve deaf students, one deaf professor, one deaf administration specialist, and eight deaf ASL instructors. The coordinator of this university's interpreting service is always bemoaning the fact that there are never enough interpreters.

Does it pay to become an interpreter? We do not wish to provide a list of salaries and hourly rates. Such figures change from time to time, and pay varies from one region to another, as well as from situation to situation. Yet, we cannot resist selecting one example that reflects the upper end of the scale. In Canada, freelance interpreters certified by the Secretary of State can earn $625 (Canadian) per day.[18] They usually work in pairs or even in groups of three, with each interpreter paid that amount. It may sound like a lot of money until one realizes that they do not work every day.

Reviewing all the demands on interpreters—the problem of thinking in two languages simultaneously, the physical and mental demands, the uncertain employment conditions, the high level of linguistic competence—one may conclude that their work has little glamour and is unfairly compensated most of the time. Nonetheless, training programs do not lack applicants, and interpreter turnover is relatively low. Interpreting does have its crowning moments.

Vocational counselors whose clients may be inquiring about interpreting as a career should consider the high job requirements. They should also be aware that pay scales often do not match the requirements. The qualifications for success as an interpreter, however, also fit other professional and managerial positions in the fields of education and rehabilitation. Many successful professionals and executives have entered their fields as interpreters. That fact should be weighed by those deciding whether or not interpreting is the career for them.

Signing to People Who Can Hear

Over the past two decades an interest has developed in using sign language therapeutically. As a result new career opportunities have opened to those who can sign, which, interestingly enough, includes deaf people. Educators have noted that some normally hearing people who had not developed speech could learn to sign. The discovery prompted a spate of research, which is by no means at an end, that has clearly established the usefulness of sign language in developing the communication abilities of children and adults with whom traditional education and rehabilitation have had little success. Furthermore, the use of sign in such cases has established a demand for care-givers who can sign, another economic reason for learning sign.

Autism

Autistic children are particularly challenging to teach, and some attempts have been made to communicate with them in sign. The results have been gratifying. Take the case of Arthur (a pseudonym). He was ten years old when he came to the Deafness Research and Training Center at New York University in 1973. Arthur had normal hearing ability, but he had never spoken. When he wanted something, he would scream. That would activate nearby adults: Was he hungry? Hot? Cold? Did he want to go to the toilet? Remedies were proffered one after the other until Arthur stopped screaming, which signaled that his wants were for the moment fulfilled. The routine obviously exhausted his parents and disgusted his younger brother, who seldom received any parental attention. Arthur's parents brought him to the center because they had heard that some autistic children learned to communicate in sign. They sought the relief that such communication would bring to their family. Oddly, they also worried somewhat that Arthur's learning to sign might interfere with his speech development. Pointing out the reality of his condition, however, alleviated those concerns enough to permit treatment to begin. A graduate student undertook Arthur's instruction over one summer. Within two weeks Arthur had learned five signs. By summer's end Arthur had mastered about twenty signs, all useful in indicating his daily wants. He learned the signs for *eat, drink, toilet,* and similar basic concepts. He could both make and recognize the signs, which greatly improved his home situation.

The literature now contains several case studies much like Arthur's, and the atmosphere for such work has changed as the use of sign is more widely accepted. Consequently, current efforts go beyond rudimentary attempts like those made in Arthur's case. Sign is now used extensively to instruct some children over long periods of time. There is adequate evidence to encourage this means of establishing a relationship between autistic children and significant adults with whom they interact.[19]

Left Brain, Right Brain

If autistic children respond to and express themselves better in sign language than speech, does that mean that their disorder is related to a left-brain deficit? Many authorities on infantile autism believe the condition has an organic basis. Does the successful use of sign language confirm the site of the organic lesion? The reasoning may be profitably extended to some severely mentally impaired individuals. Perhaps the difference lies in hemisphere dominance and in the coordination between hemispheres. The fact that severely mentally impaired children who previously learned virtually no language can learn sign language should spur research along those lines.

Mental Impairment

Some people with profound mental impairments have been able to learn sign language, though they have not learned to speak. The signs they learned, as in the case of some autistic children, have been simple but functional. The practical advantages of having some communication ability include being able to live a more independent life and develop more meaningful levels of interactions with others. One article describing the teaching of sign to groups of mentally impaired children offers this insight.

Severely mentally retarded children learned from 1 to 65 words receptively and expressively, including simple 2 and 3 word responses. Trainable mentally impaired children learned over 200 words and increased mean length of response and correct sequential order of words, including complicated sentence structure.[20]

Such results are beyond what educators typically expect. That sign language works is no longer doubted. But educators do not yet know how far they can go in developing the language abilities of these individuals or even the type of signs that yields the best results. In one study it was found that Amerind (American Indian Sign Language) signs were acquired and retained by severely to moderately mentally impaired adolescents better than were ASL signs. The investigators suggest this occurred because Amerind signs were more concrete and less complex than ASL signs.[21]

An interest in signing with mentally impaired children led to the development of the Makaton Vocabulary, which "comprises a core vocabulary of 350 concepts, which are arranged in a developmental sequence spanning 8 stages."[22] The Makaton Vocabulary selects signs from British Sign Language, the sign language of the country in which it is used. In the United States and Canada, ASL signs would be used because the key to Makaton is the concept being taught and not the formation of the sign being used. The inventors have reported considerable success in developing language in children who had very little or none.

Aphasia

Aphasia is a condition in which the afflicted individuals have lost the ability to express themselves orally. They may be able to form thoughts, but they cannot express those thoughts intelligibly. (There are other forms of aphasia, but here we will confine the discussion to expressive aphasia.) Speech therapists have found that some patients who cannot speak benefit from learning to sign. Reports of sign therapy with aphasics have shown consistent success with sign communication. Attention is being directed toward criteria for selecting patients who are more apt to benefit from sign than from the more traditional oral therapies.[23]

Schizophrenia

In addition to mental impairment, autism, and aphasia, sign may be useful in the treatment of some emotional conditions and schizophrenia. The theoretical discussion of this application has begun, but not many case reports have so far made their way into the literature. The progress in communication made by the other groups, however, encourages the broadest investigation of sign's applications to the treatment of emotional disturbances and psychoses.[24]

Physical Therapy

Physicians at the St. Michael Hospital Rehabilitation Unit in Milwaukee are recommending fingerspelling as therapy for stiffness in hands. Fingerspelling puts all thirty or so joints in the hands through their full range of motion, which is ideal exercise for osteoarthritis patients. This kind of therapy can be performed anywhere at any time of the day. The medical staff, however, cautions against patients with rheumatoid arthritis from doing these exercises because some of the fingerspelled letters may encourage joints to move into positions of deformity. In any event the hospital has uncovered one more application for manual communication.

Impediments to the Use of Sign in Therapy

Two things impede broadening the use of sign language in various therapies. One is the cultural prejudice against signing. Some parents worry about the possibility that using sign will interfere with speech development. That may seem laughable in the case of a ten-year-old child who has not yet spoken, but the fear is real enough. It may well reflect parents' apprehension that signing makes visible the shame they unjustifiably feel of having a child with a disability.

The other major impediment to the more rapid exploitation of signing for a variety of language-impaired conditions is that only a small number of professionals know how to sign. As more learn it, the use of signing in fields other than with deaf people will probably increase. For now the deaf population claims the great majority of professionals who are skilled signers, leaving few to work with other populations.

Teaching ASL

ASL's popularity has created a boom in ASL classes. At the same time there is a shortage of qualified teachers. Because this situation was discussed in chapter 5, we concern ourselves here only with the prospects for earning a living as a teacher of ASL. While teaching ASL offers considerable personal and professional satisfaction, it pays no better, and sometimes much less, than teaching positions in general. Compensation will vary with the level at which classes are taught—elementary, secondary, postsecondary—and with such other factors as location. Full-time positions for ASL instructors are relatively few in North America, though their numbers are growing. The unquestioned need for more fully qualified teachers should encourage those for whom teaching ASL matches their vocational aspirations.

The Economic Future of ASL

In our society assigning a monetary value to an activity adds greatly to its growth potential. Now that knowledge of ASL, in one way or another, can be converted into cash, its growth can be expected to soar. The impetus given to ASL by the discovery of its unique linguistic status will be sustained and possibly accelerated by its dollar value.

The Cost of Interpreting

As interpreters have gained recognition as professionals—which has led to higher rates for their services—and as the demands for their services have increased, the costs of their services have become an issue. One interpreter can communicate with dozens, even hundreds of deaf persons—as many as can see the interpreter. The more deaf people in the audience, the lower the per capita cost of interpreting.

Obviously, in a counseling situation the one interpreter will be serving only the two participants, the deaf client and the counselor. There are many other situations in which only one deaf person will be receiving the interpreter's signs; for example, in the case of interpreting for people who are deaf-blind. Under such circumstances the expense of having an interpreter can appear to be high.

Rather than defending interpreting on economic grounds, we prefer to reason that deaf people have rights to interpreting whenever the government supports the activity. What the government sponsors should be accessible to all of its citizens. Deaf people are citizens. For most activities to be accessible to them communication must be visible. Therefore, interpreters must be available in courts, public meetings, classrooms, and so on. Arguing otherwise raises criticisms about the cost of communication accommodations. Once these are seen as citizenship rights, however, the arguments no longer hold.

Signing and the Law

Strengthening the preceding reasoning about communication access are federal laws that ensure persons with disabilities their rightful place in society. These statutes are not apt to be revoked by future administrations. Some of the laws have been supplemented by state and local acts that expand the right of deaf people to full participation in a community's affairs. For that reason it is safe to assert that the demand for sign language interpreters will increase greatly over the coming decade, as will the demand for sign language instructors.

The uses of sign in therapeutic and educational settings with persons who are not deaf are only beginning to be realized. As we gain a better understanding of the value of ASL in treating language-impaired persons, we can anticipate a corresponding growth in the economic value of knowing ASL. Altogether then, learning ASL and applying it to new situations opens exciting vistas for education, rehabilitation, therapy, research, and employment.

In closing this chapter, we would like to stress that the greatest value of learning ASL has no monetary reimbursement. Learning ASL, as with learning any foreign language, contributes to intellectual growth. Studying the culture of deaf people sharpens an appreciation of one's own culture. In the economics of "feeling good," knowing ASL pays big dividends.

Notes

1. What passes for sufficient signing competence for simple communication, however, cannot satisfy the demands of a professional practice. Gaining proficiency in signing adequate for a psychiatric interview, for example, requires vastly higher standards than learning a few signs for typical in-flight situations. After one course most airline personnel and store clerks can learn enough signs for their purposes, while the mental-health counselor needs extensive study to attain a level of ASL proficiency that can satisfy the communication demands of psychotherapy.

2. Smith 1964.

3. Frederick C. Schreiber in Schein 1981, 50.

4. Sternberg, Tipton, and Schein 1973.

5. Led by New York University, NITC was made up of six institutions that had already begun to prepare interpreters: University of Arizona, California State University at Northridge, Gallaudet College (now Gallaudet University), St. Paul Technical-Vocational Institute, and University of Tennessee (Lauritsen 1976 and Romano 1975). Because the National Technical Institute for the Deaf (at the Rochester Institute of Technology) only trained interpreters for its classrooms, it declined to join the consortium. NTID's contributions to research on interpreting and to the preparation of interpreters, however, should not be overlooked.

6. While the first published curriculum for interpreter training was Sternberg et al. 1973, each NITC member contributed curriculum modifications over the five years.

7. Registry of Interpreters for the Deaf 1980, Schein and Yarwood 1990.

8. This mandate was originally known as the Education for All Handicapped Children Act or Public Law 94-142. It has been superseded by the Individuals with Disabilities Education Act of 1990.

9. Higgins 1990.

10. Chukovsky 1984, 81.

11. For more details about interpreting see Solow 1981; Frishberg 1985; and Cokely 1992.

12. Espy 1972, 203.

13. To avoid sexist language, we prefer *parentalism* to paternalism or maternalism. Both parents can be overprotective and condescending, not just fathers or mothers.

14. A provocative article by Carol Tipton (Tipton 1974) influenced the revision of RID's Code of Ethics and retains value for readers today. Copies of the current standards can be obtained from RID, 814 Thayer Avenue, Silver Spring, MD 20910.

15. Kates and Schein 1980.

16. While this critique is based on personal observation, it should be noted that the New York press did not find fault with the arrangement.

17. It is unfortunate that interpreters are at high risk with repetitive strain injuries, because their work is heavily reliant on their ability to use their hands. To make the situation worse, a majority of interpreters freelance, working when something is available. Freelance interpreters receive no medical benefits which makes theirs a medically and financially risky profession.

18. In the equivalent of U.S. dollars Canadian interpreters certified by the Secretary of State can earn about $500 per day.

19. Most of the literature contains reports of single cases of autistic children who have been aided by signed communication (e.g., Casey 1978, Cohen 1981, Webster et al. 1973, Wolf 1979). An unusual study is the report of sign used with nineteen mute autistic children (Miller and Miller, 1973, 84). All learned to sign and respond to signs; some later developed usable speech. Nonetheless, the researchers felt compelled to conclude their recitation of the excellent outcomes with a defense of sign language. "We suggest that the inability of a mute autistic child to attain meaningful speech via signs does not invalidate their use. The signs offer such children the means of understanding both signs *and* spoken language as well as the possibility of communicating with other people. Without such human contact, most mute autistic children tend to lapse into states in which they pass their days rocking back and forth and twiddling objects." A review of data on more than one hundred mute autistic children confirms their ability to acquire expressive and receptive sign, an astonishing affirmation of the value of this approach to one of psychiatry's more difficult syndromes (Bonvillian, Nelson, and Rhyne 1981).

20. Grinnell, Detamore, and Lippke 1976, 124.

21. Gates and Edwards 1989. See also Sensenig et al. 1989.

22. Walker 1986, 2.

23. Caplan 1977, Hanson 1976, Markowicz 1973, Wepman 1976, and Winitz 1976, 1981. These investigators advance evidence of the effectiveness of nonvocal approaches, generally signs, with aphasic patients. They offer several theories to explain why vocal therapies may fail where nonvocal therapies succeed, even with patients who had previously mastered speech.

24. Fristoe and Lloyd 1978 and Goodman, Wilson, and Bornstein 1978. In both books the authors reported conducting surveys that reveal the widespread use of sign communication with a variety of severe communication problems. Schaeffer (1978 and 1980) has added curricular emphases to the literature, with empirical and theoretical support for the use of sign with all nonvocal persons.

7

The Deaf Community

Up to now we have spoken about deaf people and about those who sign and those who do not sign. We have alluded to the Deaf community; we have made references to Deaf culture. But we have not defined any of these terms. Now we must.

The Deaf community consists of Deaf people who share in the preservation and further development of a culture and a distinct mode of communication—sign language. The use of the uppercase D in Deaf is in recognition of a cultural and linguistic affiliation. It distinguishes between persons who are deaf but have no cultural affiliation with others who are deaf and people who belong to the Deaf community, join Deaf clubs, participate in Deaf sport, attend Deaf churches, and involve themselves with a host of other institutions and events that bear the linguistic trademark of sign language.[1]

Deafness Defined

We can define deafness audiologically or functionally. The two definitions yield somewhat different classifications. Audiologists measure hearing by the amount of energy necessary for a sound to be detected at least half the time (called a *hearing threshold*). The more energy it takes to be heard, the greater the hearing loss. On that scale, then, zero represents normal hearing—the point at which the average person begins to hear sounds— and higher numbers indicate greater degrees of hearing loss. From an audiological standpoint, a severely deaf person has a hearing threshold for speech at or above 70 decibels (usually abbreviated dB).

In a normal conversation the human voice has peaks and valleys between 50 and 65 dB. Shout at a friend sitting directly in front of you and your voice will only reach about 75 dB. So a person with a 90 dB hearing level has little, if any, chance of efficiently handling everyday conversations even with best available amplification. And many deaf people have even higher (worse) hearing levels.

Audiologists measure hearing in another way called Speech Discrimination (SD). The audiologist presents words amplified to whatever levels are comfortable for the person being tested to see how many of the words can be correctly repeated. If the person identifies less than 40 percent of the test words correctly, the person is deaf. Given the favorable testing conditions, an SD below 40 percent is clearly inadequate for everyday communication.[2]

Another way of defining deafness is in functional terms. Being able to hear absolutely nothing is an extremely rare condition. Most deaf people can hear some sounds. But what they can hear does not allow for adequate oral communication. Being able to hear a jackhammer or a jet airplane avails one very little in this Information Age. Therefore, we concentrate on hearing speech and offer the following definition:

> Deaf people are those who cannot hear and understand speech through the ear alone, even with best-available amplification.

This definition is essential to account for those who can hear speech but cannot understand it and for those who cannot hear speech adequately but can follow a conversation under favorable conditions by using contextual and facial cues and any residual hearing they may have. For those in the first group hearing is like listening to a radio that is not quite tuned to a station: they may hear that someone is speaking, but they cannot make out what is being said. Making the speech louder "with best-available amplification" does not enable deaf people to discriminate (understand) what is being said. As for the second group, while some deaf people may seem to understand what is being said on occasion, they are not doing so "through the ear alone." *They cannot understand speech with their eyes closed.* That last statement leads to another distinguishing feature of deaf people: for communication purposes, they are visually dependent. In order to comprehend what is spoken they depend on signs, speech reading, handwritten notes, and printed text.

Cultural Deafness

In this chapter we capitalize the word Deaf to identify individuals, groups of people, events, or entities that are a part of a culture defined by the activities and beliefs of people who are deaf and who share a common sign language. Thus we have Deaf community and Deaf culture; Deaf folklore and Deaf teachers; Deaf clubs and Deaf sport; Deaf people and Deaf language. Typically, persons who are born deaf or who lost their hearing before maturity are more inclined to embrace Deaf culture than those deafened later in life. For the latter group their associations, habits, education, and more have been built during the time before they lost their hearing. In contrast, those who are born deaf are more likely to have been educated under special conditions, have Deaf friends, and have social lives that revolve around the Deaf community.[3] We will continue to use the term *deaf* in a generic sense to refer to people who have a hearing loss severe enough so that they are unable to understand speech sounds through the ear alone.

The Deaf community refers to those Deaf people who seek each others' company through organizations like the National Association of the Deaf and the Canadian Association of the Deaf. These organizations are formal self-help groups of persons who share a disability. Every developed nation, and many under-developed nations, has associations of Deaf people. In Canada and the United States every province and every state has an organization of Deaf people. Most have more than one. Notice that these are organizations *of* Deaf people. They were organized by Deaf people, they are staffed by Deaf people, and they derive their support from Deaf people. These organizations, their publications, and the numerous social and athletic events they sponsor provide tangible evidence of the Deaf community's existence; there are numerous informal, less apparent indications.[4]

You might wonder about hearing people who sign. Are they members of the Deaf community? What about hearing children of Deaf parents? Can a hearing person join the Deaf community by marrying a Deaf person? Could a Deaf person lose this cultural affiliation by marrying a non-deaf person? Some hearing adults who have Deaf parents identify themselves as being a Deaf person who happens to be able to hear. Their argument is that they grew up in a Deaf environment and learned ASL as a native language and thus, through cultural and linguistic ties, they are Deaf. We sympathize with their position but make no exceptions in our definition. We know of no Deaf people who view hearing people as core members of the Deaf community. You may wonder whether the definition can be broadened to include almost anyone who comes in contact with Deaf people. We reject such a nebulous construct and adopt a stance like that taken in defining the population involved in Deaf sport.

Deaf Like Me?

The emergence of ASL in the public domain has led to lively discussions about whom ASL "belongs to." Certainly, ASL is a strong identifying characteristic of the U. S. and Canadian Deaf communities. Some Deaf people even refuse to use ASL with hearing individuals in order to preserve its cultural and linguistic integrity. Others see a hearing individual's use of ASL as a means of putting Deaf and hearing interactions on a more equal footing. A Deaf leader summarizes his encounters with these divergent views among his fellow Deaf associates.

> I have asked a number of deaf individuals how they feel about hearing people signing like a native user of ASL. The responses are mixed. Some say that it is acceptable for hearing people to use ASL like a deaf person on one condition. The condition is that this hearing person must make sure that the deaf person knows that s/he is not deaf. Some people resent the idea of seeing hearing people signing like a native ASL user. Those who are resentful may feel sociolinguistic territorial invasion by those hearing people.[5]

Note that the author is speaking about using ASL, not signing. Most Deaf people appreciate hearing persons who use any intelligible signs, as it facilitates communication without their seeming to be trying to deceive the Deaf audience about their hearing status.

A person deafened at seventeen years of age who is only in the process of learning American Sign Language . . . can conceivably become president of a Deaf sport organization or participate in international competitions for deaf athletes. On the other hand, a hearing person who has Deaf parents, learned ASL as a native language, married a Deaf person, and works as a teacher of deaf children will at no time have a similar degree of access within the realm of Deaf sport.[6]

Some writers have dubbed gatherings of Deaf people a linguistic community. We do not need to concede that signing is the most obvious— indeed, some would say the only obvious—feature by which Deaf people are identified. Deaf people vary in height, weight, ethnicity, race, gender, and almost any other feature you can name, except two: their hearing and their communication.

How Many Deaf People?

Deaf people make up a very small part of the U. S. population. Approximately 22.5 million Americans have some degree of hearing loss, and nearly 2 million are deaf—that is, they cannot hear and understand speech through the ear alone with best available amplification. But an even smaller portion, about three hundred thousand, belong to the Deaf community.[7] In Canada the estimated size of the deaf population is about a third of the rate for the United States: 76 per 100,000 versus 203 per 100,000.[8] We compare rates, rather than actual numbers, because the two countries differ so greatly in the sizes of their populations: Canada has about 26 million people, and the United States about 254 million. Why the prevalence rate of deaf people is so much smaller for Canada than the United States is the subject for a different book. What is critical here is the relatively small proportions of both populations who are deaf. That deaf people are a numerical minority is beyond any doubt; indeed, they constitute small portions of the populations of every country in the world.[9]

How Many Signers?

People who are deafened later in life seldom use sign language. As a rule the earlier a hearing loss occurs in a person's life and the more severe it is, the more likely that the person will sign. The U. S. Bureau of the Census does not include ASL among the languages it counts. Accordingly, we must depend on other attempts to estimate the characteristics and numbers of those who use sign. One textbook notes that

> there are no figures on the number of users of signed language in the United States and Canada. Based on estimates of numbers of people who attended schools where they were extensively exposed to Deaf people and signed language, and on the number of Deaf people known to social service agencies, there are estimates in the neighborhood of a few hundred thousand.[10]

Since that book was published, Statistics Canada reported that, in 1986–87, of the 1,022,220 Canadians five years of age and older with impaired hearing, 35,355 use sign.[11] There are also some earlier studies that the authors either missed or chose to ignore. Several sources of information are used to arrive at an estimated 446,500 persons in the United States who sign[12] (Table 1). This approximation falls within the figure "a few hundred thousand" shown in the above quote. However, the rush of interest in sign that has recently occurred has probably increased that num-

Table 1. Estimates of Persons Who Sign, by Relationships to Deaf Persons:
United States, circa 1980

Group	Number
All persons	446,500
Deaf persons	360,000
Hearing members of families with a deaf member	55,000
Sign language interpreters	10,000
Teachers and staff of schools with deaf students	14,500
Ministers of churches with Deaf congregants	1,000
Others	6,000

Source: Nash 1987

ber greatly. In 1979, for example, only seven North American institutions of higher education had programs preparing interpreters. Today there are nearly ten times that number. What was noted earlier in this book about the explosion of interest in sign language gives additional impetus to arguments that the proportion of persons who can sign has grown substantially.

Another approach for estimating the size of the signing population begins with the most certain users, Deaf people. The National Census of the Deaf Population asked deaf people about their use of signs. Of those deafened before nine years of age, 94 percent said they signed. Ninety-two percent of those deafened between nine and twelve years of age said they signed, and 80 percent of those deafened between thirteen and eighteen years of age signed. The estimated total of people deafened before the age of nineteen who sign, extrapolated to 1990, is 465,000. Of those deafened at and after nineteen years of age, we estimate that 1 percent sign (mostly those deafened in their early twenties, like the current president of Gallaudet University, Dr. I. King Jordan). One percent of the number of deafened persons yields an estimate for 1990 of fifteen thousand signers. Turning to the nondeaf population, we estimate that at least one other member of a family with a deaf person signs. That figure seems too conservative when you consider that the average family headed by a deaf adult has 2.2 children. Professionals who sign and other hearing persons add nearly one hundred thousand signers; this latter group consists of present and former sign language interpreters, teachers, professionals who serve largely deaf clients (e.g., social workers, psychologists, rehabilitation counselors, and members of the clergy), and persons who learned sign out of curiosity

Table 2. Estimates of the Numbers of People Who Sign, by Group:
United States, 1990

Group	Number
All groups	1,015,000
Deaf, age at onset before 19 years of age	450,000
Deaf, age at onset at and after 19 years of age	15,000
Family members of deaf persons	450,000
Sign language interpreters, present and former	40,000
Teachers and staff of schools with Deaf students	25,000
Other professionals	20,000
Others	15,000

(e.g., Boy Scouts and hearing high-school students). The results appear in Table 2. The total of 1,015,000 signers probably underestimates the true number; certainly it is growing. It seems reasonable that Nash's estimate for 1980 would be more than doubled by 1990.

A Caution

The reader should recall the terminology that has been carefully chosen for these estimates: *signers*, not *users of ASL*. There are no reliable estimates of ASL use. It would be very difficult to obtain data on ASL, since its definition remains in dispute. Undoubtedly, some proportion of signers do not know ASL, using instead a sign code for speech (see chapter 4.) The size of that proportion is, however, unknown. What we can say with certainty is the number who sign ASL is smaller than the total number who sign.

The Deaf Community

The Deaf community does not come with a set of postal codes; it has no geographical boundaries. What makes it a *community* are, first, the common interests of its members. Second, they express their interests through their shared sign language. Further, they actively seek means by which to increase their contacts with other Deaf people, through organizations, periodicals, and social events. These tendencies, however, do not lead them to move next door to each other; it is sufficient for them to live in reasonably close proximity to facilitate their getting together frequently and comfortably. So in answer to the question, "Where is the Deaf community?" the appropriate response is, *Wherever Deaf people gather.*[13]

Although we speak of it as a single entity, there are Deaf communities in every country with a sufficiently large deaf population. Within a country the Deaf community encompasses many smaller groups, as is the case with the larger American Deaf community. It contains associations that recognize their African-American, Catholic, Hispanic, Jewish, Protestant, and other ethnic and religious heritages.[14] In many respects, then, Deaf communities are as diverse as the societies that surround them; yet they have a superordinate cohesiveness arising from their members being deaf and their use of sign language. In the remainder of this chapter our descriptions will be of the Deaf community in the United States, partly because we know so much about it and partly because we wish to keep the text in focus. While the specifics that follow are from one country, we believe most, if not all, of the generalizations apply across nations.

Roots of the Deaf Community

Surrounded as they are by people who hear, deaf people nonetheless find each other. For many the first contact with other deaf persons comes in school, since the majority of deaf children attend schools and classes with other deaf students. Most of them learn to sign in school. Until recently, the majority of schools did not permit signing in the classroom. Even today, when sign is used to some extent in the majority of schools and classes for deaf children, there are few formal efforts to teach ASL to deaf students. It has been wrongly assumed that ASL can be plucked out of the air; in other words, just put deaf children together and they will learn it from each other.

Oddly enough, there is some truth in that assumption. Put deaf children together and they will communicate in sign. They are no different than children of any language group—French, German, Japanese: they learn from each other. But what deaf students often learn is a child's version of ASL, a version that should not satisfy educators whose responsibility it is to preserve languages. Consider that in U. S. and Canadian schools English (or French in parts of Canada) is taught in each of the first twelve grades. The transmission of the language in its correct syntactical and semantic form is not left to chance encounters between children. The schools accept the responsibility for formally instructing students in their native language. Sadly, that is not the case with ASL.

Part of educators' neglect of ASL in the curriculum for deaf students stems from a hostility toward sign language or, stated more positively, from an overenthusiasm for spoken language. As noted in chapter 1, sign languages in various countries have been actively opposed on the mistaken notion that learning sign will interfere with the development of speech—a prejudice without benefit of scientific evidence. Still, despite the absence of formal instruction deaf children learn ASL from other deaf students. Thus, schools and classes that bring deaf children together plant the seeds for their social integration in the Deaf community. This is especially the case for the 90 percent of deaf children who have normally hearing parents.[15] For the first time, they meet other deaf students in school, an experience that delights most of them and greatly enhances their social and personal development.

The past three decades have seen an increase in the number of deaf students being educated in public schools. Educators refer to this trend toward placing deaf children in classes with hearing students as "integration," "inclusion," or "mainstreaming." Where the classes have no other deaf students, this placement may alter and perhaps delay the deaf student's socialization. Such delays, while affecting the individual child, will probably not have a substantial effect on the Deaf community. Most deaf people react favorably to meeting others like themselves, irrespective of their age. One deaf college student who had never gone to school with another deaf person remembers his feelings when he entered a class of deaf children for the first time: "I wanted to reach out and hug them all." Writing about the experience years later, he went on to say that "at long last I began to come home. It was literally a love experience. For the first time, I felt less like a stranger in a strange land and more like a member of a community."[16]

While the national trend is away from schools for deaf students, there are more opportunities than ever for them to meet each other at the postsecondary level. Recent federal laws bar discrimination in the higher education of people with disabilities.[17] Deaf students formerly could find few programs adapted to them; indeed, some colleges refused them admittance altogether. The situation has changed dramatically, with nearly all colleges and universities able and willing to provide the necessary support services a deaf student needs to attain access to instruction. These broadened opportunities for deaf people to meet each other will more than likely strengthen the Deaf community and invigorate its leadership.

They Only Work There

The first state school for deaf children was established in 1817. Teachers and administrators in most of these schools usually have normal hearing; many of the schools only employ a token Deaf person or two. For an institution so basic to the Deaf community the low representation of Deaf staff members brings to the surface deep resentment toward hearing staff members. The following is from an open letter written by the Louisiana Association of the Deaf ("Let's End this Conspiracy of Silence," *Deaf Life*, January 1993, 4(7), 10).

> The Louisiana School for the Deaf and the Deaf community have been a part of this state's history for 141 years. Like many other residential schools, we have had to deal with paternalistic attitudes and the generational inbreeding of state workers, their families, and local educational talent who have always worked for the deaf, not with them. Hearing people have their own culture and for the most part only work in ours. Those who "just" work here but do not really live the Deaf experience or contribute to its growth are not too far removed from the personnel of a prison—they only work there.

The United States has long held an advantage for deaf students pursuing a postsecondary education. Realizing that a deaf student's access to college-level education was limited by communication requirements, Edward Miner Gallaudet dreamed, almost from the time he came to Washington, D.C., of a college for deaf students. He chose a most unlikely time to pursue his dream. In 1863, while the country was struggling for its existence during the Civil War, Gallaudet proposed to Congress that it give his school the authority to award college degrees. He lobbied well, and in the winter of 1863, with civil war raging, Congress passed the legislation establishing the National Deaf Mute College (renamed Gallaudet College in 1880 and Gallaudet University in 1986). The first diplomas issued in 1864 were signed by the college's original patron, Abraham Lincoln. Thereafter, the college's diplomas have been signed by the President of the United States. More than one hundred years later, the United States remains the only country to have a university exclusively for the education of deaf students.[18] Today, Gallaudet University enrolls about two thousand students.

The federal government, which finances a major portion of Gallaudet University's activities, also underwrites the National Technical Institute for the Deaf (NTID) at the Rochester Institute of Technology. Established in 1968, NTID has about 1,200 deaf students. On the West Coast state-funded California State University at Northridge (CSUN) accepts about a hundred deaf undergraduates annually. With interpreters to facilitate communication, deaf students can enroll in any of CSUN's programs. In addition CSUN has had a Leadership Training Program for the Deaf at the master's level since 1964. Joining NTID and Gallaudet University, the program has become one of the principal sources of leaders for the Deaf community's organizations and the administration of special schools. Like the general community, the Deaf community seeks university-educated leaders.

The institutions of higher education that the majority of Deaf leaders attend contribute to their style of signing. Thus, for Deaf people a "Gallaudet University accent" is as identifiable as a speaker's "Harvard accent." The grasp of ASL by Deaf university graduates sets them apart from signers, though not in a pejorative sense. The style of signing particularly suits public presentations, a leader's frequent task.

Deaf Community Organizations

Deaf people seem to welcome any occasion to mingle with each other. Announce a sporting event such as a bowling tournament and they will flock to it from neighboring towns, even though they may have no interest in the sport. What they seek are opportunities to exchange news with their friends in a communication environment that is free of barriers. But social events are more than just an opportunity to get together with a few friends. Until recently, there were few if any alternatives to face-to-face dialogue as a means for gaining information of interest to the Deaf community.

The first building block for forming an organization within the Deaf community is *socialization*. This might appear a bit trite considering that all organizations bring with them some capacity to facilitate social interactions among their members. While mailing letters has always been an option for person-to-person correspondence, it is slow. Hearing people need not depend on the mail nor show up at the town hall to learn about a friend of theirs; the phone does the trick just fine. Until 1965 deaf people could only use the telephone with the cooperation of a person who could hear. Then a deaf engineer invented a modem that coupled a typing device with the telephone to send audible signals to a companion device that displayed the incoming message in print, thus enabling deaf people to use the telephone.[19] Still, using a TTY, as the device is known, requires dexterity on a keyboard. Otherwise the conversation becomes laborious and the crux of a message can easily be lost in the search for the next letter. Furthermore, not being able to use ASL on the phone or in print increases the necessity for deaf people to get together.

Hearing aids, too, have their place in the Deaf community. Not all Deaf people wear hearing aids, because they may provide little, if any, benefit to them. For others hearing aids are symbolic of a "hearing world" and reflect speech-oriented linguistic values; they shun hearing aids not only for themselves but also for their deaf children. Others treasure the benefits they gain from hearing aids, relying on them to keep in contact with the auditory environment and helping them speechread. Their use of hearing aids does not exclude their use of ASL. They expand the capacity to communicate with a wider range of people.

Visit most metropolitan areas in the United States and you will find a Deaf club. It may not be extravagant in its design and is usually lenient in its admission requirements. Simplicity rules since these clubs are financially supported by the local Deaf community, whose size is just a fraction of the larger hearing community in which it is embedded. A club may occupy rented rooms in an unfashionable part of the city, or it may be housed in a building owned by a Deaf organization. Wherever the club is, it is a safe bet that it is accessible and easily reached. If you could pop on a virtual-reality headset and explore a typical Deaf club interior you would note that the quarters are sparsely furnished but well maintained. The interior design suggests the premises' main function, to facilitate personal interactions. The walls are not covered with paintings and offer instead a display of pictures depicting the activities of the membership over the years. There will be a television set with a decoder attached.[20] Of whatever other furniture is available there is little that cannot be readily rearranged to allow for groups of various sizes to form. In many clubs you will see a bar, a kitchen, and a raised platform for stage performers or speakers. The club is clearly a place for seeing people.

Originally, Deaf clubs were strictly social centers. But the example of other minority groups in the 1950s and 1960s led Deaf people to become more active in lobbying for their civil rights. Deaf clubs have become rallying points for political activism. Deaf people may not appear as militant as some other minorities, but they are aware of their social disadvantages and of what they need to do to overcome them. The clubs form a steady base from which the members can launch themselves into the local political arena.

The state associations of Deaf people are very much like the local clubs. They too were essentially created for social purposes. Many state associations functioned solely to prepare for the next state convention. Now state associations are more active in working politically for the general welfare of their members. They are gaining the attention of their state legislatures and in several instances have succeeded in getting their states to establish commissions dealing with the concerns of deaf people.

One such organization is Michigan's Division on Deafness. Run by a Deaf director, it has been responsible for having ASL taught for foreign-language credit in elementary and secondary schools. After many years of lobbying on behalf of deaf consumers it succeeded in getting Michigan Bell to establish a twenty-four-hour-a-day message-relay center. As with many services that deaf people have had to lobby for, the telephone company was not easily persuaded that it had an obligation to provide this service. From the deaf consumer's perspective they paid for telephone service in their homes, yet they could only access those with a TTY. The telephone company countered with claims of exorbitant costs and even wanted deaf people to pay additionally for the service. Exercising vigorous leadership, the Michigan Division on Deafness won its case, making the relay service available without additional charges to its users. Federal law now mandates this service across the nation.

Most state associations of Deaf people are affiliated with the National Association of the Deaf (NAD). The NAD has represented the interests of deaf people since 1880. It is the oldest self-help group of persons who share a disability in North America. It came into being as a reaction to the Milan Conference's attack on sign language (see chapter 1). That critical point can be easily overlooked today, especially when one visits the modern office building the NAD owns in the Washington, D.C., suburb of Silver Spring, Maryland. Within the NAD nearly every administrative position is filled by a deaf person. Everyone who works for NAD, whether hearing or deaf, uses ASL.

A companion organization to the NAD is the National Fraternal Society of the Deaf (NFSD). It was founded in 1901 as a reaction to discrimination by insurance companies. At the time deaf people found themselves being overcharged for or even denied life insurance. A few Deaf leaders pooled their resources and set up a cooperative life-insurance plan. Today, NFSD fills the Deaf community's need for fairly priced life insurance and does so with a success that is the envy of the trade. NFSD has numerous chapters in the United States and Canada that serve both business and social functions. It offers scholarships to deaf students and actively fosters goodwill for Deaf communities across the nation. As in the case of the NAD, NFSD conducts its affairs in ASL.

It is not unexpected that communities of deaf people create separate organizations that cater to themselves and, most important, are managed by themselves. Their use of ASL symbolizes their self-determination. Signing reinforces the Deaf community's self-reliance.

Deaf People and Their Affiliation with English

Thus far, in describing the Deaf community we have focused on those Deaf people who use ASL and partake of cultural activities specific to their community. They are the majority, but all deaf people do not sign. Because most deaf children are born to hearing parents, they may not be exposed to the Deaf community or Deaf people who use ASL until they are adults and so do not learn ASL; some are still in the process of learning ASL. Members of the Deaf community exhibit a wide range of ASL fluency.

All deaf people learn English to one degree or another. Some deaf people, although fluent in ASL, view English as their preferred language of communication. Their choice does not mean they have not accepted their deafness. In the United States English plays a role in the lives of all deaf people as they come in contact with books, newspapers, closed-captioned television, TTYs, faxes, electronic mail, and speech. Acceptance of one language does not deny fondness for another. Like other members of bilingual communities, Deaf people are individuals, and the values they uphold and the communication they use reflect their accommodations to the complexities of the world in which they interact.

Advocacy

In the United States Deaf people have been their own best advocates. Through the NAD they have had a prominent voice before Congress in the last half of this century. State associations of Deaf people are also heavily involved in promoting for services and rights. Many state governments have established departments that are specifically responsible for

improving services, assuming the role of advocates in the case of litigation
or disputes with companies and providing information relating to education, employment, rehabilitation, and other matters relating to deaf
people. In addition to Deaf people demanding that their voices be heard,
they insist they be recognized as a culturally distinct group.[21]

The power of Deaf advocacy groups is sometimes given a lift by high-
profile or widely respected individuals. This is the case with Great Britain's
Royal National Institute for the Deaf (RNID). Originally called the National Institute for the Deaf, RNID became "royal" in 1958, when His
Royal Highness Prince Philip, Duke of Edinburgh, became its patron. In a
letter dated 23 October 1983 from the Prince's secretary to RNID Director Roger Sydenham, the appropriateness of the Duke's support becomes
clear:

> Thank you for your letter of 19th October. The Duke of Edinburgh has no
> objection to references being made to Princess Andrew and his own subse-
> quent interest in the R.N.I.D.
>
> His Royal Highness points out that Princess Andrew did not become
> deaf but was born deaf and of course that his Patronage of the R.N.I.D. was
> influenced by the realisation of the value of the work it undertakes.

For readers unfamiliar with the Royal Family, Princess Andrew of Greece
is Prince Philip's mother. (The use of the male name, Andrew, is not a
typographical error.) Prince Philip's sensitivity to the distinction between
early- and late-deafened people, as indicated in the letter, speaks highly
for his understanding of the diversity among deaf people.

Hard of Hearing and Late-deafened People

There are, of course, deaf people who do not sign. They rely on speech
and speechreading for communication. They seek ongoing contact with
each other just as Deaf people do with other Deaf people. These oral deaf
people join groups like the Oral Deaf Adults Section (ODAS) of the Alexander Graham Bell Association for the Deaf. ODAS lacks the support of
and structure associated with Deaf community organizations. Accordingly, they are not members of the Deaf community, unless they also
choose to join one of its organizations, such as the NAD, or broaden their
relationships with Deaf people.

For a long time persons who had lost their hearing during adulthood
tended to remain unorganized and largely unrepresented in the Deaf com-

munity. Many of these people refer to themselves as being hard of hearing. A hard of hearing person is someone with a hearing loss that is usually not so severe that they are unable to function effectively in the speech channel. In 1978 Self-Help for Hard of Hearing People (SHHH) was founded by a former CIA agent, Rocky Stone, who progressively lost his hearing from adolescence into adulthood. He originally sought membership in the NAD but, not knowing sign, he did not find that affiliation satisfactory. He soon attracted a large group of like-minded people and within ten years SHHH enrolled more than thirty thousand members. As an advocacy group SHHH neither opposes nor supports the use of sign language. Some of its members have at least an elementary grasp of ASL. Because most of its members do not sign, however, SHHH emphasizes communication techniques that depend on amplification and speechreading.

In 1987 the Association of Late-deafened Adults (ALDA) was founded in Chicago. Its originator, Bill Graham, awoke one day to find he could no longer hear. Like Rocky Stone, Graham saw a place for an organization with a different orientation. ALDA is proving him correct by attracting a fast-growing, nationwide group of both deaf and hard of hearing people. While ALDA takes no official stand for or against ASL, it supports those members interested in learning to sign, along with providing information about other means of improving their communication access.

The emergence of self-help groups like SHHH and ALDA sheds new light on the cultural distinctiveness of Deaf and hard of hearing people. Hard of hearing or late-deafened individuals still see themselves as occupying a niche in society that is largely defined by the norms and values of society at large. They spend a good deal of their time interacting with hearing people at work and during social activities. Yet, they do need communication aids. And regardless of the degree of their hearing loss and the ages at which they became deaf or hard of hearing, they find comfort in socializing with those who share their problems, experiences, and aspirations.

Occupations and Income

Deaf people have been employed in virtually every occupation in our country except those specifically requiring the ability to hear well. They own businesses and manage the businesses of others. They are accountants, architects, barbers, butchers, cosmeticians, dentists, lawyers, physi-

Forget Me Not!

There is no inherent reason why a person cannot be a member of both the NAD and ALDA. Membership, however, does not automatically bring with it acceptance by other members. The following plea by a deaf woman who lost her hearing when she was twenty-nine years old illustrates one reaction by Deaf people to someone who is late-deafened.[22] She learned ASL and was thirty-three years old when she wrote the following.

> Shortly after losing my hearing, I went to a Deaf Club meeting. I live in a rural area so I am not around deaf much and very much still live in the hearing world. . . . So I went to this Deaf Club meeting thinking I would be at home—accepted because we would all be deaf. That was the case until the social time after the meeting. I had about five or six people, mostly ladies, come up to me and strike up a conversation. Within three sentences it came out that I was late-deafened, and almost as soon as this was established the other person walked away from me. I was being rejected because I was not a born-deaf person. I had never encountered this before. People, please—deaf is deaf.

cians, and professors. They have often faced employment discrimination, not only at occupational entry points but also in gaining promotions. Some have compiled excellent work records and have still met with employers' opposition to further advancement. As a group deaf workers have not found remuneration consistent with their efforts. They tend on the average to earn less than their normally hearing peers in the same or similar occupations.

The reasons behind the discrimination facing deaf people are not subtle. When considering the matter at all, management usually justifies poor treatment of deaf workers on the basis of communication difficulties. They are left in entry-level jobs because it is inaccurately thought that it is too difficult to prepare them for better positions in the company. Employers claim that deaf people cannot take executive roles because such positions require use of the telephone and that they cannot be placed in work that requires rapid interpersonal communication. The excuses are many and varied and so are deaf workers' responses. The experiences of deaf executives and professionals belie the supposed insurmountability of communication barriers. One study of high-achieving deaf individuals demonstrates how well they have met and conquered the obstacles they have encountered in their work.[23] But prejudices do not disappear quickly. While they remain, they press hard on deaf people's emotional well-being and financial status.

The Americans with Disabilities Act of 1990 (ADA) forbids discrimination on the basis of disability. It requires employers to make reasonable accommodations for employees with disabilities such as providing interpreters for deaf workers attending training sessions. Of importance to traveling deaf executives and all deaf people who travel, hotels and motels must provide visual alerting systems to signal a door knock, a phone ringing, or a fire alarm. They must also provide a TTY and a television capable of showing closed captions. To what extent this federal law will improve the economic condition of deaf people, as well as that of other people with disabilities, remains to be seen. At least the law expresses a refreshing change in society's attitudes that potentially can level the playing field for people with disabilities.

Deaf Sport

Deaf sport has been called the strongest institution within the Deaf community.[24] In it Deaf people exert total control of their activities and ensure this control by restricting membership on boards of directors to themselves. The language of all Deaf sport activities is sign language, but all deaf athletes and participants are welcome, irrespective of their backgrounds and communication preferences.

The major national Deaf sport organization is the American Athletic Association of the Deaf (AAAD). It organizes and encourages competitions between local clubs. It sponsors national tournaments annually in basketball and slo-pitch that draw deaf competitors and spectators by the thousands—although, as noted earlier, many who attend come for the purpose of socializing rather than for the competition.[25] In fact, one of AAAD's stated purposes is to provide opportunities for deaf people to socialize with one another.

Most countries have their own national Deaf sport organization such as the Algeria Deaf Sports National Federation, the Estonian Deaf Sport Union, and the All India Sports Council of the Deaf. A common goal of national organizations is to select and prepare deaf athletes for competition in the World Games for the Deaf (WGD), which is patterned after the Olympics and is often referred to as the Deaf Olympics. WGD occurs quadrennially: the summer games recently took place in Los Angeles in 1985; Christchurch, New Zealand, in 1989; and Sofia, Bulgaria, in 1993. Recent winter games were held in Oslo, Norway, in 1987; Banff, Canada, in 1991; and Ylläs, Finland, in 1995. WGD and other international competitions are overseen by an international governing body called the Comité International des Sports des Sourds.

At the national level in the United States and Canada there are Deaf sport organizations for particular sports, such as the American Deaf Volleyball Association, the United States Deaf Skiers Association, and the Canadian Deaf Ice Hockey Federation. Local Deaf sport organizations sponsor a variety of sports, including darts, tennis, and racquetball. Schools for deaf students field teams that compete against other schools in their area. They also compete against other schools for deaf students from different states. The student athletes tend to move on to the adult Deaf sport leagues.

Deaf football players have left an indelible mark on the game: the huddle. It was invented so Deaf teams could hide their discussions before each play, especially when playing another Deaf team that could read their signs. Gallaudet University is generally believed to be the first college team to use the huddle in a regulation game. Although this claim has been disputed, Deaf historian Jack Gannon argues that, despite the lack of written documentation, logic is on Gallaudet's side.[26]

The emphasis on the social aspects of athletics should not obscure the fact that a number of deaf athletes have done well professionally. Perhaps the most famous one was William E. ("Dummy") Hoy, who played major league baseball for Cincinnati, New York, and Chicago. Hoy is credited with initiating the practice of umpires' signaling balls with the left hand and strikes with the right hand, so he could follow the count when at bat or in the field. His distinguished career spanned eighteen years in organized baseball and earned him a place in baseball's Hall of Fame. Eugene "Silent" Hairston is one of several highly rated Deaf boxers. Hairston won the 1946 National AAU and Golden Gloves championships and then turned professional, ranking second to Sugar Ray Robinson in the middleweight division, one of the great champions of this century. In swimming Jeff Float won ten gold medals in the 1977 WGD and then went on to win a gold medal on a U.S. relay team at the 1984 Olympics. Kenny Walker had a standout football career at the University of Nebraska. Following graduation he signed with the Denver Broncos. Shelley "Siren" Beattie is a national champion body builder. She is a favorite on television's muscle competition, *The American Gladiators* . Jim Kyte has had a long stint in the National Hockey League and last played for the Ottawa Senators during the 1992–93 season. The list goes on and on. Clearly, being deaf does not prevent superior athletic achievement.

The Nonperforming Arts

Deaf authors and artists have made significant contributions to society. Melville Ballard, for example, translated a French political pamphlet for General James Garfield, later President of the United States. The general was so impressed by Ballard's work that he rewarded him with a handsomely bound set of Caesar's Commentaries in French.[27]

Juan Fernandez de Navarrete (1526–1579) was three and half years old when he lost his hearing. He was affectionately called "El Mudo" and is famous for many paintings depicting Biblical themes such as his *The Beheading of the Apostle Saint James Mayor*. One of the foremost dry point etchers in the world, Cadwallader Washburn (1866–1965), became a war correspondent. During the Mexican revolution he succeeded in interviewing, with pad and pencil, President Madero. Earlier, Washburn had covered the Russo-Japanese conflict. In spite of these exceptional literary achievements, he made his most lasting mark with drawings rather than words.

Another renowned deaf artist was the sculptor Douglas Tilden (1860–1935). His works are prominently displayed throughout his home state of California. His massive sculpture *The Mechanics* dominates the intersection of Market and Battery Streets in San Francisco. Though he gained international acclaim by winning a prize at an exhibition in Paris, he had little commercial success during his lifetime, depending on his salary as a teacher at the California School for the Deaf. Other successful deaf artists include living painters such as William Sparks, Robert Peterson, and Kelly H. Stevens. There are many more; some have achieved commercial recognition, and others must await the judgment of history as to their long-time artistic worth.

There are increasingly more deaf writers and artists making their mark in today's society. *No Walls of Stone* is an anthology of literature by deaf and hard of hearing writers.[28] Julius Wiggins, founder and president of the popular newspaper *Silent News*, detailed his life experiences in *No Sound*.[29] A teacher from Finland, Raija Niemenen, wrote an exciting account of her work with deaf children in St. Lucia in *Voyage to the Island*.[30]

Frances Parsons has authored several books about her life, the latest being a journey through China titled *I Didn't Hear the Dragon Roar*.[31] Henry Kisor, an oral deaf adult who has been a book editor and columnist for the *Chicago Sun-Times* for the past three decades, penned a best-selling autobiography titled *What's That Pig Outdoors?*[32] Deaf poets, too, have made their mark. Rex Lowman (*Bitterweed*), Kathleen Schreiber (*Dear Beth*), and Linwood Smith (*Silence, Love and Kids I Know*) are among the currently published poets.

The Performing Arts

In the previous chapter we mentioned the increased appearance of signing on the stage, in movies, and on television. Here we discuss the parts that deaf actors have played, without sign in yesteryear and with sign today.

Gallaudet University

When Deaf people arrange entertainments, they naturally include plays, skits, and story telling. That is the case at Gallaudet University, where performances have been an important part of college life. In fact, almost from its inception in 1864 Gallaudet University has had student drama performances. These have ranged from adaptations of the classics—*The Trojan Women* and *Hamlet*—through productions of recent favorites—*Ten Little Indians, Our Town,* and *The Mikado*—to plays such as *Sign Me Alice* and *Laurent Clerc* by Deaf authors. Despite this long history the university did not offer the first drama course until 1942, and its drama department was only founded in 1969. Its drama club, however, is more than one hundred years old.[33] It was responsible for the student production in 1942 of *Arsenic and Old Lace*, then a long-running Broadway hit. The students' signed version was so well done that the Broadway producers invited the Gallaudet actors to replace the original cast at one New York performance. It was a stunt, but one that drew unusual critical acclaim (see "The Critics See Sign" below).

The Stage

A more recent Broadway success is Phyllis Frelich, a former member of the National Theatre of the Deaf and a graduate of Gallaudet University. She

The Critics See Sign

The single performance of *Arsenic and Old Lace* on Broadway by Deaf actors garnered uniformly high praise from New York's usually tough critics. *The New York Herald Tribune*'s drama critic, Helen Beebe, wrote, in part:

> If one has never seen a performance in signs—which was your reporter's case—one thing will surprise him. Somehow the actors' hands convey differences of intonation. There are the gentle, conciliatory phrases of Miss Martha and Miss Abby. There are the staccato utterances of their brother Teddy, who imagines himself to be Teddy Roosevelt. When his fingers say, "Delighted," the word is bursting with energy. When he rushes up the stairs, one hand waving the signal, "Charge," in memory of San Juan Hill, the gesture seems to shout, though there isn't a sound. When Jonathan Brewster, the arch-villain, makes his threats, his fingers are deliberate and menacing.[34]

Her counterpart on *The New York Times*, Burns Mantle, concurred in his review:

> While the greater part of the audience was composed of deaf people trained in the difficult art of reading sign language, many were present who were not deaf. These persons of normal hearing were astounded at the lucidity of the play as presented and scarcely needed the aid of a reader who spoke the lines in a monotone while the deaf actors made their speedy signs.[35]

won a Tony for her portrayal on the stage of the feisty deaf teacher in *Children of a Lesser God*. The role has been a bonanza for two other Deaf actresses: Phyllis Norman won a critics' award for her performance in the London production and Marlee Matlin won an Oscar for her portrayal in the movie version.

Aside from the road companies of the stage production *Children of a Lesser God* , other opportunities for Deaf actors have emerged on Broadway. Before Phyllis Frelich made her mark on Broadway, Bruce Hlibok, a Deaf teenager, developed a character in the off-Broadway hit *Runaways*, which later moved to a theater on Broadway. Odd as it may seem, *Runaways* was a musical, but Bruce's role was entirely pantomimed.

The magic arts have also attracted Deaf people. In 1992 the Fourth

World Deaf Magicians Festival took place in Kiev, Ukraine. Fifty-two Deaf magicians from nine countries competed for prizes in different competitions. A Deaf anthropologist, Simon Carmel, captured first place in the categories of Stage and Close-up magic.

Here and there throughout the country, regional companies of Deaf actors have sprung up. As yet, none have developed a sufficient following to permit the members to devote full time to acting, but they are finding increasingly greater outlets for their talents.

National Theatre of the Deaf

Much of the credit for the general public's acquaintance with signing goes to the National Theatre of the Deaf (NTD). Founded in 1968 to "bring to the public a new image of deaf people,"[36] NTD has performed on every continent and in all major cities within the United States. The first director of NTD, David Hays, was recruited by Dr. Edna Simon Levine, who brought the idea to the federal Office of Vocational Rehabilitation (now the Rehabilitation Services Administration). A grant was jointly given by that office and the Bureau of Education for the Handicapped, U. S. Office of Education, to hire deaf actors, provide them with instruction in theater arts, develop plays, and finance the first productions. NTD's performances have run the gamut from the classics to experimental drama, and the organization has spawned a Little Theatre of the Deaf, to introduce school-children to Deaf theater. Some former NTD Deaf employees have left to hold positions elsewhere as costumers and set designers, as well as actors. Most aspired to become actors, and a few have succeeded—possibly in the same proportion as that for all actors.

Motion Pictures

Some of the performers on the "silent screen" were truly silent. Among the Deaf actors were Granville Redmond, Emerson Romero, Louis Weinberg, Carmen de Arcos, and Albert Ballin. Few outside the Deaf community were ever aware that these performers could not hear. Some hearing actors and directors, such as Charlie Chaplin, signed well, and some could fingerspell. When the movies became "talkies," the Deaf actors lost their roles, and deaf audiences lost the subtitles that made the movies so entertaining for them.[37]

Television

In addition to her triumphs in motion pictures Marlee Matlin has also starred as an attorney in the TV series, *Reasonable Doubts*. Her fellow actors respond to her signs by answering in ways that convey their meaning to the audience that does not know ASL.

Linda Bove, a Gallaudet University graduate and former NTD member, is a regular on *Sesame Street*, in which she plays a librarian and, appropriately enough, the Deaf person on the block. Bernard Bragg, one of the most experienced Deaf actors, produced a television program for children in which he starred as a Deaf version of Superman. Earlier, Bragg, who is also a Gallaudet graduate and NTD alumnus, had a regular program on a San Francisco educational television station. Called *The Silent Man*, the program ran for two years and gained considerable popularity across the country. Other Deaf actors have won roles in regular TV series such as *L.A. Law, Barney Miller, Doogie Howser, M.D.,* and *Magnum P.I.*

The Continuing Struggle

What the above record of accomplishments fails to expose is that obtaining employment is a constant uphill battle for deaf actors. To counter prejudices against them, two organizations—Deaf Entertainment Foundation and Hands in Performance—fight for deaf actors' rights. Fighting may not always have been necessary, as this recounting of successes implies. (See chapter 6, "When Sign Turns Sour.")

What this brief summary of artistic activities exemplifies are the living, vibrant talents within the Deaf community. Being deaf does not prevent one from achievements in arts and entertainment.

Religion

Religion has had a prominent role in the lives of many deaf people. Whatever the faith, it has deaf persons among its members. Deaf congregants do not receive the same treatment from individual religious groups; some groups make extensive provisions for those who cannot hear by providing interpreted sermons or Deaf ministers who can not only sign the service but counsel their parishioners intelligibly, while others tend to ignore their

Stereotyping the Deaf Actor

Although deaf actors are winning roles in movies and television programs, many scripts still portray hearing people as knowing what is best for the deaf character. A plot summary of a recent television drama, *Doogie Howser, M.D.*, illustrates the point:

> When Julia Myatt (Terrylene), an appealing young Deaf woman, comes to the hospital emergency room with an injured knee, Doogie (Neil Patrick Harris) impresses her with his knowledge of sign language. On their first date, he tries to convince her to consult a hearing specialist about obtaining a cochlear implant, a device that (he believes) would improve her hearing—and her life. But instead of being excited about the prospect, Julia seems nonchalant.[38]

The script's patronizing tone and its implication that others know best about what is good for a deaf person, infuriate many in the Deaf community. It may be a few years before deaf people get more roles that realistically portray the diversity within their deaf community.

deaf members. Much of this ignorance could be the result of lack of exposure to Deaf people and the hesitation on the part of deaf members to request that sermons be signed.

Historically, the Catholic Church ranks at the top among religions that have given particular attention to Deaf churchgoers. As noted in chapter 1, the Catholic clergy led the early attempts to educate deaf children, freeing them from the constraints of ancient dogma. Juan Pablo Bonet, Pedro Ponce de León, the Abbé de l'Epée, and Abbé Roche-Ambroise Cucurron Sicard pioneered in the educational use of sign language. Today, in the United States the Catholic Church has several parochial schools for deaf students including St. Mary in Buffalo and St. Rita in Cincinnati. The fact that more Protestant denominations do not sponsor schools for deaf children reflects their dedication to public education more than their rejection of the children. Many Protestant groups provide Sunday school classes and other programs for deaf children, ranging from summer camps to drug treatment centers. Most religious groups also have programs for deaf adults, such as counseling, social get-togethers, and housing for the elderly.

Within the churches great variations occur in the preparation of deaf persons as ministers. By 1980 the Episcopal Church led all other denominations in the United States with forty-five priests—all of whom were deaf before ordination. At the other extreme there was only one deaf Catholic priest, Reverend Thomas Coughlin, who was ordained in 1977. Until 1985 there were no deaf rabbis; now there are two. The number of deaf ministers in other religious groups varies between these extremes, with most denominations having one or two.

The early church influences on sign language emerged through its use by the clergy in teaching deaf children, but religious use has extended well beyond the classroom. In the United States sign has become increasingly common in the conduct of church services wherever Deaf people gather in sufficient numbers. When the minister does not sign, interpreters make the service visible to Deaf congregants. Until very recently the churches were the principal employers of interpreters (most of whom, however, volunteered their services). These interpreters contributed to the shaping of signs, particularly those used in religious services.

Almost every religious concept has a few signs unique to it. The particular choice of signs depends on the religious order and, of course, the signer. For example, *baptism* is often signed as shown in Figure 7.1. This is also the sign used for *Baptists*. The sign is supposed to convey the idea of immersion, the movement reminiscent of ducking someone under water. In churches that do not subscribe to that form of baptism, the sign in Figure 7.2 might be used, since it suggests the act of sprinkling water.

Figure 7.1. BAPTISM/BAPTIST

Figure 7.2. Another sign for *baptism*.

Another sign variation is in the designation of *Bible*. A long-standing version combines the two signs shown in Figure 7.3, which separately signify JESUS and BOOK. The signs in Figure 7.4 separately mean GOD and BOOK and together BIBLE. The latter combination is preferred by some to signify the Old Testament. Other versions combine HOLY or MOSES with BOOK to achieve the same meaning of "Bible." These latter variants are relatively new.

Names for religious denominations can be amusing or, to some, offensive. The sign METHODIST (Figure 7.5) is also the gloss for EAGER and ENTHUSIASM. Methodists do not seem to object to the implied reference to their founder's evangelical spirit. Jews on the other hand dislike one

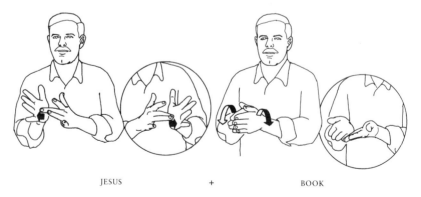

JESUS   +   BOOK

Figure 7.3. One of the signs for *Bible* is a compound of JESUS and BOOK.

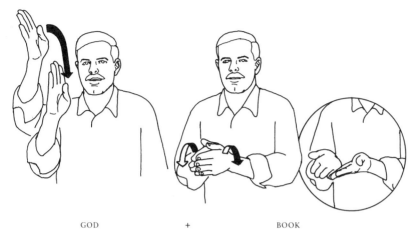

GOD   +   BOOK

Figure 7.4. Another sign for *Bible* is a compound of GOD and BOOK.

form of the sign sometimes used to designate them. The more acceptable sign is the same as the sign BEARD. The unacceptable sign also means "stingy" or "shylock" (see Figure 7.6). Obviously, neither definition is pleasing to Jewish people. It is fascinating to note, however, that the dictionary of Israeli signs uses the first sign depicted in Figure 7.6 and also glosses it as "the beards."[39] The American Congress of the Jewish Deaf has undertaken the preparation of signs for use in religious rituals. Some Judaic religious concepts, such as blowing the *shofar*, have no sign in ASL at present, though the Israelis do have such signs. Other religious groups

Figure 7.5. METHODIST

Figure 7.6. Two different signs for *Jew*.

have depended on the enterprise of interested members to compile signs relevant to their services. One such book contains more than five hundred signs.[40]

That sign has a spiritual aspect should not surprise anyone, especially if one considers its use by silent religious orders and by priests in the education of deaf children. What must be seen to be fully appreciated, however, is its singular appropriateness for religious worship. The depth of expression that can be achieved by signing defies accurate description in print. The Academy Award won by Jane Wyman in 1948 for her portrayal of a deaf girl in *Johnny Belinda* undoubtedly owed much to her beautiful (and accurate) rendering of the Lord's Prayer in ASL.

It is perhaps in the church service that the beauty of sign becomes most evident. Some churches have sign choirs. Watching the robed members sign in unison can be an awe-inspiring experience. The movements impart vigor to the service and add a spirituality that words alone do not often engender. Two Gallaudet University chaplains, Rudolph Gawlik, a Catholic priest, and Daniel Pokorny, a Lutheran minister, formed a group to present gospel songs in sign to the accompaniment of a rock band. The results brought them nine years of performances at Deaf functions, during which they never failed to arouse their audiences to high levels of participation in the "sign-sing," as well as appreciation of sign's power to make the gospel message come alive.[41]

Within the Deaf community, however, there are some members who resent sign-singing. Recently, they have spoken out, arguing that music is not part of Deaf culture. Moreover, unless one can hear the music, the signing looks superficial and may be difficult to follow. So far, their quar-

Am I One, Too?

Being a member of a religious minority does not come easy for all people. One Deaf man told the first author about his religious confusion as a child. Though Jewish, he was sent to a Catholic residential school that specialized in educating deaf children. The first night home on Christmas vacation, the boy followed the bedtime ritual he learned in school: he knelt by his bedside, folded his hands and bowed his head, and began to recite the Lord's Prayer. Without warning his mother grabbed him and, pulling him upright, said in slow words he could lipread, "Jews don't kneel!" As he later reported, "That is how I discovered I was a Jew."

Lack of information about their religion is all too common among deaf youngsters.

rels have been with sign-singing as entertainment. It is unlikely to stop the signing of songs in religious services attended by Deaf people.

Humor among the Deaf

The Deaf community is not a somber place. What is its humor like, then? In many ways what makes Deaf people laugh is as obvious and inexplicable as what makes any other group of people laugh. A major theme derives from the frustrations of being deaf in a world designed for people who can hear. Deaf people enjoy telling stories about the foolish things that happen to them because they cannot hear. One cartoon depicts a Deaf man at a bus stop being approached by a stranger obviously asking some questions. The Deaf man signals that he cannot hear. After a moment's pause the stranger circles around to the Deaf man's other ear and continues to shout his questions. Funny? Perhaps yes to those Deaf people who have repeatedly experienced that sort of situation; the display by the person telling the joke of how ridiculous it can be becomes emotionally cathartic.

Deaf people also like jokes that play on the situations that can arise from a hearing loss. One popular skit depicts a Deaf man waiting at a street corner. He is approached by a blind man, tapping along with his cane. The Deaf man is horrified by the blind man's attempts to speak with him. How can he show a blind person that he does not hear or speak? The situation is played out in accordance with the performer's skills, but the denouement is swift and always draws appreciative guffaws from the Deaf audience. The Deaf man gives the well-dressed blind man a coin and walks quickly away.

These stories play up the enjoyment of being Deaf while poking fun at mishaps that Deaf people tumble into as they go through life. They may mean little to persons outside the Deaf community (just as is true of much ethnic humor), but they serve the purposes of humor: relieving stress and making life's burdens a bit easier to bear.

Sign play is another aspect of humor in the Deaf community that parallels word play in spoken languages. Once, the first author was interpreting for a highly educated Deaf woman at a dull meeting. With barely discernible signs she signaled him to stop conveying the speaker's remarks. In response to his questioning look she signed by placing her index finger against her nose as she curled her little finger in the manner of one daintily holding a teacup. When he signed he did not know that sign and asked what it meant, she replied by spelling b-o-r-i-n-g. He protested that her execution of the sign confused him (see Figure 7.7 for the usual hand shape). Her prompt reply was that she was simply being ladylike!

In their essay on iconicity in sign, linguists Edward Klima and Ursula Bellugi recall how one elderly Deaf storyteller made sure that his viewers got the idea that a long time had elapsed. The sign is usually made by drawing the index finger along the upper surface of the arm from the wrist to the elbow. In his account the storyteller made the sign by touching his

Figure 7.7. BORING

left shoe with his index finger and bringing it through the air to a point over his right shoulder. Very long, indeed.

Punning in Sign

Similarities between signs permit punning, just as in spoken languages. Many students of ASL would consider the sign STRICT to be a sign version of American English slang, depicting "hard-nosed." The same hand position and sharp striking movement located on the opposite hand means "hard." Substituting the nose for the passive hand makes the visual pun. Otherwise, "hard-nosed" could be signed by pointing to the nose, followed by signing HARD. The correspondences are not entirely regular, but they are worth attending to when learning the language.

Creating humor out of signs is an enjoyable pastime among many Deaf people. At an early age many deaf children learn a tongue-in-cheek variation of the sign for "understand" made by signing STAND under the passive hand rather than above it (Figure 7.8). Signing MILK while moving it across the eyes becomes "pasteurized (past-your-eyes) milk." To create a pun out of "rule of thumb," punsters make the sign RULE on their thumb.

These puns do more than illustrate the humor of the Deaf community. They also highlight their *bilinguality*. Deaf people's lives demand that they acquire some degree of fluency in both ASL and English. In doing so they gain some appreciation of how words sound. They need that knowledge if they are to speechread successfully. So they learn that "pasteurized" sounds like "past-your-eyes," which leads to the sign pun. Those who pre-

Figure 7.8. UNDER-STAND, a tongue-in-cheek version of UNDERSTAND.

Hands off the Puns on Hands

The scientific approach to studying sign language has its light side. Researchers who are attracted to this field often tend to be iconoclasts and to express themselves humorously—or at least without the pedantry that dulls readers' senses in many other scientific disciplines. Consider the titles of some publications that catch the flavor of their style.[42]

> *The Case of the Missing Length*
> *Time on our Hands*
> *On the Other Hand*
> *Fingerspelling Formulae: A Word is More or Less the Sum of its Letters*
> *How Many Seats in a Chair?*
> *A Good Rule of Thumb*
> *What's Not on the Other Hand in American Sign Language*
> *Some Handy New Ideas on Pidgins and Creoles*

The puns on "hands" may pall after a while, but they are preferable to a steady diet of *Diglossic Considerations in Referential Communications Involving Implicational Lects in Fundamentally Visual Systems of Cultural Interactions*—a title that we hope is restricted to this page.

fer a deeper psychological interpretation of punning will note that by punning, Deaf people demonstrate their ability to overcome their nemesis, spoken language. Being able to play with a language is a way of demonstrating one's mastery of it. Like other aspects of humor, punning is a way of asserting oneself.

Name Signs

Proper names can be fingerspelled when they are first introduced into conversation (see chapter 3). But continual fingerspelling of a name can become tedious. (Imagine a heated discussion about Hillary Rodham Clinton.) ASL provides an economical solution to this problem. It is the name sign. Name signs signify individuals by brief gestures that usually, but not always, incorporate some prominent feature of their physiognomy or use an initial from their name. For example, a prettily dimpled lady named Enid might be given a sign consisting of the fingerspelled letter E touching the signer's face at places where dimples appear on Enid's cheeks. Likewise, a woman named Liz who works full-time as a shepherdess might be given a name sign consisting of the fingerspelled letter L moving up the left forearm in a shearing motion—which parallels the sign SHEEP in every manner except handshape. Name signs, however, are not always flattering. Among some Deaf liberals, former President Reagan's name sign is an R drawn across the throat, as if slitting it.

Name signs are not formally conferred; there is no baptismal ceremony. Name signs spring up and, if they appeal to signers, they stick to that person. Some name signs or variations of them are passed from one generation to the next or from one person to another. Mr. Williams, a long-time deaf dormitory counselor at a school for deaf students, was known by his name sign: tapping a W-handshape to the temple. Not long after Mr. Williams retired, a young deaf teacher came to work at the school. Because he looked so much like Mr. Williams he was given the same name sign although the letter W was nowhere to be found in his name. The name sign of the second author of this text is made by producing the letters D and S with both hands while crossing them at the wrist. He got his name sign when he began teaching mathematics at a school for deaf children. This name sign is derived from the sign MATHEMATICS. Although he already had a name sign before he started teaching at this school, the students preferred to maintain continuity by choosing a variation of the prior teacher's name sign, which was also based on the sign MATHEMATICS.

One researcher has identified six reasons for the way name signs are selected: "a) physical characteristics; b) inherited from older peers at residential schools; c) parental assigned; d) deaf house parents or teachers of residential schools assigned; e) peer assigned; f) separation of similar names."[43] Physical characteristics include hairstyle, dimples, and disposition.

Because name signs are such a handy solution to rapid communication, you might think all Deaf people welcome their use. We have encountered some who do not. One Deaf mother fought against her daughter's learning name signs. "When deaf children learn name signs, they don't learn each other's names, something they can only do when they spell them out," she argued. She went on to tell about Deaf students planning a reunion who could not locate many fellow students in published directories, because they did not know their names, only their name signs. Name signs do not appear in any address books. You may not accept her argument as conclusive, but it is thought provoking.

A sociologist interested in sign and the Deaf community found the majority of Deaf persons she contacted eager to investigate the topic. Her research led her to speculate that "leaders in the Deaf world might want to consider capitalizing on the positive possibilities for building identity and group identification through the encouragement and support of the notion of formal, ritualized assignment of name signs, which could reflect personal, family, and community identification and pride."[44] The free-spirited creation of name signs is so deeply ingrained in Deaf culture, however, it is unlikely that a shift toward formalizing the naming process will occur.

Name signs might also be culture-specific. In São Paulo, Brazil, the name signs of most adults and students in the Deaf community rarely involve the initials of a person's name. Each person is given a name sign based on a personal characteristic. This is in contrast to the United States

---

If This Is China, Your Name Sign Must Be . . .

Yau Shun-chiu and He Jingxian observed older children in the Guanzhou School for the Deaf assigning name signs to younger deaf children during the first week of school. The pattern for boys' name signs was PERSONAL-FEATURE + YOUNGER-BROTHER, while for girls' name signs, it was YOUNGER-SISTER + PERSONAL-FEATURE. The selection of personal features included reference to the written names of the students.

Among the nine name signs for the girls, three that make reference to the pupils' written names were created by one of the monitors, Miss Chen, a very kind and conscientious girl. These three names were YELLOW, the literal meaning of the surname Huang; PIANO, one of the definitions of the first name Qin; and the manual letter "F," for the initial letter of a first name Fen. The other monitor, a Miss Tan, a girl of fairly mischievous character, was responsible for the assignment of the name sign CRAZY, which was the least friendly of the nine name signs created for the girls.[45]

and Canada, where it is common practice to use the initials of a person's name in the creation of a name sign. In addition to the initials, however, name signs in North America also tend to include some characteristic of the person named. If as a newcomer to the Deaf community you are assigned a name sign, you may learn something about how your Deaf colleagues view you.

Dynamics of Sign

No one studying a sign language can fail to be impressed by its dynamic character. Today's ASL has moved as far from turn-of-the-century ASL as today's English has from that of Chaucer. There are several reasons why ASL has changed and why it will continue to change. For one, ASL does not have a written form. For another, it is seldom taught as a formal school subject to deaf children. Also, the bilingual/bicultural environment in which Deaf people interact makes ASL susceptible to English influences. The changes that ASL undergoes are indications of its versatility, its ability to optimize its effectiveness as a communication tool. At times the versatility of ASL is more severely tested than that of a spoken language. Spoken languages readily borrow words and phrases from each other. Open an English dictionary and count the words that have been taken recently from another tongue: atoll, blitzkrieg, cosmonaut, and zaftig.

Changing times, the emergence of new concepts, the need for additional terminology—these affect ASL as much as they do any language. English vocabulary has been greatly expanded and continues to be expanded over time. Terms are freely created to reflect new technologies or the personality of the day: teraflop, CD-ROM, Reaganomics, and Clintonite. ASL has few sources from which to borrow signs, so it often relies on fingerspelling to introduce new ideas until it creates signs for them. The creation of signs often happens in an educational setting, especially at the postsecondary level, where the subject matter requires precise terminology. There are principles that govern the creation of new signs, and only fluent ASL users should engage in this practice. New signs that come out of university classrooms are not always warmly greeted by Deaf people. Many resent tampering with their language. It is not that they wish to keep ASL in a medieval form; it is simply that over the past two decades too many people have taken the liberty of introducing new signs into the classroom. In doing so, they have often unwittingly contradicted ASL linguistic principles. What such innovators seem to overlook is that

ASL, like any language, is a social enterprise having no inherent value. It
is only when two or more persons agree on its meanings that it becomes a
useful vehicle for communication.

Today, Deaf people are proud of their ASL heritage. Where once they
hesitated to be seen signing in public, they now openly push for its use in
the education system and elsewhere. They are coming forth and challenging those linguists and others who, they believe, fail to appreciate ASL as
it is used in the community. Deaf people are asserting a right to dictate
how ASL will be presented to the general public and to professionals who
interact with Deaf people. They have shifted from a defensive posture to
a confident stance. One of the foremost leaders of Deaf people in the twentieth century, Frederick C. Schreiber, reflected the changes in an editorial
he wrote about the new attitudes toward ASL: "Of course, we are glad
that finally, after all these years of frustration and dogged determination
to keep what was ours, we have achieved recognition. We have overcome
to the extent that education finally has come to grips with the problem
and agreed that we, the deaf people, were right after all." He then reveals
the depth of feeling that language can arouse when he comments on what
he sees as outsiders tampering with ASL.

> If that were the end of the matter, it would be great. And as in fairy tales,
> we could all "live happily ever after." But that isn't all. With the acceptance
> of signs, everybody got on the bandwagon. So many people got on this
> bandwagon that there suddenly were too many and some had to be pushed
> off and guess who they were? The deaf, of course. Now everybody is in the
> business of improving sign language, everybody knows more about it than
> the people who have been using it for a hundred years and more. It was bad
> enough when we found that every Tom, Dick, and Harry was inventing
> signs for words without regard for the Deaf community and for that matter
> without regard for each other, but it became the height of the ridiculous
> when they began to "improve" on signs that were already in existence. It
> seems high time that the Deaf community ought to get up in arms and sug-
> gest politely or not so politely, if you wish, that this is our language.[46]

As executive secretary of the NAD, Schreiber's cry of "our language"
reminds others that the NAD was founded in reaction to the attack on
sign language by the delegates to the Milan conference in 1880 (see chapter 1). For one hundred years the NAD held as one of its principal aims
the preservation of ASL. Small wonder that after years of bitter struggle
Deaf leaders resent the Johnny-come-latelies who suddenly embrace ASL.

For most Deaf people the bitterness has receded. What remains is pride in their cherished language.

ASL has survived neglect and active onslaught. It has proved to be remarkably robust, growing without the nourishment of formal instruction and without the support of a written form. It flourishes in the eager hands of young deaf children; it goes cleverly to school with them; it leaps vigorously to meet the requirements of the workplace; it adapts to the shifting demands of time; and it rests comfortably in the tender care of elderly Deaf people, telling and retelling their stories of yesterday.

Linguists and others may find ASL a fascinating and rewarding language to study. Many hearing persons regard it as an object of curiosity. But for those who are deaf from childhood, ASL is simply essential.

The history of sign language augurs a secure future for it. The science of sign is developing rapidly, adding not merely to our knowledge of sign languages but to our understanding of all languages, whether spoken or signed. The high art of sign, which has always had its enthusiasts in the Deaf community, is also finding appreciation outside of it. Now, increasingly, the general society has the opportunity to observe and to learn a linguistic art form, one that cannot be called new (we have seen that) but whose wider appreciation in society is a fresh and burgeoning phenomenon.

Notes

1. Deaf people come from all walks of life and bring with them every conceivable mixture of human characteristics. One particular group of deaf people are those who lost the ability to hear and understand speech in adulthood. Are they Deaf? They are if they have come to embrace the language and values of the Deaf community. See also note 3 below.

2. Furthermore, audiologists conduct hearing tests in a soundproof booth, but we often must communicate in noise—in restaurants with the clattering of dishes; in classrooms when fire engines roar by; and in offices where phones ring, machines whir, and other voices are raised.

3. Deaf persons who have been orally trained (i.e., have been educated without the benefit of signs) may or may not choose to join the Deaf community, though the majority do. Since this text is about sign language, we do not discuss further those who do not choose to use it.

4. To read further about the Deaf community, see Padden and Humphries 1988, Schein 1989, and Stewart 1991.

5. Kemp 1992, 78.

6. Stewart 1991, x.

7. The most recent published estimates of impaired hearing in the U. S. population come from the National Center for Health Statistics. The data on the Deaf community can be found in Schein 1989.

8. The two rates are for different years: Canada in 1986–87 and the United States in 1971. For details of the research leading to these estimates see Schein 1992 and Schein and Delk 1974.

9. For further information about the relative sizes of the deaf and Deaf populations of other countries see *Gallaudet Encyclopedia* 1987; Weisel 1990. Furthermore, not everyone who is deaf belongs to the Deaf community. True, most early-deafened persons actively participate in the Deaf community, but not all do. Some deaf people never learn to sign; others do not have opportunities to meet and sustain their contacts with Deaf people. Why the small number of deaf people choose to remain apart from the Deaf community is a matter for study. Here we only note that, since deaf people are a numerical minority, the Deaf community is also small relative to the general population.

10. Padden and Humphries 1988, 4.

11. Schein 1992

12. Nash 1987.

13. For insights into the family and schooling characteristics of deaf children see Higgins 1980, Jacobs 1974, Lane 1992, Padden and Humphries 1988, Schein 1989, and Stewart 1991.

14. See Hairston and Smith 1983 and Schein and Waldman 1985.

15. The 90 percent is an average; various studies report from 89 to 94 percent of deaf children have two normally hearing parents during their formative years (Schein 1989). Where do those deaf children who do know sign learn it, if not in school? The answer for only 10 percent of deaf children is from their deaf parents.

16. The quotation is from a speech to parents of deaf children made by Frank Bowe (Bowe 1973), who never saw another deaf child until he was a college student.

17. See for example, Section 504 of the Rehabilitation Act of 1973. The law speaks clearly to the need to provide assistance by way of tuition, interpreting services, and other matters pertaining to an education at the postsecondary level. See also *The American with Disabilities Act Handbook* (December 1991), available from the U.S. Government Printing Office, SSOP, Washington, DC 20402-9328.

18. The official account of Gallaudet University's first hundred years was written on the occasion of its centennial by its then-Chairman of the Board, Albert Atwood (Atwood 1964). Another, briefer account will be found in Gannon 1981.

19. For more information about teletype communication, read Castle 1983. This device has been called variously a TTY (teletypewriter) and TDD (telecommunication device for the deaf).

20. A decoder is also known as a telecaptioning device.

21. See Bowe's 1978 and 1980 accounts of his extensive involvement in lobbying for the rights of deaf people and people with disabilities.

22. Kramer 1992, 28.

23. Crammatte 1968.

24. In Stewart 1991 the author provides a unique perspective of Deaf culture through a detailed account of the impact of sports in the Deaf community. He notes that it is within the field of Deaf sport that Deaf people are best able to assert themselves unencumbered by the interference of nondeaf people or their organizations.

25. See Stewart 1993b; Stewart, McCarthy, and Robinson 1988; and Stewart, Robinson, and McCarthy 1991 for research on the characteristics of deaf spectators, Deaf sport directors, and deaf athletes.

26. Gannon 1981. This comprehensive document contains a wealth of data on the social and cultural lives of Deaf people in the United States.

27. Over a ten-year period, Reverend Guilbert C. Braddock (Braddock 1964) wrote one hundred biographies of eminent deaf persons, Ballard among them. The collection was published by Gallaudet College Alumni Association in celebration of the centennial of its alma mater.

28. Jepson 1992.

29. Wiggins 1980.

30. Nieminen 1990.

31. Parsons 1989.

32. Kisor 1990.

33. Tadie 1978.

34. Cited in Tadie 1978, 204.

35. Cited in Tadie 1978, 205.

36. Padden and Humphries 1988, 81.

37. For further details about this aspect of Deaf life, see Granville Redmond's biography in *Gallaudet Encyclopedia of Deaf People and Deafness*, McGraw-Hill, 1987, 364–65.

38. Quoted in *Deaf Life* 1992, 5(5), 26

39. Cohen, Namir, and Schlesinger 1977.

40. Costello 1986.

41. Rudy Gawlik has left the priesthood for a career in psychological counseling; Dan Pokorny died in 1992.

42. The creators of the titles, in corresponding order, are Frishberg 1978; Frishberg and Gough 1973, Friedman 1977; Akamatsu 1983; Suppalla and Newport 1978; Battison, Markowicz, and Woodward 1975; Baker 1976; and Woodward and Markowicz 1975.

43. Jacobowitz 1991, 1.

44. Meadow 1977.

45. Shun-chiu and Jingxian 1989, 309.

46. The quotation is from Schreiber's collected papers, which were published in his biography (Schein 1981).

Appendix A: The Stokoe Notation System

Tab Symbols

1. Ø   zero, the neutral place where the hands move, in contrast with all places below
2. ∩   face or whole head
3. ∩   forehead or brow, upper face
4. △   mid-face, the eye and nose region
5. ∪   chin, lower face
6. 3   cheek, temple, ear, side-face
7. Π   neck
8. [ ]   trunk, body from shoulders to hips
9. ∖   upper arm
10. √   elbow, forearm
11. ɑ   wrist, arm in supinated position (on its back)
12. ɒ   wrist, arm in pronated position (face down)

Dez Symbols, some also used as tab

13. A   compact hand, fist; may be like 'a,' 's,' or 't' of manual alphabet
14. B   flat hand
15. 5   spread hand; fingers and thumb spread like '5' of manual numeration
16. C   curved hand; may be like 'c' or more open
17. E   contracted hand; like 'e' or more claw-like
18. F   "three-ring" hand; from spread hand, thumb and index finger touch or cross

19. G   index hand; like 'g' or sometmies like 'd'; index finger points from fist
20. H   index and second finger, side by side, extended
21. I   "pinkie" hand; little finger extended from compact hand
22. K   like G except that thumb touches middle phalanx of second finger; like 'k' and 'p' of manual alphabet
23. L   angle hand; thumb, index finger in right angle, other fingers usually bent into palm
24. 3   "cock" hand; thumb and first two finger spread, like '3' of manual numeration
25. O   tapered hand; fingers curved and squeezed together over thumb; may be like 'o' of manual alphabet
26. R   "warding off" hand; second finger crossed over index finger; like 'r' of manual alphabet
27. V   "victory" hand; index and second fingers extended and spread apart
28. W   three-finger hand; thumb and little finger touch, others extended spread
29. X   hook hand; index finger bent in hook from fist, thumb tip may touch fingertip
30. Y   "horns" hand; thumb and little spread out extended from fist; or index finger and little finger extended, parallel
31. 8   (allocheric variant of Y); second finger bent in from spread hand, may touch fingertip

Sig Symbols

32.	∧	upward movement	
33.	∨	downward movement	vertical action
34.	ᴎ	up-and-down movement	
35.	>	rightward movement	
36.	<	leftward movement	sideways action
37.	ᶻ	side to side movement	
38.	⊤	movement toward signer	
39.	⊥	movement away from signer	horizontal action
40.	⊐⊏	to-and-fro movement	

41. ɑ   supinating rotation (palm up) ⎫
42. ɒ   pronating rotation (palm down) ⎬ rotary action
43. ω   twisting movement ⎭
44. ŋ   nodding or bending action
45. □   opening action (final dez configuration shown in brackets)
46. #   closing action (final dez configuration shown in brackets)
47. ᴕ   wiggling action of fingers
48. ℗   circular action ⎫
49.)(convergent action, approach ⎬
50. ×   contactual action, touch ⎮
51. ⊐ linking action, grasp ⎮
52. †   crossing action ⎬ interaction
53. ⊙   entering action ⎮
54. ÷   divergent action, separate ⎮
55. "   interchanging action ⎭

*Appendix B: Manual Alphabets
from Argentina, Japan, and Thailand*

ARGENTINA
Argentine Hand Alphabet

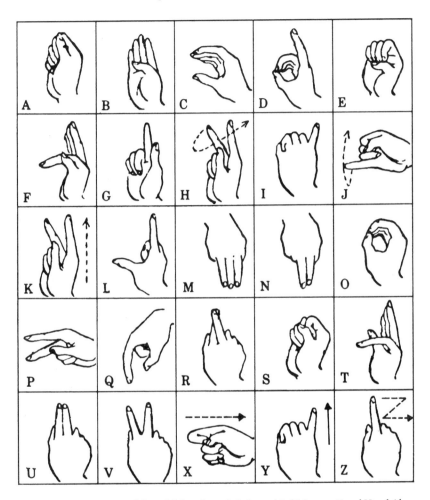

Reprinted by permission of the publisher, from S. J. Carmel (ed.) *International Hand Alphabet Charts* (1982): 1. n.p.: Simon J. Carmel.

JAPAN
Japanese Hand Alphabet

Reprinted by permission of the publisher, from S. J. Carmel (ed.) *International Hand Alphabet Charts* (1982): 75. n.p.: Simon J. Carmel.

THAILAND
Thai Hand Alphabet

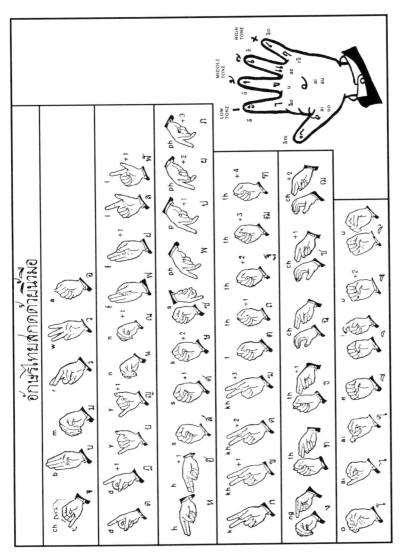

Reprinted by permission of the publisher, from S. J. Carmel (ed.) *International Hand Alphabet Charts* (1982): 47. n.p.: Simon J. Carmel.

Bibliography

Abernathy, E. 1959. An historical sketch of the manual alphabets. *American Annals of the Deaf* 104:232–40.

Ahlgren, I. 1990. Diectic pronouns in Swedish and Swedish Sign Language. In *Theoretical issues in sign language research,* ed. S. Fischer and P. Siple, Vol. 1: 167–74. Chicago: University of Chicago Press.

Akamatsu, C. 1982. The aquisition of fingerspelling in pre-school children. Ph.D. diss., Department of Psychology, University of Rochester.

———. 1983. Fingerspelling formulae: A word is more or less the sum of its letters. *Sign Language Studies* 39:126–32.

Anthony, D. 1971. *Seeing essential English.* Vols. 1 and 11. Anaheim, Calif.: Anaheim Union School District.

Atwood, A. 1964. *Gallaudet College: Its first one hundred years.* Washington, D.C.: Gallaudet University.

Babbini, B. 1965. *An introductory course in manual communication.* Northridge, Calif.: San Fernando Valley State College.

Baker, C. 1976. What's not on the other hand in American Sign Language. In *Papers from the Twelfth Regional Meeting of the Chicago Linguistic Society,* ed. S. Mufivene, C. Walker, and S. Steever. Chicago: University of Chicago.

Baker, C., and R. Battison. 1980. *Sign language and the Deaf community.* Silver Spring, Md.: National Association of the Deaf.

Baker, C., and D. Cokely. 1991. *American Sign Language: A teacher's resource text on grammar and culture.* Silver Spring, Md.: TJ Publishers, 1980. Reprint, Washington, D.C.: Gallaudet University Press, Clerc Books.

Baker-Shenk, C. 1985. The facial behavior of deaf signers: Evidence of a complex language. *American Annals of the Deaf* 130:297–304.

———. 1987a. Simultaneous communication. *Gallaudet Encyclopedia of Deaf People and Deafness.* Vol. 3:176–79. New York: McGraw-Hill.

———. 1987b. Manually coded English. *Gallaudet Encyclopedia of Deaf People and Deafness.* Vol. 2:197–200. New York: McGraw-Hill.

Barakat, R. 1975. On ambiguity in the Cistercian Sign Language. *Sign Language Studies* 8:275–89.

Barbag-Stoll, A. 1983. *Social and linguistic history of Nigerian Pidgin English.* Tubingen: Stauffenberg-Verlag.

Barrera, R., and B. Sulzer-Azaroff. 1983. An alternating treatment comparison of oral and total communication training programs with echolalic autistic children. *Journal of Applied Behavior Analysis* 16:379–94.

Battison, R. 1978. *Lexical borrowing in American Sign Language.* Silver Spring, Md.: Linstok Press.

Battison, R., and I.K. Jordan. 1976. Cross-cultural communication with foreign signers: Fact and fancy. *Sign Language Studies* 10:53–68.

Battison, R., H. Markowicz, and J. Woodward. 1975. A good rule of thumb. In *New ways of analyzing variation in English II,* ed. R. Shuy and R. Fasold. Washington, D.C.: Georgetown University.

Bellugi, U., E. Klima, and P. Siple. 1975. Remembering in signs. *Cognition* 3:93–125.

Bellugi, U., L. O'Grady, D. Lillo-Martin, M. O'Grady Hynes, K. van Hoek, and D. Corina. 1994. Enhancement of spatial cognition in deaf children. In *From gesture to language in hearing and deaf children,* ed. V. Volterra and C. J. Erting, 278–98. New York: Springer-Verlag, 1990. Reprint, Washington, D.C.: Gallaudet University Press.

Bender, R. 1981. *The conquest of deafness.* 3d ed. Danville, Ill.: Interstate Printers and Publishers.

Berger, K. W. 1972. *Speechreading principles and methods.* Baltimore, Md.: National Educational Press.

———. 1988. *New reflections on speechreading.* Washington, D.C.: A.G. Bell Association for the Deaf.

Bickerton, D. 1981. *Roots of language.* Ann Arbor, Mich.: Karoma Publishers.

Blackburn, D., et al. 1984. Manual communication as an alternative mode of language instruction for children with severe reading disabilities. *Language, speech and hearing services in the schools* 15:22–31.

Bonvillian, J. 1982. Review of the education of Koko. *Sign Language Studies* 34:7–14.

Bonvillian, J. and R. Folven. 1990. The onset of signing in young children. In *SLR 87: Papers from the Fourth International Symposium on Sign Language Research,* ed. W. Edmondson and F. Karlsson, 183–89. Hamburg: Signum.

Bonvillian, J., K. Nelson, and J. Rhyne. 1981. Sign language and autism. *Journal of Autism and Developmental Disorders* 11:125–37.

Bonvillian, J., M. Orlansky, L. Novack, and R. Folven,. 1983. Early sign language aquisition and cognitive development. In *The acquisition of symbolic skills,* ed. D. R. Rogers and J. A. Slobada, 207–14. New York: Plenum.

Bornstein, H., and L. Hamilton. 1972. Some recent national dictionaries of sign language. *Sign Language Studies* 1:42–63.

Bornstein, H., L. Hamilton, B. Kannapell, H. Roy, and K. Saulnier. 1973. *Basic Pre-School Signed English Dictionary.* Washington, D.C.: Gallaudet University.

Bornstein, H., and K. Saulnier. 1981. Signed English: A brief follow-up to the first evaluation. *American Annals of the Deaf* 126:69–72.

Bornstein, H., K. Saulnier, and L. Hamilton. 1980. Signed English: A first evaluation. *American Annals of the Deaf* 125:467–81.

Bowe, F. G. 1973. Crisis of the deaf child and his family. In *The deaf child and his family.* Washington, D.C.: Rehabilitation Services Administration.

———. 1978. *Handicapping America.* New York: Harper and Row.

———. 1980. *Rehabilitating America.* New York: Harper and Row.

Braddock, G. C. 1975. *Notable deaf persons.* Washington, D.C.: Gallaudet College Alumni Association.

Bragg, B. 1990. Communication and the Deaf community: Where do we go from here? In *Communication issues among Deaf people: A Deaf American monograph,* ed. M. Garretson, 9–14. Silver Spring, Md.: National Association of the Deaf.

Brasel, K., and S. Quigley. 1977. The influence of certain language and communication environments in early childhood on the development of language in deaf individuals. *Journal of Speech and Hearing Research* 20:95–107.

Brennan, M., and M. Colville. 1979. A British Sign Language research project. *Sign Language Studies* 24:253–72.

Brennan, M., and A. B. Hayhurst. 1980. The renaissance of British Sign Language. In *Sign language and the Deaf community,* ed. C. Baker and R. Battison. Silver Spring, Md.: National Association of the Deaf.

Brien, D., ed. 1992. *Dictionary of British Sign Language/English.* Boston: Faber and Faber.

Brito, L. 1990. Epistemic, alethic, and deontic modalities in a Brazilian Sign Language. In *Theoretical issues in sign language research,* ed. S. Fischer and P. Siple, Vol. 1:229–60. Chicago: University of Chicago Press.

Brown, D. 1973. Affective variables in second language acquisition. *Language Learning* 2:231–34.

Brown, J. 1856. *A vocabulary of mute signs.* Baton Rouge, La.: Morning Comet.

Brown, R. 1973. Development of the first language in the human species. *American Psychologist* 28:97–106.

Bruner, J., and C. Feldman. 1982. Where does language come from? *The New York Review of Books* 34–36.

Bulwer, J. 1644. *Chirologia or the natural language of the hand.* London: Tho. Harper.

———. 1648. *Philocophus, or the deafe and dumbe man's friend.* London: Humphrey Moseley.

Caccamise, F., and R. Blasdell. 1978. Distance and reception of fingerspelling, *American Annals of the Deaf* 123:873–76.

Caccamise, F., R. Ayers, K. Finch, and M. Mitchell. 1978. Signs and manual communication systems: Selection, standardization, and development. *American Annals of the Deaf* 123:877–99.

Caplan, B. 1977. Cerebral localization, cognitive strategy and reading ability. Ph.D. diss., New York University School of Education, Health, Nursing, and Arts Professions.

Carmel, S. 1982. *International hand alphabet charts.* Rockville, Md.: Studio Printing.

Carter, M. 1981. On selecting a sign language class, Part 11. *The Deaf American* 34:23–25.

Caselli, M. 1994. Communicative gestures and first words. In *From gesture to language in hearing and deaf children,* ed. V. Volterra and C. Erting, 56–67.

New York: Springer-Verlag, 1990. Reprint, Washington, D.C.: Gallaudet University Press.

Caselli, M., and V. Volterra. 1994. From communication to language in hearing and deaf children. In *From gesture to language in hearing and deaf children*, ed. V. Volterra and C. Erting, 263–77. New York: Springer-Verlag, 1990. Reprint, Washington, D.C.: Gallaudet University Press.

Casey, L. 1978. Development of communicative behavior in autistic children: A parent program using manual signs. *Journal of Autism and Childhood Schizophrenia* 8:45–60.

Chaves, T., and J. Soler. 1975. Manuel Ramirez de Carrion (1579–1652?) and his secret method of teaching the deaf. *Sign Language Studies* 8:235–48.

Chukovsky, K. 1984. *A high art*. Translated by L. Leighton. Knoxville: University of Tennessee Press.

Claiborne, R. 1989. *The roots of English*. New York: Times Books.

Clark, W. P. 1884. *The Indian Sign Language*. Philadelphia: L. R. Hammsley.

Cohen, E., L. Namir, and L. Schlesinger. 1977. *A new dictionary of sign language*. The Hague, Netherlands: Mouton.

Cohen, M. 1981. Development of language behavior in an autistic child using Total Communication. *Exceptional Children* 47:379–81.

Cokely, D. 1992. *Sign language interpreters and interpreting*. Burtonsville, Md.: Linstok Press.

Conrad, R. 1981. Sign language in education: Some consequent problems. In *Perspectives on British Sign Language and deafness*, ed. B. Woll, J. Kyle, and M. Deuchar. London: Croom Helm.

Corazza, S. 1990. The morphology of classifier handshapes in Italian Sign Language. In *Sign language research: Theoretical issues*, ed. C. Lucas, 71–82. Washington, D.C.: Gallaudet University Press.

Cornett, R. 1967 Cued Speech. *American Annals of the Deaf* 112:3–13.

———. 1973. Comments on the Nash case study. *Sign Language Studies* 3:93–98.

Crammatte, A. B. 1987. *Meeting The Challenge: Hearing-Impaired Professionals in the Workplace*. Washington, D.C.: Gallaudet University Press.

Crystal, D., and E. Craig. 1978. Contrived sign language. In *Sign language of the deaf*, ed. L. M. Schlesinger and L. Namir. New York: Academic Press.

Crystal, D. 1980, ed. *Eric Partridge in his own words*. New York: Macmillan.

Cummins, J. 1984. *Bilingual and special education: Issues in assessment and pedagogy*. San Diego: College-Hill.

———. 1986. Empowering minority students: A framework for intervention. *Harvard Educational Review* 56:18–36.

———. 1989. A theoretical framework for bilingual special education. *Exceptional Children* 56:111–19.

Cutting, J., and J. Kavanagh. 1975. On the relationship of speech to language. *ASHA* 17:500–506.

Dee, A., L. Rapin, and R. Ruben. 1982. Speech and language development in a parent-infant total communication program. *Annals of Otology, Rhinology, and Laryngology* 91:62–72.

De Francis, J. 1989. *Visible speech: The diverse oneness of writing systems*. Honolulu: University of Hawaii Press.

Deuchar, M. 1981. Variation in British Sign Language. In *Perspectives on British Sign Language and deafness*, ed. B. Woll, J. Kyle, and M. Deuchar. London: Croom Helm.

deVilliers, J. G. and P. A. deVilliers. 1978. *Language acquisition.* Cambridge, Mass.: Harvard University Press.

Diller, K. 1981. Natural methods of foreign-language teaching: Can they exist? What criteria must they meet? *Annals of the New York Academy of Sciences* 379:75–86.

Dyer, E. 1976. Sign language agglutination: A brief look at ASL and Turkish. *Sign Language Studies* 11:133–148.

Eastman, G. 1980. From student to professional: A personal chronicle of sign language. In *Sign language and the Deaf community*, ed. C. Baker and R. Battison, 9–32. Silver Spring, Md.: National Association of the Deaf.

Espy, W. R. 1972. *The game of words.* New York: Bramhall House.

Fant, L. 1972a. *Ameslan.* Silver Spring, Md.: National Association of the Deaf.

———. 1972b. The American Sign Language. *California News* 83:18–21.

Fant, L., and J. Schuchman. 1974. Experiences of two hearing children of deaf parents. In *Deafness in infancy and early childhood*, ed. Peter J. Fine. New York: MEDCOM.

Feigl, H., and M. Brodbeck. 1953. *Readings in the philosophy of science.* New York: Appleton-Century-Crofts.

Feldman, B. 1978. *An investigation of the relationship among some demographic and psychological factors and the acquisition of sign language by physically normal adults enrolled in manual communication training programs.* Ph.D. diss., Department of Communication Arts and Science, New York University.

Fine, P., ed. 1974. *Deafness in infancy and early childhood.* New York: MEDCOM.

Fischer, S., and P. Siple, eds. 1990. *Theoretical issues in sign language research.* Chicago: University of Chicago Press.

Flint, R. 1979. History of education for the hearing impaired. In *Hearing and hearing impairment*, ed. L. Bradford and W. Hardy. New York: Grune and Stratton.

Fouts, R., and. R. Mellgren. 1976. Language, signs, and cognition in the chimpanzee. *Sign Language Studies* 13:319–46.

Freeman, R., C. Carbin, and R. Boese. 1981. *Can't your child hear?* Baltimore: University Park Press.

Friedman, L. 1977. *On the other hand.* New York: Academic Press.

Frishberg, N. 1975. Arbitrariness and iconicity: Historical change in American Sign Language. *Language* 51:676–710.

———. 1976. *Some aspects of the historical development of signs in American Sign Language.* Ph.D. diss., Department of Linguistics, University of California at San Diego.

———. 1978. The case of the missing length. In *Sign language research*, ed. R. Wilbur. Special issue of *Communication and Cognition.*

———. 1985. *Interpreting: An introduction.* Silver Spring, Md.: Registry of Interpreters for the Deaf.

Frishberg, N., and B. Cough. 1973. *Time on our hands.* Paper delivered at the Third Annual California Linguistics Conference. Stanford, California.

Fristoe, M., and L. Lloyd. 1978. A survey of the use of non-speech systems with the severely communication impaired. *Mental Retardation* 16:99–103.

Gannon, J. 1981. *Deaf heritage.* Silver Spring, Md.: National Association of the Deaf.

Garnett, C. 1968. *The exchange of letters between Samuel Heinecke and Abbé Charles Michel de l'Epée.* New York: Vantage.

Gates, G., and R. Edwards. 1989. Aquisition of American Sign Language versus Amerind Signs in a mentally handicapped sample. *Journal of Communication Disorders* 22:423–35.

Gaustad, G. 1981. Review of Nim. *Sign Language Studies* 30:89–94.

———. 1982. Reply to Herbert S. Terrace. *Sign Language Studies* 35:180–82.

Gee, J. and J. Mounty. 1991. Nativization, variability, and style shifting in the sign language development of deaf children of hearing children. In *Theoretical issues in sign language research,* ed. P. Siple and S. Fischer, Vol. 2:65–84. Chicago: University of Chicago Press.

Gill, T., and D. Rumbaugh. 1974. Mastery of naming skills in a chimpanzee. *Journal of Human Evolution* 3:482–92.

Gilman, L., J. Davis, and M. Raffin. 1980. Use of common morphemes by hearing impaired children exposed to a system of manual English. *Journal of Auditory Research* 20:57–69.

Goldin-Meadow, S., and H. Feldman. 1977. The development of language-like communication without a language model. *Science* 197:401–403.

Goldin-Meadow, S. and C. Mylander. 1983. Gestural communication in deaf children: The non-effects of parental input on language development. *Science* 221:372–74.

Goodman, L., P. Wilson, and H. Bornstein. 1978. Results of a national survey of sign language programs in special education. *Mental Retardation* 16:104–106.

Gould, J. 1975. Honey bee recruitment: The dance-language controversy. *Science* 189:685–92.

Grinnell, M., K. Detamore, and B. Lippke. 1976. Sign it successful—Manual English encourages expressive communication. *Teaching Exceptional Children* 8:123–24.

Groce, N. 1980. Everyone here spoke sign language. *Natural History* 89:10–16.

Grosjean, F. 1982. *Life with two languages.* Cambridge, Mass.: Harvard University Press.

Gryski, C. 1990. *Hands on, thumbs up.* Toronto, Ont.: Kids Can.

Guillory, L. 1966. *Expressive and receptive fingerspelling for hearing adults.* Baton Rouge, La.: Claitor's.

Gustason, G. 1981. Does Signing Exact English work? *Teaching English to the Deaf* 7:16–20.

Gustason, G., D. Pfetzing, and E. Zawolkow. 1972. *Signing Exact English.* Rossmoor, Calif.: Modern Signs Press.

———. 1980. *Signing Exact English.* Los Alamitos, Calif.: Modern Signs Press.

Hairston, E., and L. Smith. 1993. *Black and deaf in America: are we that different?* Silver Spring, Md.: T. J. Publishers.

Hansen, B. 1980. Research on Danish Sign Language and its impact on the deaf community in Denmark. In *Sign language and the Deaf community*, ed. C. Baker and R. Battison. Silver Spring, Md.: National Association of the Deaf.

Hanson, W. R. 1976. *Measuring gestural communication in a brain-injured adult.* Videotape demonstration. American Speech and Hearing Association Convention.

Hewes, G. 1974a. Gesture language in culture contact. *Sign Language Studies* 4:1–34.

———. 1974b. Language in early hominids. In *Language origins,* ed. Roger W. Wescott. Silver Spring, Md.: Linstok Press.

———. 1977. A model for language evolution. *Sign Language Studies* 15: 97–168.

Higgins, D. 1923. *How to talk to the deaf.* St. Louis: Private publication.

Higgins, P. 1980. *Outsiders in a hearing world.* Beverly Hills, Calif.: Sage.

———. 1990. *The challenge of educating together deaf and hearing youth: Making mainstreaming work.* Springfield, Ill.: Charles C. Thomas.

Hill, J. H. 1974. Hominid protolinguistic capacities. In *Language origins,* ed. R. W. Wescott. Silver Spring, Md.: Linstok Press.

Hill, J. 1977. Apes, wolves, birds, and humans: Toward a comparative foundation for a functional theory of language evolution. *Sign Language Studies* 14: 21–58.

Hodgson, K. 1954. *The deaf and their problems: A study in special education.* New York: Philosophical Library.

Hoemann, H. 1975. The transparency of meaning of sign language gestures. *Sign Language Studies* 7:151–61.

Hoemann, H. 1978. *Communicating with deaf people.* Baltimore: University Park Press.

Hoemann, H., and R. Lucafo. 1980. *I want to talk.* Silver Spring, Md.: National Association of the Deaf.

Hoffmeister, R., and R. Wilbur. 1980. Developmental: The aquisition of sign language. In *Recent perspectives on American Sign Language,* ed. H. Lane and F. Grosjean, 61–78. Hillsdale, N.J.: Lawrence Erlbaum.

Holmes, K., and D. Holmes. 1980. Signed and spoken language development in a hearing child of hearing parents. *Sign Language Studies* 28:239–54.

Humphries, T., and C. Padden. 1992. *Learning American Sign Language.* Englewood Cliffs, N.J.: Prentice Hall.

Humphries, T., C. Padden, and T. J. O'Rourke. 1980. *A basic course in American Sign Language.* Silver Spring, Md.: T.J. Publishers.

Jacobowitz, E. L. 1991. Name signs in the Deaf community. *The NAD Broadcaster* December: 1,8.

Jacobs, L. 1974. *A deaf adult speaks out.* Washington, D.C.: Gallaudet University Press.

———. 1990. What is ASL? In *Eyes, hands, voices: Communication issues among Deaf people: A Deaf American Monograph,* ed. M. Garretson. Silver Spring, Md.: National Association of the Deaf.

Jamison, S. 1983. *Signs for computing terminology.* Silver Spring, Md.: National Association of the Deaf.

Jepson, J. 1991. Two sign languages in a single village in India. *Sign Language Studies* 70:47–59.

————, ed. 1992. *No walls of stone*. Washington, D.C.: Gallaudet University Press.

Johnston, T. 1993. 56 attend teachers' ASL seminar. *The Deaf Michigander* December/January:3–4.

Jordan, I. K., and R. Battison. 1976. A referential communication experiment with foreign sign languages. *Sign Language Studies* 10:69–80.

Jordan, I. K., G. Gustason, and R. Rosen. 1976. Current communication trends at programs for the deaf. *American Annals of the Deaf* 121:527–32.

Kanda, J., and L. Fleischer. 1988. Who is qualified to teach American Sign Language? *Sign Language Studies* 59:183–94.

Kannapell, B. M. 1975. The effects of using stigmatized language. In *Deafpride Papers: Perspectives and options*. Washington, D.C.: Deafpride.

————. 1980. Personal awareness and advocacy in the deaf community. In *Sign language and the Deaf community*, ed. C. Baker and R. Battison. Silver Spring, Md.: National Association of the Deaf.

Kannapell, B. M., L. B. Hamilton, and H. Bornstein. 1979. *Signs for instructional purposes*. Washington, D.C.: Gallaudet University.

Kaplan, H. 1985. *Speechreading: A way to improve understanding*. Washington, D.C.: Gallaudet University Press.

Kates, L., and J. D. Schein. 1980. *A complete guide to communication with deaf-blind persons*. Silver Spring, Md.: National Association of the Deaf.

Kemp, M. 1992. The invisible line in the Deaf community. In *Viewpoints on deafness: A Deaf American monograph*, ed. M. Garretson, 77–79. Silver Spring, Md.: National Association of the Deaf.

Kendon, A. 1975. Gesticulation, speech, and the gesture theory of language origins. *Sign Language Studies* 9:349–73.

————. 1980. The sign language of the women of Yuendumu: A preliminary report on the structure of Warlpiri Sign Language. *Sign Language Studies* 27:101–112.

Kinsbourne, M. 1981. Neuropsychological aspects of bilingualism. *Annals of the New York Academy of Sciences* 379:50–58.

Kisor, H. 1990. *What's that pig outdoors?* New York: Penguin Books.

Klima. E., and U. Bellugi. 1979. *The signs of language*. Cambridge, Mass.: Harvard University Press.

Kluwin, T. 1981a. A rationale for modifying classroom signing system. *Sign Language Studies* 31:179–87.

————. 1981b. The grammaticality of manual representations of English in classroom settings. *American Annals of the Deaf* 126:417–21.

Kramer, V. 1991. Three strikes, but I am by no means out! *Deaf Life*, January, 26–29.

Kuntze, M. 1990. ASL: Unity and Power. In *Communication issues among Deaf people: A Deaf American Monograph*, ed. M. Garretson, 75–77. Silver Spring, Md.: National Association of the Deaf.

Kushel, R. 1973. The silent inventor: The creation of a sign language by the only deaf-mute on a Polynesian island. *Sign Language Studies* 3:1–28.

Laird, C. 1970. Language and the dictionary. *Webster's New World Dictionary* 2d ed. New York: The World.

Lambert, W. 1981. Bilingualism and language acquisition. *Annals of the New York Academy of Sciences* 379:9–22.

Lane, H. 1976. *The wild boy of Aveyron.* Cambridge, Mass.: Harvard University.

———. 1977. Notes for a psycho-history of American Sign Language. *The Deaf American* 29:3–7.

———. 1980. A chronology of the oppression of sign language in France and the United States. In *Recent Perspectives on American Sign Language,* ed. H. Lane and F. Grosjean. Hillsdale, N.J.: Lawrence Erlbaum Associates.

———. 1984. *When the mind hears.* New York: Random House.

———. 1992. *The mask of benevolence: Disabling the Deaf community.* New York: Alfred A. Knopf.

Lane, H., and F. Grosjean, eds. 1980. *Recent perspectives on American Sign Language.* Hillsdale, N.J.: Lawrence Erlbaum Associates.

Lauritsen, R. R. 1976. The national interpreter training consortium. In *Seventh World Congress of the World Federation of the Deaf,* ed. F. Crammatte and A. Crammatte. Silver Spring, Md.: National Association of the Deaf.

Lee, D. 1982. Are there signs of diglossia? Re-examining the situation. *Sign Language Studies* 35:127–52.

Lentz, E., K. Mikos, and C. Smith. 1989. *Signing naturally: Teacher's curriculum—level 1.* Berkeley, Calif.: Dawn Sign.

Lewis, F. 1982. Speaking in tongues. *New York Times.* 4 February:A33.

Liddell, S. 1980. *American Sign Language syntax.* The Hague: Mouton.

Lillo-Martin, D., and E. Klima. 1990. Pointing out differences: ASL pronouns in syntactic theory. In *Theoretical Issues in sign language research,* ed. S. Fischer and P. Siple, Vol. 191–210. Chicago: University of Chicago Press.

Ling, D. 1976. *Speech and the hearing-impaired child: Theory and practice.* Washington, D.C.: A. G. Bell Association for the Deaf.

Long, S. 1909. *The sign language: A manual of signs.* Council Bluffs, Iowa: Private publication.

Lucas, C., ed. 1990. *Sign language research: Theoretical issues.* Washington, D.C.: Gallaudet University Press.

Lucas, C., and C. Valli. 1989. Language contact in the American Deaf community. In *The sociolinguistics of the Deaf Community,* ed. C. Lucas, 11–40. San Diego, Calif.: Academic Press.

Luetke-Stahlman, B. 1988a. Documenting syntactically and semantically incomplete bimodal input to hearing impaired subjects. *American Annals of the Deaf* 133:230–34.

———. 1988b. Educational ramifications of various instructional inputs for hearing impaired students. *Association of Canadian Educators of the Hearing Impaired Journal* 14:105–21.

Madsen, W. 1976a. Report on the International Dictionary of Sign Language. In

Seventh World Congress of the World Federation of the Deaf, ed. F. Crammatte and A. Crammatte. Silver Spring, Md.: National Association of the Deaf.

———. 1976b. The teaching of sign language to hearing adults. In *Seventh World Congress of the World Federation of the Deaf,* ed. F. Crammatte and A. Crammatte. Silver Spring, Md.: National Association of the Deaf.

Maestas y Moores, J. 1980. Early linguistic environments: Interactions of deaf parents with their infants. *Sign Language Studies* 26:1–13.

Mallery, G. 1881. Sign language among North American Indians. In *First Annual Report of the Bureau of Ethnology to the Secretary of the Smithsonian Institution, 1879–80,* ed. J. W. Powell. Washington, D.C.: Government Printing Office.

Markowicz, H. 1973. Aphasia and deafness. *Sign Language Studies* 3:61–71.

Mayberry, R. 1976. If a chimp can learn sign language, surely my nonverbal client can too. *ASHA* 18:223–28.

Mayer, P., and S. Lowenbraun. 1990. Total communication use among elementary teachers of hearing impaired children. *American Annals of the Deaf* 135:257–63.

McIntyre, M. L. 1977. The acquisition of American Sign Language hand configurations. *Sign Language Studies* 16:247–66.

McKee, R., and D. McKee. 1992. What's so hard about learning ASL?: Students' and teachers' perspectives. *Sign Language Studies* 75:129–58.

McLaughlin, B. 1981. Differences and similarities between first- and second-language learning. *Annals of the New York Academy of Sciences* 379:23–32.

Mead, M. 1976. Unispeak: The need for a universal second language. *Mainliner* 17–18.

Meadow, K. 1977. Name signs as identity symbols in the deaf community. *Sign Language Studies* 1:237–46.

———. 1980. *Deafness and child development.* Berkeley, Calif.: University of California.

Meissner, M., and S. Philpott. 1975. A dictionary of sawmill workers' signs. *Sign Language Studies* 9:309–47.

Michaels, J. 1923. *A handbook of the sign language of the deaf.* Atlanta: Southern Baptist Convention.

Mikin, M., and L. Rosen. 1991. *Signs for sexuality.* Seattle, Wash.: Planned Parenthood of Seattle.

Miller, A., and E. Miller. 1973. Cognitive-developmental training with elevated boards and sign language. *Journal of Autism and Childhood Schizophrenia* 3:65–85.

Mindel, E., and M. Vernon. 1971. *They grow in silence.* Silver Spring, Md.: National Association of the Deaf.

Moores, D. 1987 *Educating the deaf.* 2d ed. Boston: Houghton Mifflin.

Morkovin, B. 1968. Language in the general development of the preschool deaf child: A review of research in the Soviet Union. *ASHA* 10:195–99.

Naiman, D., and J. Schein. 1978. *For parents of deaf children.* Silver Spring, Md.: National Association of the Deaf. .

Nash, J. 1973. Cues or sign: A case study in language acquisition. *Sign Language Studies* 3:79–92.

———. 1987. Who signs to whom? The American Sign Language community. In *Understanding deafness socially*, ed. P. Higgins and J. Nash. Springfield, Ill.: Charles C. Thomas.

Neal, H. 1960. *Communication from stone age to space age.* London: Phoenix House.

Newport, E., and R. Meier. 1986. The aquisition of American Sign Language. In *The cross-linguistic study of language acquisition*, ed. D. I. Slobin, 881–938. Hillsdale, N.J.: Lawrence Erlbaum.

Nieminen, R. 1990. *Voyage to the island.* Washington, D.C.: Gallaudet University Press.

Orlansky, M. D., and J. D. Bonvillian. 1985. Sign language acquisition: Language development in children of deaf parents and implications for other populations. *Merrill-Palmer Quarterly* 31:127–43.

Packard, H. 1965. The incident of the broom handle. *Yankee Magazine* 10:17–19.

Padden, C. 1981. Some arguments for syntactic patterning in American Sign Language. *Sign Language Studies* 32:239–59.

———. 1990 Deaf children and literacy: *Literacy Lessons.* Geneva: International Bureau of Education.

Padden, C., and T. Humphries. 1988. *Deaf in America: Voices from a culture.* Cambridge, Mass.: Harvard University Press.

Paget, R. 1951. *The new sign language.* London: The Welcome Foundation.

Paget, R., and P. Gorman. 1968. *A systematic sign language.* London: Royal National Institute for the Deaf.

Pahz, J., and C. Pahz. 1978. *Total Communication: The meaning behind the movement to expand educational opportunities for deaf children.* Springfield, Ill.: Charles C. Thomas.

Parsons, F. 1988. I didn't hear the dragon roar. Washington, D.C.: Gallaudet University Press.

Pereira, M., and C. De Lemos. 1994. Gesture in hearing mother-deaf child interaction. In *From gesture to language in hearing and deaf children*, ed. V. Volterra and C. Erting, 178–86. New York: Springer-Verlag, 1990. Reprint, Washington, D.C.: Gallaudet University Press.

Poizner, H., E. Klima, and U. Bellugi. 1987. *What the hands reveal about the brain.* Cambridge, Mass.: MIT Press.

Prinz, P., and E. Prinz. 1979. Simultaneous acquisition of ASL and spoken English (in a hearing child of a deaf mother and hearing father). *Sign Language Studies* 25:283–96.

Rawlings, B., R. Trybus, and J. Biser. 1981. *A guide to college/career programs for deaf students.* Washington, D.C.: Gallaudet University.

Registry of Interpreters for the Deaf. 1980. *A resource guide for interpreter training for the deaf programs.* Silver Spring, Md.: Registry of Interpreters for the Deaf.

Riekehof, L. 1963. *Talk to the deaf.* Springfield, Mo.: Gospel Publishing House.

———. 1978. *The joy of signing.* Springfield, Mo.: Gospel Publishing House.

Romano, F. 1975. Interpreter consortium: A sign for the future. *Social and Rehabilitation Record* 2:10.

Romeo, L. 1978. For a medieval history of gesture communication. *Sign Language Studies* 21:353–80.

Rosen, L. 1981. *Just like everybody else.* New York: Harcourt Brace Jovanovich.

Rosen, R. 1993. The president signs on. *The NAD Broadcaster* May:3.

Sallagoity, P. 1975. The sign language of Southern France. *Sign Language Studies* 7:181–202.

Sandler, W. 1989. *Phonological representation of the sign: Linearity and nonlinearity in American Sign Language.* Providence, R.I.: Foris Publications.

———. 1990. Temporal aspects and ASL phonology. In *Theoretical Issues in Sign Language Research,* ed. S. Fischer and P. Siple, Vol. 1:7–35. Chicago: University of Chicago Press.

Sarles, H. 1976. On the problem: The origin of language. *Sign Language Studies* 11:149–181.

Schaeffer, B. 1978. Teaching spontaneous sign language to nonverbal children: Theory and method. *Sign Language Studies* 21:317–52.

———. 1980. Teaching signed speech to nonverbal children: Theory and method. *Sign Language Studies* 26:29–63.

Schein, J. 1968. *The Deaf community.* Washington, D.C.: Gallaudet University.

———. 1978. The Deaf community. In *Hearing and Deafness,* ed. H. Davis and S. Silverman. New York: Holt, Rinehart and Winston.

———. 1979. Society and culture of hearing-impaired people. In *Hearing and hearing impairment,* ed. L. Bradford and W. Hardy. New York: Grune and Stratton.

———. 1980. *Model state plan for rehabilitation of deaf clients* (2d rev.). Silver Spring, Md.: National Association of the Deaf.

———. 1981. *A rose for tomorrow: Biography of Frederick C. Schreiber.* Silver Spring, Md.: National Association of the Deaf.

———. 1984. *Speaking the language of sign.* New York: Doubleday.

———. 1989. *At home among strangers.* Washington, D.C.: Gallaudet University Press.

Schein, J., and S. Bushnaq. 1962. Higher education of the deaf in the United States: A retrospective investigation. *American Annals of the Deaf* 107:412.

Schein, J., and M. Delk. 1974. *The deaf population of the United States.* Silver Spring, Md.: National Association of the Deaf.

Schein, J., and M. Miller. 1982. Rehabilitation and management of auditory disorders. In *Krusen's handbook of physical medicine and rehabilitation.* 3d ed. ed. Frederic J. Kottke. Philadelphia: W. B. Saunders.

Schein, J., and L. Waldman, eds. 1985. The deaf Jew in the modern world. New York: KTAV Publishing House.

Schein, J., and S. Yarwood. 1990. The status of interpreters for deaf Canadians. Occasional Papers No. 1. Edmonton: Western Canadian Centre of Specialization in Deafness, University of Alberta.

Schlesinger, H., and K. Meadow. 1972. *Sound and sign.* Berkeley, Calif.: University of California.

Scouten, E. 1967. The Rochester Method: An oral multisensory approach for instructing prelingual deaf children. *American Annals of the Deaf* 112: 50–55.

Sebeok, T., and R. Rosenthal, eds. 1981. The Clever Hans phenomenon. *Annals of the New York Academy of Sciences* 364.

Sensenig, L. D., E. J. Mazeika, and B. Topj. 1989. Sign language facilitation of reading with students classified as trainable mentally-handicapped. *Education and Training in Mental Retardation* 24:121–25.

Serpell, R., and M. Mbewe. 1990. Dialectal flexibility in sign language in Africa. In *Sign language research: Theoretical issues,* ed. C. Lucas, 275–87. Washington, D.C.: Gallaudet University Press.

Shaw, G. 1903. *Man and superman.* London: Croom Helm.

———. 1912. *Pygmalion.* London: Routledge.

Shore, C., E. Bates, I. Bretherton, M. Beeghly, and B. O'Connell. 1990. Vocal and gestural symbols: Similarities and differences from 13 to 28 months. In *From gesture to language in hearing and deaf children,* ed. V. Volterra and C. Erting, 79–92. New York: Springer-Verlag.

Shroyer, E., and S. Shroyer. 1984. *Signs across America.* Washington, D.C.: Gallaudet University Press.

Shun-chiu, Y., and H. Jingxian. 1989. How deaf children in a Chinese school get their name signs. *Sign Language Studies* 65:305–22.

Silverman, R. S. 1978. From Aristotle to Bell and beyond. In *Hearing and deafness,* ed. H. Davis and S. Silverman. New York: Holt, Rinehart and Winston.

Siple, P., and S. Fischer, eds. 1991. *Theoretical issues in sign language research.* Vol. 2. Chicago: University of Chicago Press.

Siple, P., and C. Akamatsu. 1991. Emergence of American Sign Language in a set of fraternal twins. In *Theoretical issues in sign language research,* ed. P. Siple and S. Fischer, Vol. 2:25–40. Chicago: University of Chicago Press.

Smith, J. 1964. *Workshop on interpreting for the deaf.* Muncie, Ind.: Ball State Teachers College.

Smith, W. H. 1990. Evidence for auxiliaries in Taiwan Sign Language. In *Theoretical issues in sign language research,* ed. S. Fischer and P. Siple, Vol. 1: 211–28. Chicago: University of Chicago Press.

Solow, S. N. 1981. *Sign language interpreting: A basic resource book.* Silver Spring, Md.: National Association of the Deaf.

Sperling, G. 1978. Future prospects in language and communication for the congenitally deaf. In *Deaf children: Developmental perspectives,* ed. L. Liben. New York: Academic Press.

Spradley, T., and J. Spradley. 1985. *Deaf like me.* New York: Random House, 1978. Reprint, Washington, D.C.: Gallaudet University Press.

Statewide Project for the Deaf. 1978. *Preferred signs for instructional purposes.* Austin, Tex.: Texas Education Agency.

Stengelvik, M. 1976. Old sign language. *ASHA* 18:471.

Sternberg, M. 1981. *American Sign Language: A comprehensive dictionary.* New York: Harper and Row.

Sternberg, M., C. Tipton, and J. Schein. 1973. *Curriculum guide for interpreter training.* Silver Spring, Md.: National Association of the Deaf.

Stewart, D. 1991. *Deaf sport: The impact of sports within the Deaf community.* Washington, D.C.: Gallaudet University Press.

———. 1993a. Bi-Bi to MCE? *American Annals of the Deaf* 138:331–37.

———. 1993b. Participating in Deaf sport: Characteristics of deaf spectators. *Adapted Physical Activity Quarterly* 10:146–56.

Stewart, D., and B. Lee. 1987. Cued Speech revisited. *B.C. Journal of Special Education* 11:57–63.

Stewart, D., D. McCarthy, and J. Robinson. 1988. Participation in deaf sport: Characteristics of deaf sport directors. *Adapted Physical Activity Quarterly* 5: 233–244.

Stewart, D., J. Robinson, and D. McCarthy. 1991. Participation in deaf sport: Characteristics of elite deaf athletes. *Adapted Physical Activity Quarterly* 8: 136–145.

Stewart, L. 1990. Sign language: Some thoughts of a Deaf American. In *Eyes, hands, voices: Communication issues among deaf people: A Deaf American monograph,* ed. M. Garretson, 117–24. Silver Spring, Md.: National Association of the Deaf.

Stokoe, W. 1971. *Semantics and human sign languages.* The Hague, Netherlands: Mouton.

———. 1972. A classroom experiment in two languages. In *Psycholinguistics and total communication: The state of the art,* ed. T. J. O'Rourke. Washington, D.C.: American Annals of the Deaf.

———. 1976. The study and use of sign language. *Sign Language Studies* 10: 1–36.

———. 1978. *Sign language structure.* Rev. ed. Silver Spring, Md.: Linstok Press.

———. 1980. Afterword. In *Sign language and the Deaf community,* ed. C. Baker and R. Battison. Silver Spring, Md.: National Association of the Deaf.

———. 1987. Sign languages: Origin. In *Gallaudet encyclopedia of deaf people and deafness,* ed. J. V. Van Cleve, Vol. 3:35–37. New York: McGraw-Hill.

———. 1991. Semantic phonology. *Sign Language Studies* 71:107–14.

———. 1993. Dictionary making: Then and now. *Sign Language Studies* 79: 126–46.

Stokoe, W., D. Casterline, and C. Croneberg. 1965. *A dictionary of American Sign Language on linguistic principles.* Washington, D.C.: Gallaudet University.

Strong, M., and E. Charlson. 1987. Simultaneous communication: Are teachers attempting an impossible task? *American Annals of the Deaf* 132:376–82.

Supalla, T., and E. Newport. 1978. How many seats in a chair? In *Understanding sign language through sign language research,* ed. P. Siple. New York: Academic Press.

Tadie, N. 1978. *A history of drama at Gallaudet College: 1864 to 1969.* Ph.D. diss., New York University School of Education, Health, Nursing, and Arts Professions.

Taylor, L., J. Catford, A. Guiora, and H. Lane. 1971. Psychological variables and the ability to pronounce a foreign language. *Language and Speech* 14:146–57.

Terrace, H. 1979. *Nim.* New York: Knopf.

———. 1982. Comment on Gaustad's review of Nim. *Sign Language Studies* 35: 178–80.

Tervoort, B. 1975. *Developmental features of visual communication.* New York: American Elsevier.

Tipton, C. 1974. Interpreting ethics. *Journal of Rehabilitation of the Deaf* 7: 10–16.

Tomkins, W. 1937. *Universal Indian Sign Language of the Plains Indians of North America.* San Diego, Calif.: Private publication.

Umiker-Sebeok, D., and T. Sebeok. 1978. *Aboriginal sign languages of the Americas and Australia.* Vol. 1. New York: Plenum.

Unification of Signs Commission, World Federation of the Deaf. 1975. *Gestuno: International sign language of the deaf.* Carlisle, England: British Deaf Association.

U.S. Equal Employment Opportunity Commission and U.S. Department of Justice. 1991. *American with Disabilities Act handbook.* Washington, D.C.: U.S. Government Printing Office.

Valli, C. 1990. A taboo exposed: Using ASL in the classroom. In *Eyes, hands, voices: Communication issues among deaf people,* ed. M. Garretson, 129–31. Silver Spring, Md.: National Association of the Deaf.

Van Cantfort, T., and J. Rimpau. 1982. Sign language studies with chimpanzees and children. *Sign Language Studies* 34:15–72.

Van Cleve, J. 1987. George William Veditz. In *Gallaudet encyclopedia of deaf people and deafness,* ed. J. V. Van Cleve. New York: McGraw Hill.

Veinberg, S. 1993. Nonmanual negation and assertion in Argentine Sign Language. *Sign Language Studies* 79:95–112.

Vernon, M. 1974. Effects of parents' deafness on hearing children. In *Deafness in infancy and early childhood,* ed. P. Fine. New York: MEDCOM.

Volterra, V. 1983. Gestures, signs and words at two years. In *Language in signs,* ed. J. Kyle and B. Woll, 109–15. London: Croom Hill.

Volterra, V., S. Beronesi, and P. Massoni. 1990. How does gestural communication become language? In *From gesture to language in hearing and deaf children,* ed. V. Volterra and C. Erting, 205–16. New York: Springer-Verlag.

Volterra, V., and M. Caselli. 1985. From gestures and vocalizations to signs and words. In *SLR '83: Proceedings of the third international symposium on sign language research,* ed. W. Stokoe and V. Volterra, 1–9. Silver Spring, Md.: Linstok Press.

Volterra, V., and C. Erting, eds. 1994. *From gesture to language in hearing and deaf children.* New York: Springer-Verlag, 1990. Reprint, Washington, D.C.: Gallaudet University Press.

Walker, M. 1986. *Illustrations of the signs for the revised Makaton Vocabulary: New Zealand version 1986.* Porirua, New Zealand: Makaton Vocabulary New Zealand Resource Centre.

Wampler, D. 1971. *Linguistics of visual English.* Santa Rosa, Calif.: Early Childhood Education Department, Santa Rosa City Schools.

Washabaugh, W. 1980a. The organization and use of Providence Island Sign Language. *Sign Language Studies* 26:65–92.

———. 1980b. The manufacturing of a language. *Sign Language Studies* 29: 291–330.

———. 1981. The deaf of Grand Cayman, British West Indies. *Sign Language Studies* 31:117–34.

Washington State School for the Deaf. 1972. *An introduction to Manual English.* Vancouver, Wash.: Private publication.

Watson, D. 1964. *Talk with your hands.* Winneconne, Wis.: n.p.

Webster, C., H. McPherson, L. Sloman, M. A. Evans, and E. Kuchar. 1973. Communicating with an autistic boy by gestures. *Journal of Autism and Childhood Schizophrenia* 3:337–49.

Wepman, J. M. 1976. Aphasia: Language without thought or thought without language? *ASHA* 18:131–36.

Wescott, R. W., ed. 1974. *Language origins.* Silver Spring, Md.: Linstok Press.

Wiggins, J. 1970. *No sound.* New York: Silent Press.

Wilbur, R. B. 1979. *American Sign Language and sign systems.* Baltimore: University Park Press.

Winitz, H. 1976. Full-time experience. *ASHA* 18:404.

———, ed. 1981. Native language and foreign language acquisition. *Annals of the New York Academy of Sciences* 379.

Wolf, E. 1979. Development of improved communication skills in autistic children through use of sign language. *Tijdschrift voor Zwakzinnigheid, Autisme en andere Ontwikkelingsstoornissen* 16:50–54.

Woll, B., J. Kyle, and M. Deuchar, eds. 1981. *Perspectives on British Sign Language and deafness.* London: Croom Helm.

Woodward, J. 1973. Some characteristics of Pidgin Sign English. *Sign Language Studies* 3:39–46.

———. 1978. All in the family: Kinship lexicalization across sign languages. *Sign Language Studies* 19:121–38.

———. 1979a. *Signs of sexual behavior.* Silver Spring, Md.: TJ Publishers.

———. 1979b. The selfishness of Providence Island Sign Language: Personal pronoun morphology. *Sign Language Studies* 23:167–74.

———. 1980. *Signs of drug use.* Silver Spring, Md.: TJ Publishers.

———. 1987. Universal constraints across sign languages: Single finger contact handshapes. *Sign Language Studies* 57:375–85.

Woodward, J., and T. Allen. 1988. Classroom use of artificial sign systems by teachers. *Sign Language Studies* 61:405–18.

Woodward, J., and S. DeSantis. 1977. Two-to-one it happens: Dynamic phonology in two sign languages. *Sign Language Studies* 17:329–46.

Woodward, J., and H. Markowicz. 1975. *Some handy new ideas on pidgins and creoles.* Paper delivered at International Conference on Pidgin and Creole Languages. Honolulu.

Yarnall, G. 1980. Preferred methods of communication of four deaf-blind adults: A field report of four selected case studies. *Journal of Rehabilitation of the Deaf* 13:1–8.

Yau, S. 1990. Lexical branching in sign language. In *Theoretical issues in sign language research*, ed. S. Fischer and P. Siple, Vol. 1:261–78. Chicago: University of Chicago Press.

Youguang, Z. 1980. The Chinese finger alphabet and the Chinese finger syllabary. *Sign Language Studies* 28:209–16.

Index